C000023074

ENGLAND'S HIGHEST PEAKS

ENGLAND'S HIGHEST PEAKS

A Guide to the 2,000ft Summits

ALASDAIR DIBB

MAINSTREAM
PUBLISHING

EDINBURGH AND LONDON

Copyright © Alasdair Dibb, 2000
All rights reserved
The moral right of the author has been asserted

First published in Great Britain in 2000 by
MAINSTREAM PUBLISHING COMPANY (EDINBURGH) LTD
7 Albany Street
Edinburgh EH1 3UG

ISBN 1 84018 353 5

No part of this book may be reproduced or transmitted in any form or by any
means without written permission from the publisher, except by a reviewer who
wishes to quote brief passages in connection with a review written for insertion in
a magazine, newspaper or broadcast

Maps drawn by the author and digitally prepared by
Woodlands Reprographic Services Ltd, Maidenhead.
All photographs by the author.

A catalogue record for this book is available from the British Library

Typeset in Garamond and Gill Sans
Printed and bound in Great Britain by Butler and Tanner Ltd, Frome and London

'MOUNTAINS ARE THE BEGINNING AND

THE END OF ALL NATURAL SCENERY'

John Ruskin (1856)

Contents

Acknowledgements

During the time in which I have been writing this book, I have received help from many people. I owe special thanks to Colin Dibb for his company whilst walking and checking the routes in all weathers and Christina Skaife for her great effort in reading and editing the typescript.

In addition, I would also like to thank the following, in no particular order: Professor Michael Barnes, Professor of Scandinavian Studies at University College, London, and Dr Gillian Fellowes-Jensen of the Institute of Name Research at the University of Copenhagen, both for their help with placenames; Mr S.C. Rowarth, of Youngs Chartered Surveyors; Stephen White, Local Studies Librarian at Carlisle Library; Richard Turner and Peter Wilkinson of the Alston Moor Historical Society; Mary Philip; Hazel McIntosh; Susan Antal; the residents of Forest Head, Cumbria, and anyone else who I have unintentionally overlooked mentioning.

Finally, I hope all those who read this book and follow in my footsteps have as many happy days in the hills as I did when writing it.

Alasdair Dibb
Reading, Spring 2000

Introduction

There are, in Britain, seven hundred and fifty-two distinct and separate summits above 2,000ft (610m) in altitude. Of these peaks, fifty-two lie in England and qualify as some of the most popular mountains within the United Kingdom. Names include old favourites such as Pillar, Scafell Pike, Helvellyn, Skiddaw and Ingleborough, but equally pleasant and less well-known names also appear, such as Mickle Fell, Wild Boar Fell, Tarn Crag, Place Fell and High Willhays.

The fifty-two English peaks are distributed across the country although they are to be found mainly in the north. Only at two points in Southern England, at the highest point on Dartmoor and on the border with Wales, does the relief exceed an altitude of 2,000ft (610m). Of the rest, approximately half lie in the Pennines while the others are to be found within the much smaller area of the English Lake District.

With the exception of the North Pennines (Section 9), all the summits lie in or just out of National Parks. England's first National Park was the Peak District (Section 3), created in 1951 as a result of the public's demand for access to the wild and high moors. This movement first came to a head with the famous mass trespass on Kinder Scout (Section 3) in 1932 when only 0.8 per cent of the Peak District's moorland had adequate public access. Today, there is, in most places, little resistance to ramblers walking the high and uncultivated moorland and, in the Lake District, there is virtually none whatsoever. Perhaps the new 'right to roam' legislation will finally oblige unwilling landowners outside of the National Parks, such as in the North Pennines, to allow walkers onto the moors. However, in the vast majority of cases, and certainly where this guide is concerned, it will make very little difference to the current voluntary situation.

It was Sir Hugh Munro in 1891 who published the first 'list' of hills. Munro's list defined all the summits in Scotland above 3,000ft (914m) which he himself considered to be separate.

Today, the majority of British hills and mountains have been included in some list or another, culminating with Alan Dawson's list of his so-called 'Marilyns' in 1992. By then, all the summits which rise more than 500ft (150m) from their surrounding landscape had been included, although all the individual lists are remarkably different.

The way in which the lists differ is in their definition of what makes any given summit separate from another. As already mentioned, Munro made a personal decision on this, but since then, the majority of authors have defined at least one criterion to define the summits on their list. John Rooke Corbett was the first to do this when compiling his list of the Scottish mountains between 2,500ft (762m) and 3,000ft (914m) in altitude. He said that each summit on his list must have a drop of at least 500ft (150m) on all sides to detach it from a neighbouring peak. Later lists also adopted this criterion, including Fiona Graham's list of the Scottish summits between 2,000ft (610m) and 2,500ft (762m) in height and Alan Dawson's list of his 'relative hills' of Britain.

The need for a descent of 500ft (150m) on all sides clearly defined what made a mountain. However, some other authors in England and Wales, where there is less high ground, have chosen a smaller descent, sometimes of less than 100ft (30m). The difference between the two types of list is clear; whereas the former contains separate mountains, the latter includes a multitude of dull and bleak shoulders of higher mountains, which, if they were not on a list, would attract little attention in their own right.

However, the obvious differences between the two types of list have not prevented people mistakenly drawing misleading comparisons between the two. This has, rather unfortunately, created the impression that the Scottish mountains are far superior to the English ones, which, by contrast, are dull and bleak. In fact, contrary to this view, if like is compared with like, the percentage of 'dull' Scottish summits which have a small descent of 100ft (30m) on all sides is roughly equal to the percentage of like 'dull' English summits when the same descent criterion is applied. In the same way, the percentage of interesting English summits with a descent of 500ft (150m) on all sides is roughly equal to those in Scotland again with the application of the 500ft (150m) descent rule.

In dealing only with the English mountain summits as defined by a 500ft (150m) descent on all sides, this book excludes all those dull, boring and bleak tops whose inclusion have plagued so many previous lists. Therefore, the mountains described here are those that no guidebook should omit (even though some do). In the collection, there is a huge variety of scenery, landscapes and mountain forms. There are routes that can be comfortably undertaken by the whole family on a summer's afternoon, as well as much more challenging full-day expeditions into the wildest and most remote scenery that England has to offer. Each route ascends the mountain by what I consider to be the most interesting route. It should be stressed that this is not necessarily the shortest or easiest route or indeed a route which necessarily includes several separate summits, but each route has been carefully planned so as to show the best features and most interesting views of the mountain and its neighbours.

For many who find the challenge of the two hundred and seventy-seven Scottish Munros (summits above 3,000ft (614m) as defined by the most recent edition of *Munros' Tables*) or indeed the six hundred and forty-seven Scottish hills above 2,000ft (610m) that have a descent of 500ft (150m) on all sides, these fifty-three English hills provide the ideal answer. Unlike the Munros, it is quite possible to complete the ascent of these hills comfortably within a few years and most people could certainly aim to achieve them in a lifetime even with other commitments.

Needless to say, as a result of applying the 500ft (150m) descent rule, there were prominent and well-known casualties, but there would be whatever criterion is applied. Scafell missed out to its higher neighbour Scafell Pike, as did Bowfell and the Crinkle Crags, while the fine summit of Yewbarrow failed by a narrow margin to become a separate summit and instead remains as a top of its distant neighbour Pillar. Other summits, such as Mellbreak and Haystacks, fail to reach 2,000ft (610m) despite being such prominent and beautiful viewpoints. Where possible, I have included these lesser summits along with the routes on their higher neighbours and, in the case of Bowfell, an extra route has been described, as to exclude it from a book of England's major mountains would be a severe omission.

It is a well-known fact in Scotland that the Ordnance Survey can magically declare that a mountain has gained or lost many feet or metres of altitude between editions of maps. However, in England this is less of a problem and one can be fairly certain that the summit heights and col heights are fairly accurate (the one exception to this rule is Potts Moor (Section 4) which may or may not just cross the magical 2,000ft (610m) mark). However, there are a few summits over 2,000ft that fall just short of inclusion and these are listed on the next page. Those with a star are visited on the described route to their higher neighbours.

SUMMIT	HEIGHT	SECTION	NEAREST
			'SEPARATE' SUMMIT
Harter Fell* (Mardale)	778m / 2,552ft	5	High Street
Bowfell*	902m / 2,959ft	6	Scafell Pike
Wetherlam*	763m / 2,500ft	6	The Old Man of Coniston
High Spy	653m / 2,133ft	6	Dale Head
Yewbarrow	627m / 2,057ft	6	Pillar
Great Calva	690m / 2,264ft	7	Knott
Chapelfell Top	703m / 2,306ft	9	Burnhope Seat
Hedgehope Hill	714m / 2,342ft	10	The Cheviot
Cushat Law	615m / 2,018ft	10	The Cheviot

In addition, the following do have a descent of 500ft on all sides but narrowly miss the 2,000ft (610m) mark:

SUMMIT	HEIGHT	SECTION
Calf Top	609m / 1,999ft	4
Illgill Head	609m / 1,998ft	6
Black Combe	600m / 1,970ft	6
Peel Fell	602m / 1,975ft	10

Included in the fifty-three summits is Snaefell, the highest point on the Isle of Man. Despite being above 2,000ft (610m) in altitude, it is often omitted from guidebooks, as it does not really fit in with the summits of any other region or area. Geologically, the Isle of Man fits best with the rocks of the English Lake District and it is from England that most ferry services depart. Indeed, until very recent times geologically, the island was actually linked to the mainland by a land bridge.

The routes

In writing this book, I have accepted that due to the decline in public transport, particularly in rural areas, many walkers will use cars to reach the mountains that they wish to climb. As such, the routes all start and finish at the same point where car-parking space is available. However, in some places space may be limited and this is mentioned in the text where appropriate.

With this in mind, every walk is circular except in a few cases where this is not possible, specifically Great Knoutberry Hill (Section 4) and Mickle Fell (Section 9). As already mentioned, each walk climbs the mountain in the most interesting way. While this may not necessarily be the quickest, shortest or easiest approach, it is assumed that for most, quality will come above other factors when ascending to a summit.

Most mountainous areas in England are also either National Parks or other popular tourist areas. Therefore, there is usually no shortage of accommodation of any kind. However, accommodation is less plentiful in the North Pennines (Section 9) and it may be advisable to make arrangements in advance. Also, the Lake District is always very busy in the summer and it is becoming increasingly important to pre-book accommodation, especially on the eastern side in popular places such as Grasmere, Ambleside, Windermere, Coniston and Patterdale.

Each route begins (and ends) at valley level, often in or very close to a village or town. It may in some cases be possible to drive to a higher altitude and take an alternative route from there. However, few would argue that it is really possible to catch the train up Snowdon or the chairlift up Cairngorm and then claim to have climbed to the summit. Similarly, commencing the ascent after driving half-way to the summit is not really 'climbing' the mountain. This angle also ties in with the idea of quality being the determining factor as it is generally much more satisfying to have climbed to any given summit from a natural valley level, or the closest practicable point to it, than it is to ascend from a higher altitude.

In the most popular areas, there is no shortage of footpaths but in some of the less frequented areas and less popular hills, footpaths are simply not formed or are not designed for mountaineering purposes, instead contouring around high ground to provide an easy link between settlements. In these cases, it is assumed that a compass is carried to aid navigation even in quite clear weather.

However, footpaths and routes described may not be public rights of way; this is not often a problem on high moorland but care should be taken not to abuse this trust. It is important to remember that the hills are 'extensions' of estates and farms and the following code is recommended to minimise conflicts between walkers and landowners or farmers.

A hillwalker's code (based on the Countryside Code)

1. Avoid damage to fences, gates and walls. When fences and walls must be crossed, use stiles and gates where possible.

2. Boundaries have an important function, to keep livestock either in or out. Keep closed gates closed. Conversely, gates may have been left deliberately open to make larger fields, so leave them as you find them.

3. Keep to footpaths and other rights of way where this is possible. Do not damage crops. Keep to restored footpaths even though they may be difficult to descend in places – they are almost certainly better than the loose and unsightly alternatives.

4. Respect other people's belongings; leave farm machinery alone.

5. Keep dogs under control. Always have your dog on a lead, especially on the open fell or in fields containing livestock. Dogs pose a threat not only to livestock but also to wild animals. Remember, they live there throughout the year, it is their home – do not disturb them. Also remember that it is within a farmer's legal rights to shoot a dog found worrying his sheep.

6. Do not leave litter. Dispose of organic debris such as tea bags discreetly under stones or, better still, take them home. Organic matter does not biodegrade as quickly on mountains as it is colder and, too often, orange peel is left lying around a summit cairn, detracting from the scene. Do not dispose of human waste, liquid or solid, in places where people may require shelter (under or near to boulders and in shelter cairns). Take special care with cigarettes, matches and anything else that could cause a fire. Dry moorland and the underlying peat can burn very easily and quickly out of control.

7. Keep to the right and in single file when walking on country roads – face oncoming traffic.

8. Do not pick wild flowers – it may be illegal and they can be enjoyed by all if they are left where they are.

9. Tread carefully on eroded paths. Do not create erosion scars by short-cutting hairpin bends, moving stones downhill with you ('scree running') or widening wet or muddy footpaths. If a footpath is too wet or boggy to walk on, do not walk on the edge, which will cause erosion, but on vegetated ground a few yards away on either side.

10. Heather moors are often used for grouse shooting, which begins on 12 August and continues throughout the winter. Do not disturb a shoot or get shot! Heather moors are often carefully managed for grouse so do not damage them (see 6). Moorland is sometimes used for military training and, where applicable, this is mentioned in the text. Be aware of this and check when firing is taking place.

11. Do not build extra cairns – too many can be a hindrance rather than a help. However, conversely do not demolish any existing ones, as someone else may be relying on them. Cairns on summits, however, are different as they are an indication of the highest point and a measure of achievement.

Adhere to this code – other people's livelihood and enjoyment depend on your doing so.

Note

Attacks by cattle upon humans are becoming increasingly common. While it is illegal to keep a dairy bull in a field with a public right of way running through it, it is perfectly legal to keep a beef bull with a herd of cows in a field to which the public have access. When with cows, bulls are normally not interested in passers-by although it is still wise to check for a bull, avoid it and keep an eye on it at all times. Young bullocks and heifers may express an interest in walkers but usually this is nothing more than curiosity. Cows with calves pose a more serious problem. A cow will attack any person or animal (particularly dogs) that she sees as a potential threat to either her or her calf. The vast majority of recent attacks, most of which have led to either serious injury or in some cases death, are due to dog owners being attacked as they try to help their dog.

Cattle are to be frequently found in the high pastures of the North Pennines (Section 9) and in many other places in Section 4 particularly. If you must walk your dog through a field with cattle then keep your dog on a lead and keep as far away from the herd as is possible. Keep an eye on the cattle and keep close to a boundary that you can cross if necessary. If your dog is attacked by cattle then leave the dog and get away as quickly as possible – dogs are smaller and more agile and certainly much less likely to come to harm than you are. The important thing to remember is that well-behaved dogs on leads can provoke cattle, as well as those that are unleashed.

Technical difficulty

I have tried to resist the temptation to include scrambling in the routes. Occasionally, very short and simple scrambles have been included where they improve the climb or make it more interesting. However, inexperienced walkers may well take their hands out of their pockets (in theory making it scrambling) on other routes as many are steep and arduous – not simple country strolls. Most of the simple scrambling can be avoided by longer and generally less interesting alternatives.

Scrambling is (at its highest level) one of the most dangerous of mountaineering pastimes as it is largely done over difficult terrain unroped. Even on very simple scrambles, such as Helvellyn's Striding Edge, the consequences of a slip would be severe and these routes are best done in good, dry conditions except by the experienced. At the back of the book, there is a section of alternative scrambling routes upon some mountains for those who wish to undertake them. However, the inexperienced should read the introductory notes to that section, make their own judgement as to which ones are safe for them to undertake and if in doubt err on the side of caution.

At-a-glance grids and the grading system

A grid accompanies each route, showing the difficulty of terrain, difficulty of navigation and quality. The name, metric and imperial heights, OS grid reference, OS Landranger Sheet number, distance, time and starting point are also shown.

The timings are calculated by assuming that for every 1,000ft of ascent undertaken, an average walker could cover 2 miles on the level. It is also assumed that the average walker does so at an average speed, including stops for views, photographs on the summit, lunch and other breaks for food, of 1½ miles per hour. If, however, you intend to undertake some of the shorter routes in just an afternoon, you may wish to take off 20 minutes to half an hour to compensate for the lunch break, which presumably would not be taken. A difference of 10 per cent is then given on either side to allow for the differing speeds of walkers; times are then rounded to the nearest half hour. Guidebooks that give timings that do not allow for stops are somewhat impractical. Everyone will need to stop sometimes and therefore timings that do not include such breaks are bound to be inaccurate for most individuals.

TERRAIN GRADINGS All the routes shown are walks or simple scrambles so therefore there is little difference in technical difficulty. However, terrain does differ considerably and the grading is based upon the table below. It is fair to comment that Grade 1 routes are suitable for all the family in good conditions, Grades 2 and 3 walking and Grades 4 and 5 simple scrambles.

1. Easy terrain.
2. Steep and/or arduous over short distances.
3. Appreciable sections of rough, difficult ground.
4. Some handwork may be required in places.
5. Longer unavoidable sections of simple scrambling.

NAVIGATION GRADINGS It is assumed that other than for odd occasions where a compass bearing is given in the text, there will be no problem with navigation in clear weather. However, mountain weather does change quickly and a compass should always be carried. The gradings listed below are the worst possible, i.e. in misty conditions. Under a covering of snow, grades 1 to 3 become 4, and grade 4 becomes 5.

1. Clear paths; easy to follow in mist.
2. A few pathless sections but a compass is unlikely to be used.
3. Some pathless sections on which a compass may be needed.
4. Long pathless sections over which a map and compass are necessary.
5. Featureless – a high standard of navigation required in bad weather.

QUALITY GRADINGS Quality is very subjective so there will be many different opinions. I base quality on a range of factors including mountain scenery, mountain structure, archaeology and views.

1. Generally bleak and uninteresting.
2. Some interesting parts.
3. Interesting.
4. Fine views and rock architecture or consistently interesting.
5. Excellent, a wide variety of scenery and views.

Routes given a Grade 5 are the very best, those that can compare with the wildest and grandest places in Britain, for example An Teallach, Lochnagar, Snowdon and Tryfan.

However, as the quality gradings are based on a wide range of factors, some readers may wish to see the hills indexed by subjects of interest and this is shown on the next page.

(Numbers in brackets are section numbers)

ARCHAEOLOGY Ingleborough (4), Great Whernside (4), Seatallan (6).

ARÊTES Helvellyn (5), Skiddaw (7), Blencathra (7).

CAVES AND POTHOLES Whernside (4), Ingleborough (4), Great Whernside (4), Pen-y-ghent (4), Great Coum (4).

GEOLOGY Black Mountain (2), Pen-y-ghent (4), Fountains Fell (4),

Scafell Pike (6), High Stile (6), Skiddaw (7), Mickle Fell (9), The Cheviot (10).

IMPRESSIVE SCENERY All routes given a grade 4 or 5 for quality.

LAKES AND TARNS Fountains Fell (4), Fairfield route (5), Place Fell (5), High Raise (6).

LIMESTONE PAVEMENT Ingleborough (4), Fountains Fell (4).

MINING AND QUARRYING Buckden Pike (4), Great Knoutberry Hill (4), Fountains Fell (4), The Old Man of Coniston (6), Dale Head route (6), Rogan's Seat (8), Cold Fell (9), Snaefell (11).

RAILWAYS Whernside (4), Cold Fell (9).

SPECIAL INTEREST –

BOTANY High Willhays (1), Ingleborough (4), Cold Fell (9).

WATERFALLS Buckden Pike (4), Tarn Rigg Hill (8), The Calf route (8), High Raise scrambling alternative (6). Many other routes have minor waterfalls and to list them all here would be impractical. Those that are listed support large cataracts or a sustained number of smaller ones.

A frequent question asked of me is what would I consider to be the finest mountain of the fifty-three in England and the Isle of Man. I find this a very difficult question to answer as the quality of a mountain ascent depends upon the route. However, I have listed below, in order, the mountains that I consider to be the ten finest in the book:

1.   Scafell Pike (6).
2.   Pillar (6).
3.   Blencathra (7).
4.   Helvellyn (5).
5.   High Stile (6).
6.   Skiddaw (7).
7.   High Street (5).
8.   Pen-y-ghent (4).
9.   The Old Man of Coniston (6).
10. Ingleborough (4).

Directions

Points of the compass and compass bearings are often given to indicate direction. Compass bearings begin at north (0°) and run through east (90°), south (180°) and west (270°). Any directions such as left and right refer to the direction of travel and walkers following the routes in reverse may have considerable difficulty in following the description. In reference to the banks of rivers and streams, the phrases 'true left' and 'true right' are not used and 'left bank' refers to the left-hand bank and 'right bank' the right-hand bank, both in the direction of travel and not necessarily the direction in which the water is flowing.

How to use this book

Each area is given an introduction in which accommodation, transport and geology are discussed. A map of the region showing the mountains, starting points and important roads is included to give an understanding of how the mountains all link together. Each route is given a description and a map to give the reader an idea of the route while reading the text.

Beginners and novices may like to read the pages on GENERAL ADVICE that follow and those readers with little or no geological knowledge may find the geological descriptions of each section a little more meaningful after reading the GEOLOGICAL INTRODUCTION. Any terms that may be unfamiliar are explained in the GLOSSARY at the back of the book. The section on useful telephone numbers lists those of all places mentioned in the text and Tourist Information/National Park Centres. In addition, the section on scrambling routes is intended to supplement the main route descriptions for those who are sufficiently experienced to undertake them. Also, there is a PERSONAL LOG for your own records and a section on ENGLISH MOUNTAIN NAMES AND THEIR MEANINGS for those interested in their derivations. Due to the access difficulties in Sections 9 and 10, there is also a separate section that discusses whom to contact in order to acquire the necessary permissions. A complete list of the English mountains and tops is also given towards the back.

Walking routes in reverse

There are very few routes that can be reversed without some loss of quality. The routes are planned so as to keep the most impressive views of the mountain ahead rather than behind. Also, use is made of simple grassy descents at the end of long days rather than steep, awkward stony tracks where possible. Indeed, many of the descriptions will be difficult, if not impossible, to use in reverse as what may appear very obvious in one direction may be far from obvious in the other. Therefore, the walking of routes in reverse is not recommended.

The descriptions

Too often, in my opinion, guidebooks tell you little more than that which can be seen from a 1:25 000 map. 'Follow the south ridge from the car-park to the summit' is not an adequate description unless the route is very obvious indeed. I have tried to give clear and detailed descriptions to help those using the book. Some authors claim that if the descriptions are too detailed, then some walkers will feel that they have lost the sense of wilderness. Personally, I see the purpose of a guidebook as being to guide; perhaps those who do not wish to be guided should not use a guidebook. It should be stressed, however, that a 1:50 000 map should be carried at all times to aid navigation if the route is lost in mist or bad weather.

The maps

The route maps are drawn approximately to a 1:50 000 scale (2cm = 1km; 1¼ inches = 1 mile) and show only important information to avoid clutter. They are provided to give an idea of the route, not for navigation on the ground, as they are not as accurate as an Ordnance Survey map. The section maps are drawn approximately to a 1:250 000 scale (2cm = 5km; 1 inch = 4 miles). Again, unimportant information is excluded to avoid clutter. ALL THE MAPS HAVE NORTH AT THE TOP. A list of symbols is provided overleaf. The scales of some maps do vary slightly to allow them to fit on a single page. However, the differences in scale are minor and unlikely to cause confusion.

Accompanying maps

As I have already mentioned, this guide alone is not satisfactory; a map and compass and knowledge of how to use them are essential. An Ordnance Survey 1:50 000 scale Landranger map of the areas involved will suffice but, alternatively, all but one of the mountains, Snaefell (Section 11), are covered by the Ordnance Survey's Outdoor Leisure Series at a 1:25 000 scale.

Therefore, the following Landranger sheets will be required: 74, 86, 89, 90, 91, 95, 96, 98, 110, 161 and 191.

Alternatively, they could be replaced with the following Outdoor Leisure sheets: 1, 2, 4, 5, 6, 7, 13, 16, 19, 28, 30, 31 and 43.

KEY TO ROUTE MAPS:

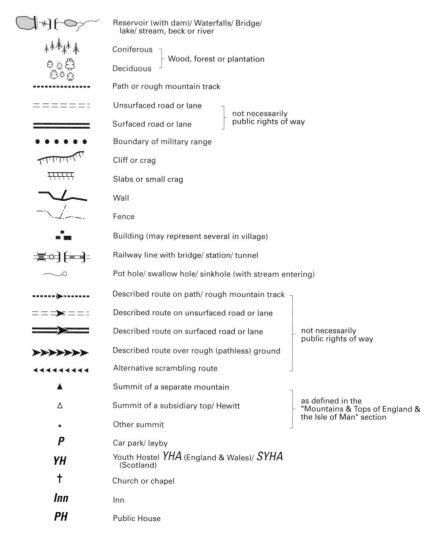

	Reservoir (with dam)/ Waterfalls/ Bridge/ lake/ stream, beck or river
	Coniferous ⎤ ⎱ Wood, forest or plantation
	Deciduous ⎦
	Path or rough mountain track
	Unsurfaced road or lane ⎤ not necessarily
	Surfaced road or lane ⎦ public rights of way
	Boundary of military range
	Cliff or crag
	Slabs or small crag
	Wall
	Fence
	Building (may represent several in village)
	Railway line with bridge/ station/ tunnel
	Pot hole/ swallow hole/ sinkhole (with stream entering)
	Described route on path/ rough mountain track ⎤
	Described route on unsurfaced road or lane
	Described route on surfaced road or lane ⎱ not necessarily
	Described route over rough (pathless) ground ⎱ public rights of way
	Alternative scrambling route ⎦
▲	Summit of a separate mountain
△	Summit of a subsidiary top/ Hewitt ⎤ as defined in the "Mountains & Tops of England & the Isle of Man" section
•	Other summit ⎦
P	Car park/ layby
YH	Youth Hostel *YHA* (England & Wales)/ *SYHA* (Scotland)
†	Church or chapel
Inn	Inn
PH	Public House

KEY TO SECTION MAPS:

○	Settlement
A 65	A Road
B 6265	B Road
	Unclassified Road
△	Summit of a seperate mountain
	Significant lake/ tarn/ reservoir
	Boundary

General Advice

Walking in the hills and mountains is a very different experience to walking in more lowland and 'tame' areas. Most mountaineering accidents are caused by walkers and climbers who stray onto the hills without adequate preparation or tackle routes which are beyond their technical ability. As such, I would urge novice walkers to take careful note of this section before undertaking the routes that follow.

Winter walking is once again completely different from walking in the same place in summer. Not only do the very low temperatures lead to a greater energy expenditure but also when snow and ice are underfoot they bring their inherent dangers and navigational problems.

Weather conditions

Mountainous regions often have their own microclimates, which are generally of a wet and windy nature! Most English mountains lie in the west and these attract the most rain, even in the south on Dartmoor. Those in the eastern parts of the Yorkshire Dales, for example, are often drier, although there may still be a lot of mist and low cloud, the rain being deposited over their western neighbours.

This said, nothing can be taken for granted and a weather forecast should always be consulted before departure. Most national television, radio and newspaper forecasts are unreliable above valley level, although ITV Teletext does have a climbing forecast. A detailed climbing forecast should always be sought locally before departure. These are available at Youth Hostels and most National Park information centres, or by recorded telephone answering services in the more popular areas. Even a good weather forecast cannot be relied on as mountains often 'produce' and 'attract' showers while everywhere else is dry and sunny. Some form of waterproof clothing should be carried at all times.

Wind in mountain areas is often one of the most dangerous factors. It may in theory be coming from, say, the north-west, but in practice it will gust around mountainsides and up valleys. A walker on a leeward (sheltered) slope can often get a nasty surprise when the summit (and wind) is reached. Winds are particularly strong on summits, ridges and passes and can often be up to twice their strength when they funnel through low gaps. These so called 'gap winds' are therefore potentially very dangerous. Another point worth remembering is that wind blows from different directions at different altitudes, which should be mentioned in climbing forecasts. Wind should not be relied upon for direction except as a last resort as it can be over 90° out as it gusts around peaks and through passes.

Lightning is again much more dangerous on mountains than elsewhere. Lightning usually strikes the highest point around and if you are standing on a mountain top, that's you! Keep your feet close together and do not lie down, only crouch. The greater the distance between your extremities, the higher the potential voltage. Get rid of metal equipment (including frame rucksacks) and crouch on your rucksack to help insulate you. Seek low ground and depressions (not containing water). Do not stand under lone trees or on or near summits, rock peaks or pinnacles. Move immediately if you hear crackling (as in touching a television screen) or you feel your hair stand on end. Keep a check on thunderstorms. Time the difference in seconds between the lightning flash and hearing the thunder. The bigger the gap then the further away the strike is; if there is no difference then the storm is overhead (very dangerous).

Winter weather in England is not as bad as is often thought, especially given the recent trend for milder winters when there is little snow. If you can choose to go when the weather is good, you can enjoy the charm of the popular areas when they are almost deserted. Remember, though, that winter and summer mountaineering are completely different. Showers often fall as snow, sleet or hail and things can quickly turn into a 'white-out'. Knowledge of compass use is essential in these circumstances given that only a few centimetres of snow can quickly obliterate landmarks and turn fell tops into 'arctic' landscapes. If there is lying snow, take an ice-axe, and if there is hard snow, take a pair of crampons and know how to use them – snow is very slippery and a slide can be very difficult to stop with bare hands and can prove fatal. Make sure you know how and where avalanches occur and also know what to do if you or somebody else is caught in one – you will have only seconds to act to determine your or somebody else's ultimate survival. Carry gloves, scarves, bobble hats and spare jumpers. A polybag (insulated 'sleeping-bag') is a good idea in case of injury.

Boots

A good pair of boots is a precondition to successful mountaineering. Shoes and trainers do not have the necessary grip, are not strong enough and are not waterproof when it comes to crossing mountain streams or bogs. Wellington boots do not have a good enough grip either. A pair of flexible, broken-in, well-fitting leather boots is essential. Buy a pair with some bend in them, but not too bendy so that a pair of flexible crampons can be fitted if desired. Fabric boots are rarely as waterproof or sturdy as leather boots. Rock shoes are out of the question unless you are a rock-climber and rigid plastic boots are far too uncomfortable unless you are planning on going ice climbing. Make sure your boots are well dubbed (carry a spare tin of dubbin) and most importantly of all make sure they fit and are broken in! All too often a pair of badly fitted boots ruins a walking holiday when they cause blisters. However, that said, carrying plasters and a blister kit is always a good idea since however well your boots may fit you, there is always a first time.

Rucksacks

Almost as important as boots is a rucksack, which is an essential walker's tool. It keeps equipment dry and should provide a safe and comfortable way of carrying it. However, several things can be wrong. Frame rucksacks cannot be recommended, as they are big, heavy and bulky and are easily wedged in tight, difficult situations. A mesh next to the back is a good idea. This allows air to circulate and helps stop the back from becoming too hot and sweaty. Chest and waist straps are also important to look out for. Although most rucksacks now have waist straps, they do not all have chest straps, which are very helpful in distributing weight and load. Outside pockets are another consideration. A good selection of pockets and hoops, which are easily accessible, is very important, as it is very awkward to store small things that are in frequent use in the main compartment where they fall to the bottom and become lost among larger, bulkier items.

Perhaps the best piece of advice is to buy what feels comfortable in the shop. If possible put some weight in it and walk around. If it is not comfortable in the shop, it certainly will not improve at 2,000ft. As for size, many walkers find between 25 and 30 litres adequate for day expeditions. However, I am always to be found with a 60-litre rucksack as I find it difficult to fit large bulky jackets and waterproofs into the smaller sizes along with my other equipment.

Whatever it may say on the label, very few rucksacks are actually waterproof and although sandwich bags will suffice for the outside pockets, a rucksack liner is a good investment for the main compartment since it saves wrapping up items individually.

Clothing

Clothing is certainly very much dependent on the time of year. Mountain clothing consists of three layers – (i) next-to-skin layer, (ii) insulating layer and (iii) outer shell.

1. **NEXT-TO-SKIN LAYER** This is very important and possibly the most critical of the three layers. Except in *very cold* weather, climbers will sweat quite a lot. The layer next to the skin must 'wick' this sweat away from the skin and also off itself and onto another outer layer. If a cotton garment is worn next to the skin, it will become waterlogged and damp, leaving the climber's back cold and clammy. Cotton is sometimes called 'death cloth' because of its notorious reputation for causing hypothermia.

   The best clothing to wear in this layer consists of 100 per cent polyester. Clothing such as this is quite expensive and is not easy to find in the high street but is available in many outdoor shops. However, as they wick well, they can be washed and dried quickly so you will not need many.

2. **INSULATING LAYER** The primary function of this layer is to keep the climber warm. Jumpers, sweatshirts and particularly climbing fleeces may be used. Even though you may feel cold to start with, it is a mistake to put too much on too soon. You will soon get hot when you start walking and will end up hot and sweaty and then unable to take any of it off. Instead, add it as you feel you need it. It is always necessary to keep one or two extra layers to put on when you have stopped for any length of time.

3. **OUTER SHELL** The function of this layer is to keep you dry – not warm. A breathable fabric, such as Goretex, is essential. It must keep the rain and wind outside but also let perspiration out. It need only be put on when the rain starts and must consist of waterproof trousers as well as a jacket with a hood. Remember, a weather forecast which

promises a fine day does not guard against heavy showers which are easily generated on apparently fine days in the mountains.

Ice-axes and how to use them

The situations in which ice-axes are needed are becoming increasingly rare in England but this trend may not be permanent. An ice-axe is used either to prevent a slide or to stop one once it has started. Everyone knows that ice is slippery on level surfaces and it is even worse on steep mountainsides. Hard snow is just as bad as ice in terms of its slipperiness. The chances of a successful self-arrest (stopping a slide) using an ice-axe is about 50 per cent; without an ice-axe this will be dramatically reduced.

There are two types of hand-held ice tools; ice-axes and ice-picks. Walkers will want an ice-axe of about 70 centimetres in length. Shorter tools are for use by ice climbers finding their sport on vertical ice faces where they need much more intimate contact.

As well as an axe, a wrist-leash will be required which, when tied to the axe and attached to your wrist, will prevent the axe from being lost during self-arrest.

Walkers will use the pick of their ice-axe very little, mainly using the spike and sometimes the adze but this again more rarely.

There are two methods of holding an ice-axe and techniques associated with them.

SELF-BELAY is used to prevent a fall from occurring in the first place. Hold the axe with the spike pointing down and place your palm on top of the adze. Put your thumb and index finger under the upper reaches of the pick and your other fingers under the adze. To operate self-belay, plunge the spike into the snow ahead of you and then step up to it, remove it, plunge it in again and so on. If you slip, grab the top of the shaft with your other hand and, providing that the snow is hard enough, the axe should hold you. If it does not, you will have to instantaneously change your grip to one suitable for self-arrest. Whilst it is possible to self-belay using the self-arrest grasp, it is uncomfortable.

SELF-ARREST is used to stop a fall once it has started. Assuming you are sliding feet first, on your back, grasp the bottom of the shaft with your left hand and place your right palm on the pick with your thumb and index finger underneath the adze and your other fingers under the pick (the opposite to self-belay). To self-arrest, fall to your right, *away from the shaft*, plunging the pick into the snow and getting your body pushing down on top of it. Push your feet (unless you are wearing crampons), knees and face down into the snow. Many self-arrests are not successful because people are too reluctant to get their faces down into the snow. If you are sliding head first, then you will need to dig the pick in as before and then be 'swung around' so that your head is uphill before digging in your feet, knees and face. Self-arrest is a difficult technique to learn so practise it beforehand because it could save your life.

The other purpose of an ice-axe to a walker is to cut steps on steep sections. Swing the adze down ahead of you to cut the steps, and then use self-belay whilst you climb up them before cutting some more. This method is very slow and difficult and if there are long steep sections then a pair of crampons will be a good investment.

Crampons and how to fit and use them

Crampons can be a great aid to a walker in hard snow and ice but are not a substitute for an ice-axe, merely an aid.

There are four types of crampon – ten-point crampons and twelve-point crampons and then each can be either flexible or rigid. Unless you have plastic boots and are an ice climber then forget rigid ones; for walking purposes flexible crampons are fine. Every crampon has ten points on the bottom and most also have an extra two points on the front giving twelve points in total, which are recommended because they are more versatile.

Before choosing crampons, you will need to be sure that your boots will fit crampons. Do not be fobbed off by being told that you have to buy a new pair of boots. If your boots are stiff enough, so that they do not bend in half, like a slipper, they will fit a pair of flexible crampons fairly well.

A flexible crampon does not have a firm frame underneath from toe to heel but instead has a movable joint in the middle which means that it will fit any size of boot. Rigid crampons fit particular boots and when you change your boots then you must also change your rigid crampons. Crampons attach to boots by a system of straps and this should be explained in the instructions otherwise a shop assistant will be able to demonstrate.

There are two ways of using crampons and which you use will depend to a large extent on how steep the ground is.

PIED PLAT (FLAT FOOTED) On ground, which is between 20° and 40°, 'pied plat' will definitely be used. Between 40° and 60°, pied plat is advised, but front pointing could also be used, but above 60° front pointing is essential. 'Flat footed' is exactly what pied plat is. All ten points on the base of the crampon should be firmly in the snow or ice with your boot touching the slope from toe to heel. This does put a strain upon the ankles but all ten points must be in the snow to gain satisfactory purchase and grip.

FRONT POINTING is a technique more commonly used by ice climbers but can be used over *short* distances by walkers with flexible crampons. Using this method, the two front points are plunged into the snow and that is all. This is more comfortable for the walker but it does put a terrible strain on the crampon, which, if used for too long, will break under the pressure. Front pointing can only be done using twelve-point crampons.

A final point to remember about crampons: in self-arrest do not jam your feet into the snow otherwise a point is likely to catch and catapult you up into the air.

The Dangers of Snow

AVALANCHES The risk of being caught in an avalanche is the single biggest danger to winter walkers. Avalanches occur on slopes between 25° and 60° but are most likely between 30° and 45°. Over the period of time in which the snowpack forms, several different snowfalls may occur and some of these may have existed on the surface long enough to become hard and consolidated. Also, the surface may have temporarily thawed and then refrozen forming another type of hard layer. Wind, of course, moves vast volumes of snow around and even when there has not been any fresh snowfall, a brisk breeze may have mimicked one by blowing snow over a ridge and forming a much softer layer which can then be consolidated itself.

When there is bad bonding between layers in the snowpack an avalanche can occur. What happens is the top layers simply slide off the bottom ones and the trigger for this is generally movement on the slopes: victims usually cause the avalanches in which they are trapped. It is wise to be prudent by evaluating the risk before crossing a slope of a gradient in the danger zone. Plunging a ski-pole or ice-axe shaft down into the snow will give you an idea of its strata and any hard layers to which the snow may be less well bonded.

CORNICES form when the wind blows snow up a slope and over a ridge. A lip of snow forms on the leeward side, which, although almost completely flat on top, is usually considerably undercut. Any reasonably sharp ridge can form a cornice and if there is a crag on the leeward side then it may pose a particular danger. The key is to assume that any ridge is likely to be corniced and not to risk walking too close to the edge. If this is unavoidable, however, the best thing is to probe the ground with a ski pole or ice-axe shaft before each step and if it breaks through, retreat immediately.

The key point about both avalanches and cornices is to understand the weather patterns in the days and weeks leading up to your walk and, if necessary, seek local knowledge before departure.

Geological Introduction

Much of what is written about the geology in the introductions to the individual regions in this guide is self-explanatory and any terms which may be unfamiliar to some readers are to be found in the glossary on page 275. However, some knowledge is assumed and that is explained here.

There are three types of rock: sedimentary, igneous and metamorphic. Sedimentary rocks form most of the mountain ranges of England and they are mainly formed from sediments on a sea floor, such as muds or the skeletons of dead sea creatures. These are then compacted by further sediment that is deposited above them and they turn into rock. Often the carcasses of sea creatures are muddled up in the mud rather than forming the rock totally or being crushed beyond recognition. These appear in cliffs and other exposures and are called fossils. The knowledge of where and when they lived allows geologists not only to date the rock but also to predict the conditions in which it was deposited. Limestones, shales and mudstones are all usually fossiliferous rocks that are formed on the sea floor.

However, sedimentary rocks do not only originate under the sea; some identical rocks are formed in inland lakes and lagoons. Others are formed on dry land or beaches. Sandstones and gritstones are examples of a rock formed on a beach. The process of compaction is the same as that under the sea but this rock will contain no marine fossils. Other sandstones are formed in deserts. Where plants grow profusely, such as in tropical swamps, their remnants collapse into wet ground and are not decomposed normally. Instead, they form peat, which is then compacted into coal, a fossil fuel.

Igneous rocks are lavas which may have erupted from a volcano or been forced under pressure into existing rocks; when this happens it is called an igneous intrusion. All igneous rocks begin as magma in the Earth's mantle, which is forced to the surface as a result of movements in the crust, often close to a tectonic plate boundary. The type of rock formed will depend not only on whether it formed above or below ground but also on its chemical composition. All igneous rocks are made up of crystals and contain no fossils. The size of the crystals is dependent upon the speed at which the rock cooled. If it erupted under the sea, it will have small crystals because the seawater cooled it rapidly, but if it intruded into other rocks and cooled underground it will have cooled much more slowly and larger crystals will have been able to form. Finally, if it erupted onto dry land, it will have medium-sized to small crystals. However, some igneous rocks with large crystals are now exposed at the surface in areas such as Dartmoor. Here, the rocks into which it intruded have since been worn away. Granite, gabbro, dolerite and basalt are all examples of igneous rocks.

Where an igneous rock came into contact with a sedimentary rock, the igneous rock baked the sedimentary rock, which was melted before crystallising out. This type of rock is known as metamorphic. Metamorphic rocks are also formed when other types of rock are subjected to intense pressure. Marble is the metamorphic version of limestone, while slates are the metamorphic version of shales.

Most of the sedimentary rocks that are seen today, however, were deposited in very different conditions to those in which they now sit. Coal, for example, was deposited in tropical swamps, limestone in tropical shelf-seas and on coral reefs and some sandstones in desert conditions. The reason for this is that Britain, hundreds of millions of years ago, lay just to the north of the equator. In fact, 270 million years ago, all the continents of the Earth formed one huge land mass known as Pangaea. They have since diverged due to the movement of the Earth's tectonic plates, which are subdivisions of the Earth's crust able to move independently; Britain lies on the Eurasian plate.

Since Britain moved to its current northern latitude, successive changes in temperature have caused the melting of ice in hotter periods and the spread of ice in colder periods; these cold periods are called ice ages. Britain in many ways leads a charmed life in its current position. Despite lying on the same latitude as the frozen wastes of Siberia (Russia) and Labrador (Canada), Britain experiences a much milder, temperate climate. This is due to a warm ocean current, known as the Mid Atlantic Drift, which, along with the Gulf Stream, brings tropical water northwards from the Bay of Mexico. It is, in fact, a convection current; warm, less dense water on the surface is drawn northwards from the Bay of Mexico to replace cooler, denser water which has sunk further to the north around the west coast of Britain and Ireland. This cold water is then, at depth, drawn back in the opposite direction to replace the warm water that moves northwards from the Gulf of Mexico. This process is the same as what happens in a room when a radiator or fan heater is turned on.

However, for this process to work, the water must be salty. If a large amount of fresh water enters the North Atlantic, for example from the bursting of a massive continental lake or much higher rainfall, the convection current ceases and the seas around north-western Europe suddenly become much colder. Contrary to historical opinion, this change does not necessarily happen over hundreds of years but in fact can take place in a lifetime.

As Britain is quite a small island, its climate is very dependent on the oceans surrounding it. As a larger amount of energy is required to heat water than ordinary soil, water retains its heat in winter and remains cool in summer (water has a higher specific heat capacity). This is why Britain can never experience the extremes of temperature that can be felt in places at the centre of large continents, such as Moscow, which has freezing winters and very hot summers. Therefore, while the sea is warmed by the Mid Atlantic Drift, Britain's climate is not only stable but warm as well. However, when the sea is not warmed, Britain's climate suddenly changes to one that is still stable but very cold.

These 'freak' events that release the amount of fresh water necessary to interrupt the Mid Atlantic Drift occur very infrequently but given the geological time-scale (mentioned below) these events have occurred several times in the past. The last ice age was known as the Dimlington Stadial, which lasted for about 10,000 years, and, together with a minor readvancement of the ice, the Loch Lomond Stadial, this period is referred to as the Ice Age. In fact, during the Middle Ages, between AD 1450 and AD 1850, with its peak about 1680 when 'frost fairs' were held in London on the frozen Thames, there was a cooling of the climate known as the Little Ice Age. This was caused by a reduction in the amount of water convected in the Mid Atlantic Drift due to the presence of a largish amount of fresh water in the North Atlantic, which, although not large enough to stop the convection current altogether, did weaken it sufficiently to cool Britain's climate severely. Despite this, however, Britain currently enjoys the climate of a warmer or interglacial period.

It is rather ironic that, with global warming, Britain may enter another ice age in the very near future. One of the effects of global warming will be an increase in rainfall over the North Atlantic (including Britain). This, coupled with the melting of the Arctic ice sheets, would introduce a huge amount of fresh water into the North Atlantic. Scientists disagree as to whether this will actually reach the critical quantity necessary to interrupt the Mid Atlantic Drift but what is generally agreed upon is that it will come very close. So whether Britain only enters another Little Ice Age or a full-blown ice age is disputed, but what is clear is that it is very

ERA	PERIOD		AGE (MILLIONS OF YEARS)	OVERVIEW OF THE FORMATION OF MOUNTAINS
	QUARTERNARY	HOLOCENE	0	THE ICE AGE ALTERS THE LAND-SCAPE INTO THAT SEEN TODAY.
		PLEISTOCENE	2	
TERTIARY (CENOZONIC)	NEOGENE	PLIOCENE	7	SUBSIDENCE OF THE NORTH SEA BASIN PUSHED UP THE WESTERN PENNINES AND THE TORS OF DARTMOOR WERE EXTENSIVELY WEATHERED.
(ALPINE MOVEMENTS)				
		MIOCENE	26	
	PALAEOGENE	OLIGOCENE	38	
		EOCENE	54	
		PALAEOCENE	64	
MESOZOIC	CRETACEOUS		136	FINAL DOMING OF THE LAKE DISTRICT.
	JURASSIC		190	
	TRIASSIC		225	SANDSTONES DEPOSITED OVER THE OTHER SEDIMENTS. TODAY THESE CAN BE SEEN ON THE CUMBRIAN COAST, THE ISLE OF MAN AND IN THE EDEN VALLEY. FURTHER FOLDING IN THE LAKE DISTRICT
	PERMIAN		280	
(ARMORICIAN MOVEMENTS)				
PALEZOIC				
(CALEDONIAN MOVEMENTS)				
	CARBONIFEROUS		345	LIMESTONES, SHALES, GRITS, SANDSTONES AND COALS DEPOSITED OVER THE ORDOVI-VIAN AND SILURIAN MOUNTAIN SYSTEM. IGNEOUS INSTRUSIONS UNDER DARTMOOR AND THE NORTH PENNINES.
	DEVONIAN		410	OLD RED SANDSTONES DEPOSITED IN BRECON BEACONS AND BLACK MOUTAINS. LARGE-SCALE INTRUSIONS OF GRANITE INTO ORCDOVIN AND SILURIAN MOUNTAIN SYSTEM AND EXTENSIVE FAULTING AND FOLDING DUE TO THE CALE-DONIAN EARTH MOVEMENTS.
	SILURIAN		440	BASEMENT ROCKS OF NORTHERN ENGLAND DEPOSITED IN A MOUNTAIN CHAIN THAT LINKED THE ISLE OF MAN AND NORTH-EAST ENGLAND. VOLCANIC ACTIVITY IN THE LAKE DISTRICT IN THE UPPER ORDOVICIAN PERIOD.
	ORDOVICIAN		530	
	CAMBRIAN		570	

likely that Britain's climate is going to become very much colder during the next few hundred years and possibly enter another major ice age soon.

The geological time-scale

When geologists talk of time, what they are talking of is time in relation to a geological scale, spanning 3,750 million years of the Earth's history. As such, what they may consider to be a short period of time may be 10,000 years and quite easily more.

Names are given to separate periods in the Earth's history, some of which have meaning; for example, Carboniferous means coal-forming. The table on the previous page shows those more recent periods that have affected the geology of Britain as seen today.

Section 1 – Dartmoor

That area of high ground in south-west England surrounded by lines drawn between the towns of Exeter, Okehampton and Plymouth and bounded to the south and east by the English Channel and Exe Estuaries.

NAME	HEIGHT	IN SECTION	IN ENGLAND	IN BRITAIN
High Willhays	621m/2,038ft	1 of 1	50 of 53	724 of 751

The northern part of Dartmoor forms the highest ground in southern England but there are several other moors in Devon and Cornwall, such as Bodmin Moor, which exhibit similar characteristics. Indeed, like

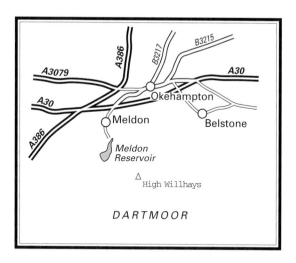

Dartmoor, much of the south-west has a volcanic origin; the rare Serpentine rock, a soft dark-green rock, which chemically is hydrated magnesium silicate, is found on the Lizard peninsula in Cornwall and is fashioned into decorative rock ornaments.

Dartmoor itself is basically part of a Carboniferous granitic intrusion, which stretches from here all the way to the Scilly Islands off the Cornish coast at Land's End. Being formed under the Earth's surface, it cooled more slowly and therefore has developed large crystals and a coarse texture. Since it was deposited, the overlying sedimentary deposits have been eroded and today the granite is covered by a thick coating of wet peat, except where it is exposed in tors.

However, mineralising solutions within the granite have deposited material around the edges of the moor. One of the main deposits was of the aluminosilicates of potassium, sodium and calcium, which form the mineral feldspar, characterised by its large, white crystals. This has since weathered into a fine powder known as kaolin or china clay, kaolinite $(Al_2(OH)_4Si_2O_5)$ being one of the main constituents. Deposits of china clay are to be found on the south-western edge of the moor as well as throughout Cornwall close to where the granitic intrusion has been exposed, particularly in the St Austell area, where they have been extensively mined.

The tors themselves have formed where the surrounding rock has been weathered away. As granite cools, cracks appear as a result of both horizontal and vertical shrinkage, which are collectively known as Pseudo-Joints. In the Tertiary period, rain collected in these cracks and wore away the rock into sand and gravel, which developed, between the tors where more resistant rock with fewer joints existed. The sand and gravel have since been washed away and the tors left isolated. However, a process known as exfoliation has also weathered the larger domes. This is where, in the desert conditions that existed in the Tertiary and Permian periods, the extreme heat by day caused the rock to expand while the extreme cold of night caused it to contract. After a while, the outer layers of rock began to flake, giving the rock an 'onion-skin' appearance. It then disintegrated into granite blocks, which can be seen today on the hill slopes and are known as clitter.

The tors were further weathered by the Ice Age. Although the glaciers did not reach this far south, the cold temperatures allowed a large amount of freeze-thaw weathering. As water collected in the smallest cracks, it expanded and, over time, pushed the rock apart. However, others maintain that the biggest single factor in the development of the tors was the warm Tertiary rainfall which disintegrated the bedrock to a depth of around 65ft (20m).

Access

Okehampton lies on the A30 dual carriageway, which connects Launceston, Bodmin and the rest of Cornwall with Exeter and the M5 to the east. Although there is a railway line to Okehampton, there are no regular passenger services, only goods trains *en route* to and from Meldon Quarry. However, at the time of writing, a private company is operating a Sunday service from Exeter St Davids (which can be reached by train from London Paddington and Bristol) to the old station in Okehampton. There are also bus services to and from Exeter.

Accommodation

There is plenty of accommodation in the towns and villages surrounding the moor, including Okehampton, Tavistock and Bovey Tracey. On the moor itself, the Two Bridges Hotel at Two Bridges and a number of bed and breakfast establishments in and around Widecombe-in-the-Moor offer accommodation. The popular holiday resorts of Torquay and Paignton and the conurbations of Exeter and Plymouth are not far away and offer all the customary services. There are youth hostels at Exeter, Maypool (near Torbay), Plymouth, Dartington, Bellever, Steps Bridge (near Dunsford) and Okehampton.

High Willhays

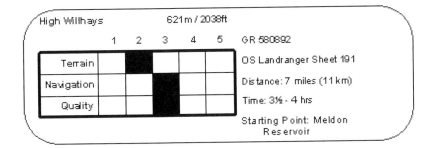

High Willhays and Yes Tor are the two highest points on Dartmoor. Situated near Okehampton, they can be climbed either from Okehampton Camp or Belstone, but by far the best approach is from Meldon Reservoir. The summits lie within the Okehampton military firing range, which, at the time of writing, is open to walkers every Saturday, Sunday and public holiday and other popular periods. However, walkers should telephone the Commandant of Dartmoor Rangers' telephone-answering service on (01837) 52939. Even though live firing may not be taking place, dry training could be in progress. This is training without live ammunitions. Simulations of battle noises take place and sentries may ask you to avoid certain areas of the moor.

To reach Meldon Reservoir, leave the A30 at Okehampton. For those approaching from the west, turn off the dual carriageway at the first Okehampton turn and bear right across the bridge. Those approaching from the east must turn off before Okehampton and go through the town since westbound traffic cannot leave at the junction previously recommended for eastbound traffic. Once through Meldon village, the car-park is signposted, although a left turn immediately after a railway bridge is easily missed.

Leave the car-park by the steps next to the toilet block. Cross straight over the road and go through a gate, signposted 'Sourton and the Moor'. After 50 yards, turn left on a grassy track, signposted 'Reservoir Walk'. This runs high above the reservoir to its head. After passing through a kissing-gate, turn left and after a short descent do not go down steps on

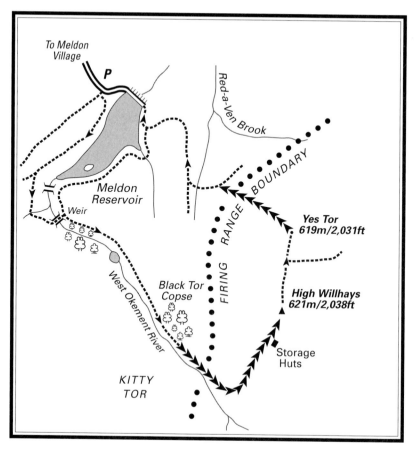

the left but keep straight on, signposted 'Reservoir Walk (Longer Route)'.

After passing round an acutely angled bend, descend to cross the river by a small weir slightly upstream. After crossing the grassy meadow straight ahead, turn right, following an ascending track running obliquely across the hillside. After a while, a small weir and walled enclosure is passed, beyond which lies a bog. The path and driest progress is to be found near the riverbank.

Shortly, the path enters the trees of Black Tor Copse. This is a National Nature Reserve because it is a rare example of high altitude oak woodland. Another example can be found north of Two Bridges, named Wistman's Wood. It takes about one hour to here. Continue through the wood, then through the open, then through the wood again to emerge near a line of red and white poles running across the valley marking the boundary of the firing range. A hundred yards or so further upstream, a stunted, multi-branched tree will be found on the opposite bank. From here, ascend up a small path, unclear at a distance, running up the hillside, through bracken, between bands of rocks to emerge within site of the flagpole at Fordsland Ledge. On closer inspection, two storage sheds will also be found.

After Fordsland Ledge, aim for the nearest rocky knoll (the right-hand one); there are traces of a vague path. Once at the rock knoll, the objective will be seen a few yards further, with a large white cairn.

When finished here, continue along a clear track to the slightly lower summit of Yes Tor. To survey the route onwards, cross to the west summit and locate the flagpole on Longstone Hill (302º). An easy route to the track running across Longstone Hill can be found on a bearing of 276º. Depending on exactly where you walk, you may find another track before crossing the intervening stream, which can either be followed to the left, or a beeline can be made to meet the main track on Longstone Hill. Turn right, and follow it down to the footpath by the reservoir at which point a right turn leads back to the dam, on the other side of which is the car-park.

Section 2 – The Black Mountains

That part of the county of Hereford and Worcester on the union border between England and Wales.

NAME	HEIGHT	IN SECTION	IN ENGLAND	IN BRITAIN
Black Mountain	703m/2,306ft	1 of 1	32 of 53	581 of 751

The Black Mountains and the Brecon Beacons form one massif, the highest point of which, Pen y Fan, rises to 2,906ft (886m). Although mostly in Wales, the current union border runs along the furthest eastern south–north running ridge of the Black Mountains. The summit named Black Mountain therefore lies in both England and Wales, although the range as a whole should be considered as entirely Welsh.

The range is the only one in Britain constructed entirely from Devonian Old Red Sandstone. It forms a huge upland plateau, deeply incised by valleys, which exhibit some fine sandstone crags in the Pen y Fan area. Steep escarpments are particularly prominent in the east where they are less broken by corries, known in Welsh as cwms. It has resisted erosion due to horizontal layers of tough, pebbly Lower Old Red Sandstones, separated by layers of flaggy mudstones and horizontal grits. These layers can be seen on many of the scarp slopes, which rise steeply for up to 2,620ft (800m). The exact type of rock deposited depended upon the environmental characteristics at that time, the sandstones being deposited in semi-arid conditions, whereas the mudstones were deposited in beds in wetter times.

The Carboniferous period saw some subsidence of the region causing the sandstones to be covered in a warm, shallow sea. This saw the deposition of limestones and then, as the area became a beach, rocks of the Millstone Grit Facies (grits, shales and sandstones). Most of this covering has since been eroded but the highest summits still have a capping of limestone, covered by a protective layer of Millstone Grit.

However, south of the range where a syncline has developed, all the rocks deposited above the sandstone can be seen where they disappear

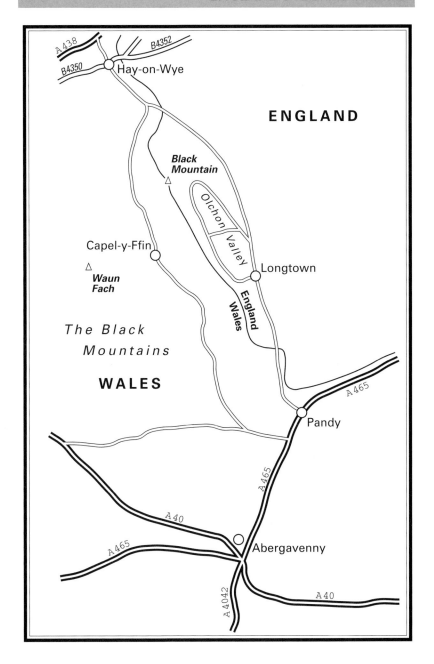

below the surface and then where they reappear. From the syncline, it can be seen that above the Old Red Sandstones, several layers of Carboniferous rocks were deposited. First, as already mentioned, were the Carboniferous limestones and the rocks of the Millstone Grit Facies, but they were followed by coal measures, the Pennant Sandstone and more coal. The coal was deposited in tropical swamps that obviously existed in this region during the Carboniferous period. It was by virtue of this syncline that the South Wales coal industry developed, for had the syncline not existed then the coals here would have long since been eroded, like those which lay above the sandstone elsewhere. The Old Red Sandstone reappears to the south in the small hills of the Vale of Glamorgan and in many of the hills, such as Cefn Bryn, of the Gower peninsula as well as underlying most of Herefordshire.

At the end of the Carboniferous period, when the seas had retreated, a vast plateau existed; subsequent erosion stripped it of its highest rocks but the final formation of this most dramatic of landscapes would not be until the Ice Age. Ice separated the range from its surroundings and formed the Usk Valley, essentially splitting the range into two, the Brecon Beacons lying to the west and the Black Mountains to the east. However, there are large differences between the eastern and western ends of the range and this also was due to the Ice Age. Current rainfall is highest at the western end of the range and, in the Ice Age, snowfall was higher here also, which, when compacted into ice, scooped out the cwms which indent the smooth escarpments that are so prominent at the eastern end of the range. However, they did allow the development of the fine sandstone crags mentioned above on the headwalls of the cwms. However, as the sandstone is less prominent in the west, the range here has been named the Black Mountains, a name derived from their covering of dark heather and bilberries rather than the red sandstone rock from which they are constructed. One other praised characteristic of the Black Mountains are the monolithic hills which stand on its fringes, examples being Mynydd Troed, the Sugar Loaf above Abergavenny and Ysgyryd Fawr.

Access

There is a good road network in the region, based largely upon the A40 and M4. From the west, the best route lies down the A40 from Fishguard and Carmarthen as far as Brecon. From the south, the M4 crosses the River Severn on the recently constructed Second Severn Crossing just to the north of Avonmouth and obligatory return tolls are payable when travelling into Wales, though it is free when returning to England. From northern England, the M50 leaves the M5 at Junction 8 and then joins the A40 which should be followed as far as Abergavenny or Brecon. From North Wales, the A470 runs from Llandudno all the way down to Brecon before continuing onwards to Cardiff.

There are no rail services to the northern side of the hills but the southern towns are well served. There are frequent daily local services from Cardiff Central to both Merthyr Tydfil and Rhymney. There are also trains from Liverpool Lime Street and Manchester Piccadilly, calling at Stockport, Crewe, Shrewsbury, Hereford and Abergavenny before continuing to Cardiff Central. Services to Wales from London Paddington, calling at Reading and Bristol Parkway, call or terminate at Cardiff Central. There are also fast services from London Paddington to Hereford, calling at Oxford, although it may be necessary to change at Great Malvern onto a service from Birmingham New Street, especially at weekends. There are buses from Hereford to Hay-on-Wye, from Merthyr Tydfill to Brecon and from Newport and Abergavenny to Brecon.

Accommodation

Accommodation is sparse in the old mining towns of Merthyr Tydfill and Abergavenny in the south but it is plentiful in the north in the towns of Hay-on-Wye and Brecon and in farmhouses nearby. The best base for both the Brecon Beacons and the Black Mountains would be Brecon, although those only interested in the Black Mountain itself could do worse than to stay in either Hay-on-Wye or one of the small farmhouse bed and breakfast establishments in the Olchon Valley around Longtown. There are youth hostels at Ystradfellte, in the upper Neath Valley; at Llanddeusant, in the west of the Brecon Beacons; at Llwyn-y-Celyn, near Brecon, at the foot of Pen y Fan; at Ty'n-y-Caeau, near Brecon and at Capel-y-Ffin in the Black Mountains.

Black Mountain

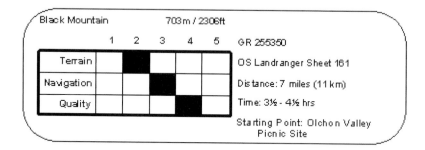

Black Mountain						703m / 2306ft
	1	2	3	4	5	GR 255350
Terrain		■				OS Landranger Sheet 161
Navigation			■			Distance: 7 miles (11 km)
Quality				■		Time: 3½ - 4½ hrs
						Starting Point: Olchon Valley Picnic Site

King Offa of Mercia realised the strategic importance of the long, steep-sided ridge forming the eastern extremity of the Black Mountains when he built his famous dyke in the eighth century. The ridge rises almost vertically from the lush valley pastures of England and commands good views in all directions. Although the highest point on the ridge is not named on Ordnance Survey maps and the summit unadorned by either a cairn or a trig point, it makes a worthwhile excursion, best completed from the Olchon Valley.

Park at the picnic site at GR 288328 at the end of a dead-end road, easily reached from Longtown along narrow lanes, where there is room for about five or six cars. Begin by walking back down to the valley loop road and turn left. After about a hundred yards or so, a footpath, signposted, drops downhill into a hazel coppice on the right. Beyond, it leads down to Blackhill Farm through the woods, entering the farmyard through a gate. It leaves through a stile at the very bottom (ignore a gate on the left) and then continues down, waymarked, to cross the river on a footbridge.

On the other side, the path is again well waymarked and continues up to the loop road on the other side of the valley. Follow the road to the left, shortly turning right up another tarmac lane. Just after a left-hand bend, a footpath runs back to the right, soon crossing a stile and then running up an old green lane. Ignore a stile on the right after about a quarter of a mile; instead, continue up the green lane until a fence bars progress. Here, a stile on the right marks the continuing route and

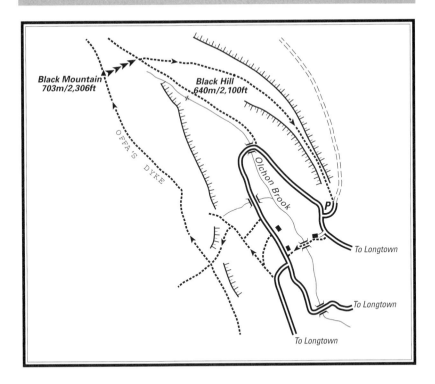

beyond, the path runs along the headland of a first field before continuing along another green lane along the bottom of a second field.

Before long, access onto the open, bracken-covered hillside is gained by crossing a gate acting as a stile on the left. The path then runs to the right before striking off up through the tall bracken, making a rising traverse of the fellside to meet another track ascending straight up from the road further along. This track bends to follow the line of the existing route before hairpinning back to the left and this should be followed in preference to the small path ahead. After passing some sandstone craglets and running high above a sizeable spring, the path gains the ridge and meets the Offa's Dyke Path at a marker stone.

Turn right along the distinct and worn path (shortly to be paved) passing over a subsidiary knoll before starting the long, slow ascent up to the summit. When it levels off, there are two high points about three hundred yards apart, both traversed by the path and both apparently of equal height; the first is actually the higher of the two, although there is nothing on the ground to show it. However, continue onto the second and then leave the path on a bearing of 92° descending down to the head of the valley where a path will be picked up running from left to right after crossing some areas of extensive denudation.

When found, follow the path to the right and up onto the shoulder on the eastern side of the valley, ignoring a less distinct path that descends down into the valley itself. Beyond the trig point on Black Hill, the ridge narrows in spectacular fashion, making a fitting end to the walk. There are no problems and the best route lies along the crest itself, although at a few points there is a traverse path on the eastern side. Eventually, the crest ends and the ridge drops steeply down to the picnic site and car-park.

Section 3 – The Peak District

That area of the Pennines south of the Huddersfield Narrow Canal, linking Huddersfield and Manchester through Marsden, and to the north of a line drawn between Stoke-on-Trent and Derby.

NAME	HEIGHT	IN SECTION	IN ENGLAND	IN BRITAIN
Kinder Scout	636m/2,088ft	1 of 1	49 of 53	706 of 751

The Peak District forms the southernmost block of the Pennines. From the south, the lowlands of the Midlands abruptly end and the landscape rises up onto an elevated limestone plateau, known as the White Peak, before turning into a higher and much darker, typically Pennine, moorland landscape, known as the Dark Peak. The Peak District was the first British National Park and is the most popular, lying within easy reach of the industrial towns of South Yorkshire and the Manchester area and also because it supports a wide variety of landscapes and leisure activities.

The Peak District rock formations are very similar to those in the rest of the Pennines (Sections 4, 8 and 9). In the lower Carboniferous period, the land here was covered by a warm, shallow shelf-sea in which many tiny organisms thrived. Their dead bodies sunk to the sea floor and have built up and been compressed to form the limestone rock of the White Peak. Coral reefs also developed and these reef limestones form most of the small hills which exist on the limestone plateau, notable examples being Chrome Hill in Upper Dovedale to the south of Buxton and Thorpe Cloud at the southern entrance to the main part of Dovedale, its famous limestone gorge.

However, rivers from a landmass situated far to the north (where Scotland is now) were discharging into this sea and forming a large delta. This encroached upon the sea and different rocks began to be deposited, namely shales and sandstones. Shales were formed from the mud, which appeared first, and then, as deltaic conditions became more firmly established, sandstones accumulated from beach sediments. On

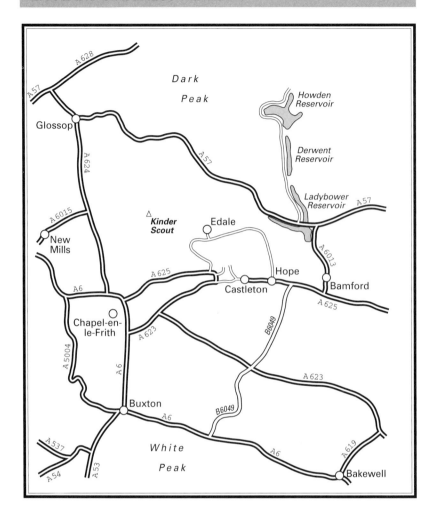

occasions, lagoons formed and tropical swamps existed, the plant remains being compressed into coal. However, due to subsidence and the lateral movement of delta channels, shales and sometimes even limestones began to be deposited once more, and then the sandstones again. This process occurred several times and led to the cyclical succession of rocks that is found today. These cyclical sequences, or cyclothems, are known here as the Mam Tor Beds, although they are similar to the Yoredale Beds, discussed in Section 8.

By the upper Carboniferous period, deltaic conditions had become firmly established and, due to a gradual uplift of northern Scotland, coarser material was being brought down and deposited, namely rocks of the Millstone Grit Facies (grits, shales and sandstones). Finally coal formed from swamps that covered the whole area. Much of the coal and Millstone Grit has since been worn away but the Millstone Grit is well seen in the north as a protective capping on hills, such as Kinder Scout, where it forms gritstone edges. To shape the rocks into those that are seen today, a folding of the Carboniferous sediments took place. This is attributed to the intrusion of a granite mass at depth which had the effect of uplifting the White Peak area into a dome about 10,000ft (3,050m) high. Erosion has since removed the higher layers to leave the limestone exposed on the surface. Around the edges of the limestone, steeply angled rocks of the Mam Tor Beds and Millstone Grit Facies are to be found, although they do level off in the north. This has given rise to the surround of shales and sandstones which enclose the White Peak; these can be seen at Lud's Church (a large fissure formed by land slippage) and the gritstones seen in The Roaches, a popular climbing area; both are to be found on the southern side of the Dane Valley, to the south of Buxton.

Hot mineralising solutions originating from the molten granite rose into cracks (tension faults) in the limestone, depositing their minerals there, such as galena (lead ore), in veins. This has given rise to the mining activity in the White Peak. The individual minerals found are discussed in more detail in Section 9. However, one of the minerals deposited, fluorspar (calcium fluoride – CaF_2), has been coloured by natural oils into a banded blue, purple and white gemstone, known as Blue John. This expensive stone is found only in one other place in the world and its unusual name is thought to derive from the French, bleu-jaune (blue-yellow). The story is that miners working at Castleton sent a sample to the French who were, at that time, the leading authority on gemstones. Baffled, the French, who had never seen anything like it before, named it blue-yellow from its appearance. Very small samples of the rock can be bought in the Castleton area for a reasonable price and larger ornaments for much larger prices. Exposures of the rock can be seen in the Blue John Cavern and Treak Cliff Cavern, both at Castleton.

Unlike further north, the Ice Age had little effect this far south, so the massive limestone scars of the Yorkshire Dales (Section 4) are not replicated. Most of the erosion hereabout was done entirely by water. Limestone is weakened by vertical joints and horizontal bedding planes that allow rainwater to percolate into it. As rainwater is a weak form of carbonic acid, derived from carbon dioxide in the atmosphere, it reacts with the limestone, slowly wearing it away. This has given rise to huge cave systems in the Castleton area, including three show caves – Peak Cavern, Treak Cliff Cavern and Speedwell Cavern. Speedwell is truthfully a mine but the workings did break through into a cave system and visitors are taken to it by boat along an underground canal. Other small holes can be found in many places but Thor's Cave, near Weeton, above the Manifold Valley, is another notable example that can be visited by foot free of charge.

Limestone dales also formed as rivers excavated huge gorges into the limestone, although some, such as Cave Dale at Castleton, are in fact large caves where the roof has collapsed. Several such dales exist including Monsal Dale and the Manifold Valley, although Dovedale is probably the most famous. A visit to Dovedale is recommended to all visitors to the district. It is possible to park near Ilam at the foot of the dale and walk up past the dominating Tissington Spires as far as Milldale before returning. Walkers should look out for the following: (i) a natural arch, known as Reynold's Arch high up on the east side of the gorge (it is possible to walk up to and through the arch and enter a short cave behind it) and (ii) a number of cave entrances on the east bank near the mouth of Hall Dale (the only sizeable valley between Ilam and Milldale which enters on the western side).

Due to the permeability of limestone and despite its verdant appearance, the White Peak is very dry. Water has always been available in wells, which gave rise to the tradition of well-dressing in villages such as Tissington but, as time progressed, it became necessary to pump water up from valleys, such as Dovedale. As such, an old pumping station can be seen in Dovedale between Ilam and Dove Holes that originally served the village of Tissington.

Access

From the north and west, it is best to approach the region from the M6 around Manchester's motorway ring from which the A6 runs south-east to Buxton. From the north-east, an approach by the M1 and then through Sheffield onto the A625 to Castleton would be best. From the south, the A515 runs from Lichfield, just up the A38 from Birmingham, and continues all the way through Ashbourne to Buxton. The road network in the Castleton vicinity is quite complicated. The A625, which formally linked Chapel-en-le-Frith and Sheffield, has been blocked below Mam Tor by an extensive landslide and has not been reconstructed for fear of further earth movement. A small, narrow and steep road has been constructed up the narrow, spectacular gorge of Winnats Pass. This, apart from a longer route via Edale, provides the only way out of the valley above Castleton.

The Peak is also well served by rail services. There are regular daily trains between Buxton and Manchester Piccadilly and Bolton although, on occasions, it may be necessary to change at Stockport. The line between Sheffield and Manchester Piccadilly (some trains continue to Liverpool Lime Street) has regular daily services and stations at Hathersage, Bamford, Hope, Edale and Chinley (near Chapel-en-le-Frith), although only local trains stop there. There are also regular services between Manchester Piccadilly and Glossop and Hadfield (not Sundays). There are bus services between Buxton, Castleton and Sheffield and from Buxton into most parts of the White Peak. On Friday evenings, between four and eight, all trains at Edale station are met by a courtesy bus from Edale Youth Hostel for those wishing to stay there.

Accommodation

The best base for both the White and Dark Peaks would be Buxton and accommodation of all types is plentiful here. If Kinder Scout only or just the Dark Peak are the sole objectives, then Castleton or Edale may be a better location. However, it should be said that apart from a campsite and a couple of bed and breakfast houses, accommodation is scarce in Edale and the same has to be said about Castleton, although some accommodation may be found away from the main street. In the White Peak, youth hostels are located at Ilam Hall, Meerbrook (near Leek), Gradbach Mill (near Flash), Buxton, Ravenstor (near Miller's Dale), Bakewell, Youlgreave, Matlock, Shining Cliff (near Ambergate), Elton and Hartington. There are youth hostels in, or appropriate for, the Dark Peak at Edale, Castleton, Hathersage, Eyam and Bretton, although Buxton and Ravenstor (near Miller's Dale), which are firmly in the White Peak, would also be good bases.

Kinder Scout

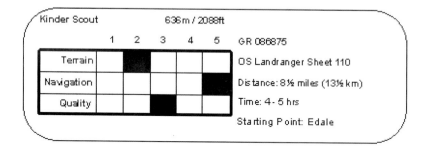

Kinder Scout			636m / 2088ft			
	1	2	3	4	5	GR 086875
Terrain		■				OS Landranger Sheet 110
Navigation					■	Distance: 8½ miles (13½ km)
Quality			■			Time: 4 - 5 hrs
						Starting Point: Edale

Kinder Scout is the only separate summit in Derbyshire and is certainly a very interesting mountain with steep slopes and a flat and wet summit plateau, drained by countless steams. The easily accessible trig point on Kinder Low is not actually the true top, which is to be found in one of the wildest parts of the bog. Also here, there is a population of mountain hares on the summit, which stand out well against the black peat when they are dressed in their white winter coat. This walk must be done on a clear day when the pathless route over the bog can be surveyed in advance (a compass is of little help), and certainly not in reverse because to find the route from Kinder Low to the real top is impossible except to someone with an intimate knowledge of the area.

Begin by parking in the car-park at Edale by the station. After paying and displaying, leave by the steps near the toilet block and walk up the road to the right until the village pub is reached, which is also the official start of the Pennine Way. Instead of walking left on the Pennine Way, go straight up a track, which soon leads to a pair of white gates. Here, follow a narrow path slanting right (signposted Grindsbrook) which crosses the beck and runs through the fields on the other side of the gill with a paved surface, eventually gaining access to the open hill after passing through a wood.

The path then climbs on the right-hand side of the clough, eventually coming very close to the stream (almost into it) as the clough narrows in its upper reaches. Eventually, near the top, there is a confluence. The main stream comes in from the right but the path climbs up the shorter, steeper gill coming down straight ahead. Towards the top, quit the gill for

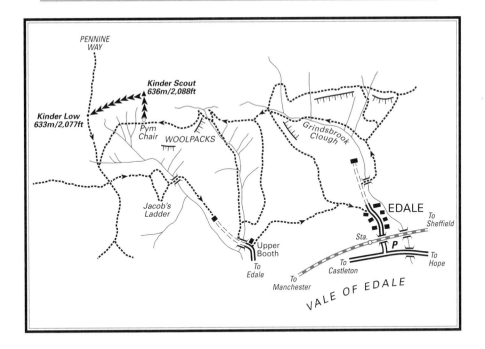

the rocks on the left. On arriving on the summit plateau, a large cairn will be found a few yards to the right.

From the cairn, continue ahead on the same bearing as the gill, following its headwaters. A reasonable path runs by the stream where it has eroded the peat down to the bedrock. Care should be taken at the first fork in the stream to keep left and from here until the head of the stream the route is cairned. When the stream ends, bear half left and a wide, distinct track will be found running from left to right. Turn right on the track and, after a short dip, where a stream will be crossed, climb up again to reach the remarkable 'woolpacks' of Millstone Grit (note that at the stream crossing, a path does run slightly left on the level, but this should be ignored).

When at the final woolpack, known as Pym Chair, stop to survey the ground ahead. Ignore the path and look half right to some flat slabs of Millstone Grit, which are the next destination. Therefore, leaving the path, cross the peat half right, which involves crossing three deepish peat 'gullies'. Luckily, however, the peat is not as wet as it might seem. At the slabs, again stop and look half right (therefore at right angles from the original path) and a cairn and stake will be seen in the bog. Continue onwards to this point. This cairn is the actual summit as the trigonometric point away to the left, which looks higher, is actually 10ft (3m) lower.

From the cairn, the trig point on Kinder Low is the next objective and the bog is not actually as fearsome as it may seem. The rocks, on which the trig point is built, are the only dry pieces of ground around, apart from the woolpacks. Leave Kinder Low going due south on the Pennine Way until the low point is reached where there is a crosspaths. Here go left and follow Jacob's Ladder down into the valley and down to the buildings at Lee Farm. From here follow the drive down to the head of the public road where there is a telephone box. Opposite the telephone box, turn left (signposted 'Edale'). The path rises quite steeply on grass over a small hill then falls away onto a paved section before descending by a stream back to the pub in Edale, from where the car-park is only a short distance away to the right.

Section 4 – South Yorkshire Dales

That part of the Yorkshire Dales bounded by the Rivers Ouse and Ure from Cawood to Garsdale Head, the Clough River and then the River Lune to Kirkby Lonsdale, the A65 from there to Ilkley and then the River Wharfe to Cawood.

NAME	HEIGHT	IN SECTION	IN ENGLAND	IN BRITAIN
Whernside	736m/2,416ft	1 of 10	24 of 53	508 of 751
Ingleborough	724m 2,376ft	2 of 10	26 of 53	537 of 751
Great Whernside	704m/2,309ft	3 of 10	31 of 53	580 of 751
Buckden Pike	702m/2,302ft	4 of 10	33 of 53	588 of 751
Pen-y-ghent	694m/2,278ft	5 of 10	34 of 53	602 of 751
Great Coum	687m/2,255ft	6 of 10	36 of 53	616 of 751
Great Knoutberry Hill	672m/2,205ft	7 of 10	40 of 53	644 of 751
Dodd Fell Hill	668m 2,192ft	8 of 10	42 of 53	653 of 751
Fountains Fell	668m/2,191ft	9 of 10	43 of 53	654 of 751
Potts Moor	610m/2,001ft	10 of 10	53 of 53	750 of 751

When most people think of the Yorkshire Dales, the visions they have are largely contained within the boundaries of this section. The Three Peaks, Ingleborough, Whernside and Pen-y-ghent, dominate the landscape around Ingleton and Ribblesdale, while to the east lie Malham and the long limestone valley of Upper Wharfedale. The rocks that are seen here were mainly formed in the Carboniferous period, about 345 million years ago, and are sedimentary in nature, limestone being the most evident but also grits, shales and sandstones.

However, these carboniferous rocks are laid down on a base of older Ordovician and Silurian sediments. These are unseen within the mountains themselves but are shown on the southern edges – in Ribblesdale, from Horton-in-Ribblesdale to the Stainforth area, and in Crummackdale (Austwick). The join is shown quite clearly by the resurgences of Austwick Beck Head and, at Horton-in-Ribblesdale,

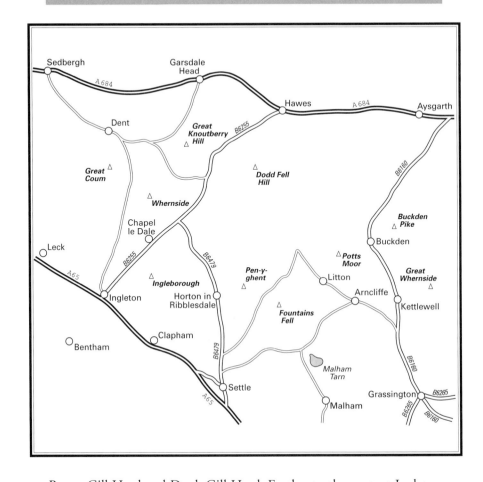

Brants Gill Head and Douk Gill Head. Further to the west, at Ingleton, the rocks are exposed once more at the top tiers of its famous waterfalls and in the Doe Valley above. The oldest deposits are the Ingleton Group (lower Ordovician in age), which consists of greywacke (fine to coarse sandy particles cemented together by clay) and highly slanting slates. A small fault, specific to the Ingleton area, then thrust down a calcareous mudstone of the Coniston Limestone Group (see Section 5), formed in the late Ordovician period and eroded elsewhere before the Carboniferous rocks were deposited. The rocks formed in the late Ordovician and Silurian period are present in Ribblesdale and Crummackdale. All these pre-Carboniferous rocks were formed as part of a huge mountain system stretching from the north-east of England to the Isle of Man and sizeable exposures can be seen both on the Isle of Man and in the Lake District. In total, these rocks are about 2,500ft (760m) thick.

An intrusion of granite at depth then pushed up the Ordovician and Silurian deposits, with cracking at the edges, to form a block of elevated land, higher than the Craven Lowlands to the south. The southern boundary is marked by the Mid-Craven Fault and the western boundary by the Dent Fault. The block underlying Sections 4 and 8 is known as the Askrigg Block, named after the village in Wensleydale. Due to the elevation of the land, it escaped the early deposition of the Lower Carboniferous period but as the warm, tropical sea encroached further, the block was submerged. As such, the shales and reef limestones of the Clitheroe region are absent here, deposition only beginning in the Arundian period or cycle three of the Dinantian (Lower Carboniferous) era. In total, there were six cycles of the Lower Carboniferous period with different rocks or beds being deposited in each. The Great Scar Limestones were deposited in cycles three, four and five, therefore, the mid to late part of the Dinantian era. The limestones hereabout are extremely pure, about 98 per cent calcium carbonate, which gives them a very white colour, which contrasts with the deeper yellow colour of the limestones in places such as the Cotswolds. Although limestone is a fossiliferous rock, there are few fossils visible to the naked eye in the area. There are, however, bands of shale amongst the limestone that, although rarely seen on the surface, do give rise to the Aysgarth Falls in Wensleydale (see Section 8) and can be seen in pothole shafts.

However, the warm shallow shelf sea in which the limestone was deposited was not to last. A river delta encroached from the north bringing about completely different conditions, which led to the deposition of different rocks. These are known as the Yoredale Beds, named after Wensleydale ('Uredale'). They are discussed in more detail in Section 8 where they are more prominent but it is sufficient to say that the beds consist of a cyclical succession of limestone, shales, siltstones, sandstones and thin coal seams. The type of rock deposited depended upon the conditions at the time; for example, the limestones were deposited in a shallow shelf sea whereas the coal was deposited in the tropical swamps that existed on the delta top. It is these coal seams that have given rise to the mining activity to the north of the South Craven Fault (a line between roughly Ingleton and Settle, following approximately the course of the A65). Examples include the shafts and bell-pits of Fountains Fell and the bell-pits on Great Knoutberry Hill.

However, in the Upper Carboniferous period, deltaic conditions were firmly established and rocks of the Millstone Grit Facies (grits, shales and sandstones) were deposited and above that the Coal Measures. Most of this thick coating (and all of the Coal Measures) has since been worn away but all of the main summits (particularly those, such as Dodd Fell Hill, further to the north) have a protective capping of Millstone Grit, as seen in the summit crags of Ingleborough. However, it is the southern end of Pen-y-ghent that displays the succession best. When viewed from Horton-in-Ribblesdale or Fountains Fell, two 'steps' in the ridge can be seen. The summit plateau itself is constructed of rocks of the Millstone Grit Facies whereas the drop itself shows some of the upper cyclothems of the Yoredale Beds (see Section 8). The top of each step is protected by a covering of more resistant rock (Millstone Grit at the top and shale in the middle), below which the limestone wears away readily. Two limestones of the Yoredale Beds can be seen. Below the middle step, there is an exposure of the Middle Limestone whereas below the top step there is an exposure of the Main Limestone (see Section 8). Other small bands of limestone are present but all cease at the foot of the steps as that point marks the upper boundary of the Great Scar Limestone Group. This contrasts with Section 8 where there are lower beds of the Yoredale Series in place of some of the Great Scar Limestones.

Therefore, at the end of the Carboniferous period, all the rocks that form the landscape that is seen today had been deposited. However, it would have been completely unrecognisable as there were several massive upheavals yet to come. It all stems from the subsidence of the North Sea basin. This caused the western Pennines to rise and also caused considerable activity along the Pennine boundary faults. This uplift caused the strata of all the rock beds to sink to the north-east and rise to the south-west. This partly explains why the Great Scar Limestones, which are so prominent around Malham and Ingleborough, appear only very low down in Wensleydale, to the east of Aysgarth, at levels less than 600ft (180m) in direct contrast to the southern end of Ingleborough where there are Great Scar Limestones as high as 1,450ft (440m).

This uplift caused massive upheavals along the unstable southern boundary of the Askrigg Block as well as along the Dent Fault to the west. At the Dent Fault, the rocks to the west were uplifted to a level much higher than that of the Dales; however, subsequent erosion has removed the Carboniferous rocks from their summits (see also Section 8). As such, the rocks lying to the west of Ireby and Barbondale have a much older origin than the Carboniferous sediments deposited to the east. Although Calf Top (the hill to the west of Barbondale) is often thought of as a part of the Dales, it is an intruder geologically.

At Bullpot Farm (GR 663814), the two series of rocks are thrown into a convenient juxtaposition. To the west of the farm lies Barbon Low Fell, a wet and boggy environment, but by the farm itself there is a series of shake holes, pot-holes and swallow holes forming a part of the vast Aygill and Easegill Caverns, the largest cave system in Britain. The line of the fault can be clearly seen between Lower Easegill Kirk (seen on the Great Coum route), where the subterranean waters of the Easegill and Leck Fell systems are forced into daylight, and Bullpot Farm. Here, on and to the east of the straight line between the Kirk and the farm, there is a series of limestone features that are not replicated on the western side; this line marks the fault. Again, by following the straight line into Barbondale, shake holes and pot-holes abound to its east, eventually all the way across the valley, but to the west there is nothing.

However, whereas there was an uplift along the Dent Fault, there was a massive down thrust along the Craven Faults to the south. The Mid Craven Fault is responsible for the formation of the fault scarps of Malham Cove and Gordale Scar and it is the oldest of the three Craven Faults. The coating of Upper Carboniferous rocks, Grassington Grits and Bowland Shales, which cover it, shows this. At Ingleton and Malham, erosion has exposed the pre-Carboniferous basement rocks above the line of faulting. These rocks are shown in Thornton Force (Twiss Valley, Ingleton) and in the existence of Malham Tarn, which would not otherwise exist upon a limestone upland. However, to the south of this at Swilla Glen (Twiss Valley) and Malham Cove/Gordale Scar (Malham), the limestones of the Great Scar group reappear.

This is due to the North Craven Fault which runs parallel to the west bank of the River Twiss at the head of Swilla Glen where it turns from north to north-west to the south of Pecca Quarry and, at Malham, where the outflow from Malham Tarn sinks underground. In Wharfedale too it is present in Linton Falls and also in Catrigg Force (Ribblesdale). However, it is the South Craven Fault that finally buries the limestone. This follows roughly the line of the A65 and is prominent in features such as Giggleswick Scar, just to the west of Settle. Again, a massive down thrust occurred here and, at Ingleton, the line of the fault lies at the foot of Swilla Glen (River Twiss) and the southern edge of Storrs Common.

To the south of the fault lie the only remnants of the Upper Carboniferous Coal Measures which once overlay the Millstone Grit Facies over the whole of the area. Here, the same strata which exists on the summit of Ingleborough, 1,970ft (600m) higher, lies buried hundreds of feet underground. The fault is still unstable; the epicentre of a 1944 earth-tremor in Settle was found to lie on the South Craven Fault.

Much of the characteristic Dales limestone scenery has been caused by erosion. Although limestone itself is a non-porous rock due to its crystalline character, vertical joints break it as well as horizontal planes. This means that vertical erosion can weather the rock into the clints and grikes of limestone pavements and that potholes can form, but also that lateral erosion can form caves with their bases along the horizontal planes. Of course, it is erosion that has removed the Upper Carboniferous rocks to expose the Great Scar Limestone below from which the characteristic dry limestone walls can be constructed. The lime-rich soils give rise to verdant green pastures, even though the soil is quite dry, and the woodlands of ash and other lime-loving trees, particularly prevalent in Littondale and Wharfedale. However, in the valley bottom of Wharfedale, oak woods have developed on the heavier, more acidic soils relating to the older basement rocks above which the limestone has been completely worn away.

The Ice Age also changed the landscape, carving out many of the valleys seen today. The limestone scars along valley sides were also formed as a result of freeze-thaw weathering which was commonplace in the arctic conditions surrounding the main period of glaciation. This is where rainwater collects in a crack and then freezes. As water freezes, it expands which pushes the crack further apart until the rock shatters, ending up as scree and leaving a scar or small cliff face behind. However, as the glaciers retreated they left behind a coating of pebbles and soil, which is commonly known as boulder clay or glacial drift. In many valleys, this was deposited very thickly and completely covers the rock below.

The Three Peaks Walk

This section would be incomplete without some mention of the marathon walk which links the ascent of all three peaks, Whernside, Pen-y-ghent and Ingleborough, into a single day's walk. It is tough and difficult but not impossible and below is a description of the route. The description is not as detailed as others in the book as it is not really a recommended route but the description is good enough to be followed on the ground. There are three main reasons why it is not as good as the ascent of the three mountains individually: the caves, potholes and resurgences of Chapel le Dale are not seen; the fine limestone scenery of

Ingleborough Cave, Trow Gill and Gaping Gill are not seen; and whichever mountain is left until last (or in some cases second last as well) will not be fully appreciated due to aching limbs. However, as an additional route or a challenge, it is highly recommended.

There are two decisions to be made before starting, namely, where to begin and in which direction to do it. The two normal starting points are the Hill Inn at Chapel le Dale or Horton-in-Ribblesdale but the direction of the walk and the start/finish point are closely intertwined. The worst part of the walk is the long drag between Pen-y-ghent and Whernside, which is therefore best done early in the day. If starting from the Hill Inn, it will therefore be necessary to ascend Whernside first or, if starting at Horton-in-Ribblesdale, Pen-y-ghent. The problem with starting from the Hill Inn up Whernside is the very steep start from Bruntscar, which takes the steam out of most people and may well make the difference between completion or failure. Therefore, it is recommended that the start be made from Horton-in-Ribblesdale to ascend Pen-y-ghent first.

There are a number of different opinions as to the exact route and the one described here avoids the tarmac for the most part and aims to be as interesting as possible. However, at some points, where there is a difference of opinion, what is in my opinion the best route is described but the 'direct' alternatives are described in the footnotes, rejoining the described route where the text is marked * and **. The whole route is covered by map sheet 98. Its gradings are: terrain 2, navigation 3 (navigation 1 following the footnotes), quality 3 (quality 2 following the footnotes). In total the walk is 39 km (24½ miles) in length (38 km (23½ miles) by 'direct' alternatives) and involves 5,624ft (1,714m) of ascent (5,558ft (1,694m) by 'direct' alternatives). Allow 13–15½ hrs (12½–15½ hrs by 'direct' alternatives). This effectively rules out the walk on short winter days and do not be tempted to try because walking over limestone country in the dark can be extremely dangerous, especially so if the path is lost.

Start at the National Parks pay and display car-park in Horton-in-Ribblesdale and follow the route of ascent of Pen-y-ghent (see page 80) to its summit. From the summit, cross the ladder stile on the left and follow the path ahead which runs along the edge of and then obliquely across the escarpment, before running down to a stile. Before the next stile is reached, Hunt Pot will be found on the left. There is not too much to see other than a deep black slit but it is well worth a visit. Once over the next stile, walk down to the bottom of the small valley and turn right.

In about two hundred yards, Hull Pot will be found quite suddenly and unexpectedly.

Unlike Hunt Pot, Hull Pot is a huge amphitheatre 60ft (20m) deep with a fine waterfall at the back over which the water falls in wet weather before running across the floor and disappearing. The best view can be obtained from the left-hand side. In dry weather, the water sinks into the streambed a little further upstream. Follow a track on the left-hand side of the pot up the valley until a path, crossing the beck on a set of stepping stones, is met which should be followed to the left. It traverses Black Dub Moss before crossing a track, the Pennine Way, and then continuing onwards to meet a track coming in on the right at the top of a slightly wooded valley containing Birkwith Cave (a stile lower down the wall gives interested walkers access).

Keep straight ahead down the track, crossing straight over the farm road between High Birkwith and Old Ing, to join another track in the far corner of the field. It continues onwards, over God's Bridge, to Nether Lodge.[2] Go through the buildings and onto the farm road but, rather than following it to the left, keep straight on along a small path, waymarked by yellow-topped stakes. Go over a stile and then slightly left over Crutchin Gill to a barn, a right turn at which, along the far side of the wall, leads in time to Black Hools Barn.

Turn left beyond the barn and follow the wall until it turns away to the right, at which point strike off across the field on the same line to a small traditional packhorse bridge over the small limestone gorge of Thorns Gill, beyond which the wall should be followed all the way to the road. From here, take off direct for the right-hand end of the Ribblehead Viaduct. The country now crossed is pierced by pots and caves, some of which, unless you are desperately unlucky, will inevitably be seen.

Keen enthusiasts will probably wish to know that the pots are set a discreet distance back from the edge of the small scar and the caves at its base. At the right-hand end of the viaduct, a track will be found, which, if followed to the right, leads up to the signal box at Blea Head, at which point the route up Whernside (see page 67) should be joined. Follow that route up to and over the summit of Whernside and then down to Bruntscar. Here, instead of turning right, keep straight ahead along a lane to the Hill Inn, a good stop for sustenance before tackling the final stretch over Ingleborough.

A path, signposted to Great Douk Cave, leaves the main road a short distance above the Hill Inn and then crosses three stiles. After the third, turn left up to the small crater in which lies Great Douk Cave and on the moor just beyond it, Little Douk Pot. The path leads on past a pair of caves at Middle Washfold, to reach a wall running up the slope. Follow the path on the near side of it all the way to the top of the escarpment. Here, a right turn leads along the top of the scarp before finally climbing up onto the summit plateau of Ingleborough. By maintaining the line that has been followed, the triangulation point and shelter will soon be reached.

To begin the final descent, return to the western end of the summit plateau, following a line of cairns, and then follow the ascent track, which drops sharply before forking. Take the right-hand fork, which crosses Simon Fell Breast, before crossing two walls on ladder stiles. After the second wall crossing, where the track forks, a signpost points down the left fork to Horton-in-Ribblesdale. The route continues onwards through an area of limestone pavements where it crosses another track. It eventually drops down into the inbye and runs below Beecroft Hall, to cross the railway in the vicinity of the station, before meeting the main road just beyond. Keep straight ahead along the main road, crossing the Ribble, and then following it sharply around to the right over another bridge (Brants Gill), to reach the car-park on the right.

---

[1]   When the track turns sharply left at the foot of the escarpment, follow a track half-left which continues to cross the Hull Pot Beck above the pot on a set of stepping stones (awkward in wet weather).

[2]   Go through the buildings and onto the farm road, following it around to the left, across the Ribble and through the buildings at Lodge Hall to reach the road. Turn right and plod up the tarmac to the Ingleton to Hawes road. Straight ahead, a track leads along the near side of the viaduct and then up by the railway line to the signal box at Blea Head, at which point the route up Whernside (see page 67) should be joined.

Access

The area is easily accessed from the east via Skipton (A59 from York; A650 and A629 from Bradford) and the Lake District along the A65. From the south, leave the M6 at junction 31 and follow the A59 through Clitheroe, turning up to Settle on the A682 at Gisburn. Hawes is best reached from the A1 along the A684 from Leeming Bar and from junction 37 of the M6 along the A684 through Sedbergh.

There are also good rail connections; there are stations at Gargrave (about 10 miles south of Malham), Giggleswick, Clapham and Bentham (about 5 miles south of Ingleton) on the Leeds to Lancaster and Morecambe line and on the Settle to Carlisle line at Settle, Horton in Ribblesdale, Ribblehead, Dent (about 8 miles from the village) and Garsdale (about 7 miles from Hawes) – trains depart Carlisle and Leeds. At the time of writing, both lines have a Monday to Sunday service. A Sunday special between Preston (sometimes Blackpool North) and Carlisle runs along the Settle–Carlisle route from Hellifield northwards and then returns. It is possible to connect with this service from Manchester Victoria by changing at Clitheroe.

Accommodation

Towns such as Hawes, Settle, Ingleton and Skipton all offer a wide variety of accommodation as do many of the villages, such as Dent and Kettlewell. Perhaps the best base would be somewhere around Settle or Ingleton as all parts of the area are easily reached from there. Sedbergh would also be quite good for the fells to the west and around Dentdale as well as being a good location for the fells in Section 8. There are Youth Hostels at Malham (Airedale), Stainforth (Ribblesdale), Hawes and Aysgarth (Wensleydale), Kettlewell and Linton (Wharfedale), Ingleton and Upper Dentdale.

Whernside

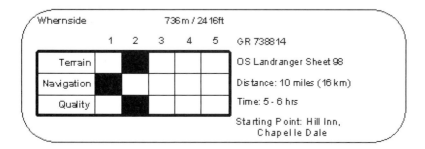

Whernside			738m / 2416ft			
	1	2	3	4	5	GR 738814
Terrain		■				OS Landranger Sheet 98
Navigation	■					Distance: 10 miles (16 km)
Quality		■				Time: 5 - 6 hrs
						Starting Point: Hill Inn, Chapel le Dale

The highest of the three peaks and the highest in Section 4, Whernside rises steeply on all sides, being prominent in the view from Chapel le Dale, Ribblehead and Dentdale. The most interesting circuit is from Chapel le Dale and this is the route described here.

Park in the Hill Inn car-park (for the sum of twenty pence) just north of the hamlet of Chapel le Dale on the Ingleton–Hawes road. A few yards to the south, on the main road, a small side lane takes off across the fields to a snack bar at Philpin. Soon, the road bends sharply to the left and begins rising slightly; at this point, turn right (signposted 'Bridleway') along a sunken lane (actually the dry riverbed). After leaving the streambed through a gate on the left, another gate is passed through to arrive at a large rocky depression on the right that is marked very prominently on Ordnance Survey maps. By climbing down into this small pot-hole, the stream will be seen emerging from a cave and then sinking innocuously into the boulder floor.

However, continuing onwards, pass through another gate and after crossing the dry streambed, the path begins to rise. Look to the left at this point and the stream will be seen to sink into its bed. After passing through another gate, the path joins another small tarmac lane. Keen explorers at this point may wish to visit the resurgence at Gatekirk. To do this, walk to the left down to the dry streambed and, after negotiating the stock barrier, follow the stream down until it becomes wet. To the right, in amongst trees, there is another cave with much more water coming out, which is, in many ways, similar to that seen earlier. Return to the

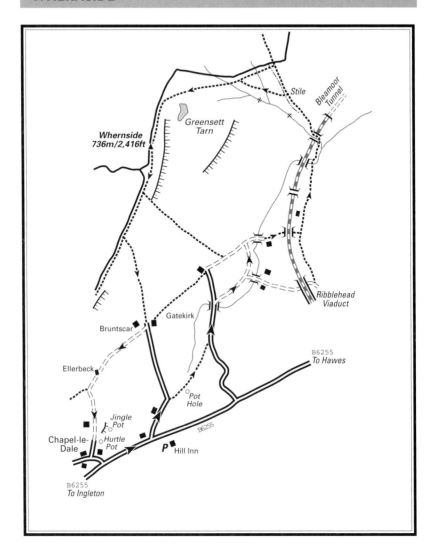

road, turn left and follow it up until it crosses the dry streambed.

A few yards further on, pass through a gate on the right and follow another tarmac lane across the fields, passing some farm buildings on the right, until it ends at a bridleway. Here turn right and, after passing Winterscales Farm, cross a bridge and walk up, through a gate, onto the moor to reach a tunnel underneath the Settle to Carlisle line. Turn left and follow a much-improved path (the Three Peaks Route) past Blea Head Signal Box and up the Blue Clay Ridge to cross the railway on a conjoint bridge/aqueduct close to the mouth of Bleamoor Tunnel. Ignoring a right-hand fork, follow the path past the fine waterfall on the left in Force Gill and up the side of a fence. Cross the fence at a stile (signposted 'Whernside') and continue on the path all the way to the summit, set above the pretty blue waters of Greensett Tarn.

After visiting the trig point on the other side of the wall (access provided), descend the southern ridge until after two sharp descents, the main path turns left downhill. Until now, the standard of footpath restoration has been very good, indeed a model example; here this ends, as the restoration changes to badly placed cobbles and stones.

After crossing a ladder stile, the path leads down to a gate at Bruntscar. Turn right here, instead of going straight ahead directly to the Hill Inn. Follow this path through the hamlet and the next farmyard at Ellerbeck, beyond which a tarmac road leads down to the left through some interesting limestone pavement formations. Following this lane, it leads past the pretty cottage at Gill Head before reaching the mighty hole of Hurtle Pot on the left. Walk down the nearside and at the bottom of the slope, a path, with some rough steps and a helping rope, leads down the steep, muddy slope to the pool of water at the bottom in a fantastic surrounding which cannot be fully appreciated from the top. However, the temperature difference between the top and the bottom is very noticeable, so an extra layer would not be a bad idea!

By following the dry streambed up to the left, another massive hole appears under a cliff on the left. This is Jingle Pot, and, although not massively deep, cannot be descended without a rope; indeed all that can be seen is a slope running down into a hole beneath the viewing platform. Return to the road and walk down into the hamlet of Chapel le Dale, passing the Methodist Chapel on the left. Turn left at the T-junction and walk out onto the main road, a left turn on which leads back up to the Hill Inn.

Ingleborough

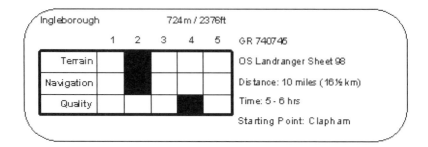

Ingleborough			724m / 2376ft			
	1	2	3	4	5	GR 740745
Terrain		■				OS Landranger Sheet 98
Navigation		■				Distance: 10 miles (16½ km)
Quality				■		Time: 5 - 6 hrs
						Starting Point: Clapham

Ingleborough is perhaps the most striking of the Three Peaks with its easily distinguishable flat top, which was the biggest Iron Age hill fort in the Pennines and, today, is managed by English Heritage as an ancient monument, although there is little for the untrained eye to see.

Park in Clapham village, either in the National Park pay-and-display car-park, or on the lane just outside for free if there is room. The car-park is signposted from the old road through the village, which now forms a loop off the A65 bypass. Walk up the road and cross the stream almost immediately on a small bridge on the left, continuing up the road on the other bank until it swings to the left, at which point a brown sign points walkers to the right to Ingleborough Cave into what looks like a work-yard. It is here that the grounds of Ingleborough Hall are entered for which a small sum is payable; currently forty pence for adults and twenty pence for children, payable to a machine which issues a ticket.

If you object to paying the money, the alternative is to follow the road a little further on and then follow the right of way up a track to Clapdale Farm on the hillside before dropping back down into the valley, on a path, beyond the grounds of Ingleborough Hall. However, assuming the route through the grounds is followed, after a hairpin bend, the track runs alongside the lake, which was constructed by the Farrer family, who owned the Hall, in 1833. Beyond the lake, the track climbs to bypass some waterfalls and then emerges from the wood and the estate grounds to meet the public right of way descending from Clapdale Farm. A short distance further up the valley, on the left, is Ingleborough Showcave.

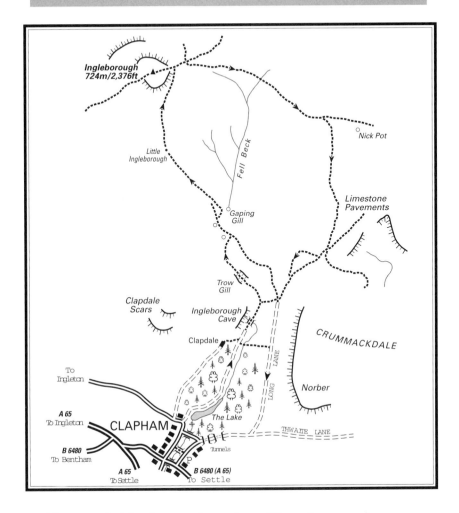

The tour inside the cave lasts about fifty minutes and costs two pounds for children and four pounds for adults; there are concessions also for senior citizens. Allow about half an hour for the walk from Clapham to the cave and tours depart on the hour from ten in the morning until late afternoon. The tour is very interesting and well worth while for anyone with an interest in geology. The cave itself was first discovered in 1837 when the entrance was enlarged and several lakes behind drained.

Continuing up the valley, a small bridge is crossed almost immediately over the beck, which emerges from a cave on the left-hand side. This water originally flowed through Ingleborough Cave until the water level dropped and formed the cave through which it now runs. It is here that the streams that sink into the moor in and around Gaping Gill emerge once more into daylight.

Following the valley up, the track soon curves around to the left and enters the massive gorge of Trow Gill, formed by melt water at the end of the last ice age. The gorge narrows to a small neck at its head and the path ascends through this up a boulder ruckle. The dry valley continues at the top becoming increasingly shallow until the path leaves it to the left over a pair of ladder stiles. It now continues around the base of a small hill on the right and then forks. Take the right-hand fork, which runs across the moor towards a fenced area and notice-board. This is Gaping Gill. A notice-board at the far side describes the journey of a raindrop from Ingleborough's summit to Clapham, although somewhat inaccurately as it does infer that the water actually flows down through the showcave itself.

The notice-board errs a little on the cautious side by stating that the presence of an experienced person is essential to pass this point, although with a shaft 340ft (110m) deep, perhaps that is no bad thing. However, providing that you are reasonably careful, there is no reason why the descent should not be made into the shake hole and then to the edge of the pot, the best view being gained where, rather unnervingly, a small piece has fallen away.

What can be seen is quite magnificent, a trail of water and spray falling into the blackness, but if any readers are feeling over-ambitious in looking into the hole, it is worth remembering that, however far you lean, only about a seventh of the distance to the boulder floor below will ever be seen. Indeed, it makes the journey of the French potholer E.A. Martel to that boulder floor even more remarkable when it is considered that in the summer of 1895, all he had was a very long rope ladder and a field telephone to communicate with his helpers at ground level.

Today, cavers descend the shaft in three pitches, a short one to begin with to a small ledge and then another two beyond to reach the bottom. It is possible for the general public to follow Martel's journey to the foot of the shaft by petrol winch on special dates, available from the local tourist information centres. On these dates, one of the major potholing clubs sets up a winch and, for a fee, currently about seven pounds, the public are winched down individually, harnessed into a chair. It is thoroughly recommended for all who are interested in geology and who enjoy visiting showcaves and it is certainly worth the money.

A pair of waterproofs is recommended as although the stream has been diverted it can still be quite damp and those who are scared of heights will be pleased to know that it is very difficult to look vertically downwards from the chair. The chamber below is the largest in Britain, large enough to contain York Minster or St Paul's Cathedral, and supports a spectacular waterfall, even when the stream has been diverted away from the main shaft.

However, cross the beck away from the shaft and follow a path onwards which joins with the direct route to climb all the way to the summit of Little Ingleborough ahead. A fairly flat ridge then follows before the final ascent is made across Ingleborough's face to the western end of the summit plateau. A walk half left leads to the summit cairn, triangulation point and wind shelter.

To begin the descent, return to the western end of the summit plateau, following a line of cairns, and then follow a track, which descends steeply before forking. Take the right-hand fork, which crosses Simon Fell Breast before crossing two walls on ladder stiles. After the second wall crossing, where the track forks and a signpost points down the left fork to Horton-in-Ribblesdale, follow the right fork which crosses over the limestone pavements hereabouts to reach a staggered crosstracks. Turn right and soon the green track forks. Follow the right fork which contours around the slopes of the hill ahead before crossing a ladder stile into a field and then another into a lane. Shortly, a further ladder stile is seen on the right-hand wall.

Some readers may wish to cross this and make the short descent into the valley below to rejoin the route of ascent at the foot of Trow Gill. Otherwise, continue along the aptly named Long Lane, which follows almost an exact straight line for over a mile, before bending to the right and ascending to meet the Austwick to Clapham bridle road. Follow this downhill to the right, through some tunnels under the grounds of Ingleborough Hall (the first one is long enough almost to require the use of a torch), to reach the church and tarmac road at Clapham. Turn left in front of the church and follow this road the short distance back to the car.

Great Whernside

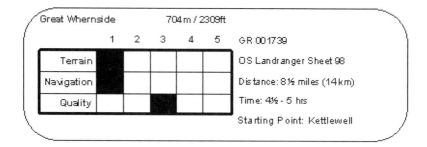

Great Whernside is the highest point of the Wharfedale–Nidderdale watershed. The nearest village is Kettlewell in Wharfedale and indeed an approach from the Nidderdale side is dull and impracticable. An interesting variation of the normal route via Hag Dike is one that involves a visit to Providence Pot and this is described here.

Park in the free car-park in Kettlewell, by the main bridge over the Wharfe. Begin by walking to the left on the road to the top of the car-park and turn right (off the main road) onto a minor road signposted to the church. Shortly, the village square is reached; here turn left until the road turns left again and crosses the river. Instead of crossing the bridge, walk straight ahead and follow this lane until it comes to cross the river as well. Turn right here and follow a track signposted to 'Hag Dike' and 'Providence Pot'. Shortly, this crosses a small tributary and, immediately across it, before a gate, turns right up the water's edge as far as the next gate. Once through the gate, turn right and follow a clear path up the left-hand side of the narrowing valley past various springs issuing from small sources by the path. When at the head of the valley, a 'manhole cover' will be found in the middle of the stream with a small hole in it. This is Providence Pot and under the cover is a ladder descending into the blackness.

Turn sharply back left, taking another path climbing out of the valley and then making a gently rising traverse to the house at Hag Dike. Here, turn right and climb up the short, steep slope to a multitude of cairns, from where various paths lead on, eventually coming together at the foot of the final steep climb to the summit. A triangulation pillar and large cairn grace the summit.

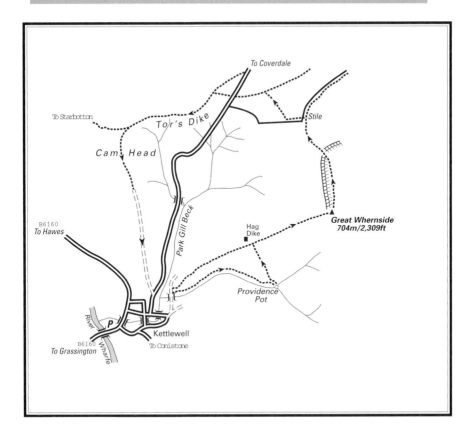

From here, follow a track running parallel to the edge of the small crag to the left. This continues before starting to descend shortly after a pair of hollow cairns. Continue the descent until a wall is found coming up from the left and turning along the ridge. Here, turn left over a stile and descend on the far side of the wall before turning to the right by a stile on the left. Now a steep descent begins in many short, steep gullies before running out into a bog. The path continues to a gate in a wall. Go through here and follow the path half right to the road by a signpost.

While at this point it is possible to follow the road left to Kettlewell, it is much more pleasing to continue around the head of the valley. Directly ahead is a private track and 100 yards along it a triangular enclosure. This is the point that will be reached by legally following the road 500 yards to the right and then following a bridlepath 400 yards back to the left.

From the triangular enclosure, continue on the bridleway, which passes through a gate and contours along the earthwork of Tor's Dike before dropping back down to the wall and through another gate. Continue straight on for 100 yards until a path runs left at a signposted junction. Follow this path, signposted 'Kettlewell', until after about 2 miles it comes down to the road above the village. Follow this road down to the Post Office, where a left turn brings you back to the church, square, toilets and car-park.

Buckden Pike

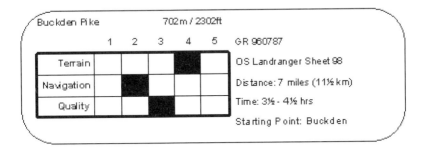

Buckden Pike — 702m / 2302ft

	1	2	3	4	5
Terrain				■	
Navigation		■			
Quality			■		

GR 960787
OS Landranger Sheet 98
Distance: 7 miles (11½ km)
Time: 3½ - 4½ hrs
Starting Point: Buckden

Buckden Pike is almost a twin to Great Whernside and this ascent is very similar to that of Great Whernside via Providence Pot. Many guidebooks of the area pass little reference to Buckden Beck – the stream descending the prominent steep-sided valley behind the village – perhaps due to the slippery nature of the rocks after rain and the fact that some minor scrambling is involved. However, as the route is far more interesting in my opinion than that via Rakes Wood, the Buckden Beck route is described here.

If you do not wish to ascend to the lead mine by Buckden Beck, leave the car-park by the gate at the opposite end from the toilet block and ascend the track (signposted to 'Buckden Pike') and turn right after about half a mile up a track which leads eventually to Buckden lead mine (add 1 mile (1½km) and add between 20 and 25 minutes).

However, if limestone scars, waterfalls and deep valleys are appealing, leave the car-park by the same gate mentioned above and then, almost immediately, turn right (signposted 'Buckden Lead Mine'). Follow a faint path in the grass over a stile and down to the beck by the water treatment works. Now, turn left and skirt the buildings, following a small track above the beck and past Buckden's water intake. Ahead is the first obstacle, a fine 30ft cascade. The track climbs up the scree on the left in good time to a holly bush on the limestone scar.

Despite the scar's intimidating appearance, an 'easy' gully lies hidden behind the bush, running back up the face, and this is the most difficult section of the ascent. The track keeps above the beck in a small copse, climbing to the foot of the next scar. At its base again another hidden

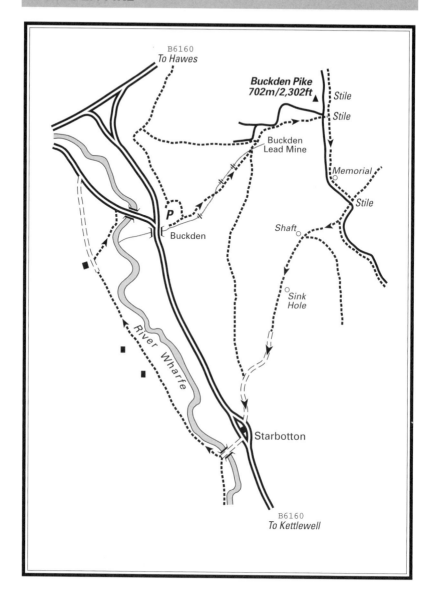

easy gully, under an overhanging ash tree, avoids the obstacle. The path running straight on, from the foot of the scar, continues to the foot of another waterfall and is not an alternative ascent route. Once above the scar, however, the track runs back along its very edge to the head of the third waterfall. This is muddy and slippery after rain, which renders this section dangerous in such conditions.

Now the track crosses to the right-hand side of the beck and continues to the next (fourth) waterfall. Here, there is no large scar on the right bank, only grass with a little rock near to the top. Above the small fifth waterfall, ignore a track running left across the beck and continue straight on over a stile and up the spoil tip to the mine.

After exploring the derelict mine buildings and looking at the level from the outside, follow the wall left at the foot of the mine workings and almost immediately follow another wall running up the hill to the right. After 20 yards, the path leaves the wall and runs back, above the workings and all the way up to the gate in the summit wall. Turn left and follow the wall a short distance to a ladder stile over which the summit is only yards away.

After visiting the summit, return to the gate in the summit wall. However, instead of crossing back over it, continue straight on along the wallside to a memorial cross commemorating five Polish airmen who were killed here when their plane crashed in January 1942. The fox's head on the base of the cross represents the fact that the only survivor reached the valley by following the tracks of a fox in the snow. Continue by the wall side and, after a short descent, go through a gate in the wall on the right. Continue on by another wall and shortly pass through another gate.

The path now passes a small enclosure on the right and starts the main descent through a wet area, down to a wall at the head of the valley, shortly after passing a mine shaft, immediately by the path, covered partly by timber beams. The path continues through an area of shake holes with a small sink on the left, before turning into a track and passing through a number of gates and stiles as it drops down to Starbotton.

When the track reaches a small tarmac road at the back of Starbotton, turn left and cross a stream on a bridge. Once over the bridge, ignore a road on the right and go straight on over a small crossroads following the road round to the right just after the old schoolhouse. When a T-junction is reached, turn left to reach the main road over which a walled track, signposted to 'Buckden' and 'Kettlewell', leads down to and crosses the Wharfe on a footbridge. Here, turn right and follow the obvious and well-signposted path/track up the valley to Buckden Bridge (also the Dales Way). Here turn right and walk up towards the village, taking a small track on the left-hand edge of the green, which leads to the main road only a few yards to the south of the car-park entrance.

Pen-y-ghent

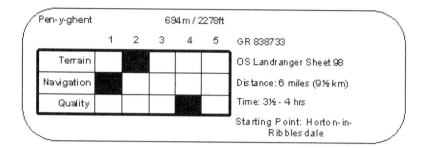

Pen-y-ghent						694m / 2278ft
	1	2	3	4	5	GR 838733
Terrain		■				OS Landranger Sheet 98
Navigation	■					Distance: 6 miles (9½ km)
Quality				■		Time: 3½ - 4 hrs
						Starting Point: Horton-in-Ribblesdale

Pen-y-ghent has a dominating appearance when viewed from Horton-in-Ribblesdale and demands attention. While Ingleborough may be higher, it is scarred by quarries and hidden by distance. A very pleasant circular walk can be made from Horton-in-Ribblesdale in either direction but is best in the direction described because it keeps the dominating south end of Pen-y-ghent in view.

Begin from the National Park car-park in Horton-in-Ribblesdale (pay and display; toilets). Walk to the right down the road towards Settle until the wall of the churchyard is found on the left. Go through a gate and across a field by a narrow tarmac path and through another two gates to gain access to a small lane. Here, turn left, before turning right over a small bridge. Turn left again once over this and walk past the school (at weekends, it may be possible to park here for free), continuing up the road to the farm at Brackenbottoms. Here, a path (signposted 'Pen-y-ghent Summit') climbs up the hill, crossing a number of stiles and climbing a succession of small limestone scars. When the final stile has been crossed and the ridge and Pennine Way have been reached, turn left and begin the steep pull up onto the summit plateau. The clear, well-defined path, which is steep and rocky, leads directly to the triangulation point on the summit.

Cross the ladder stile on the left and follow the path ahead which runs along the edge of and then obliquely across the escarpment before running down to a stile. Before the next stile is reached, Hunt Pot will be found on the left. There is not too much to see other than a deep black slit but it is well worth a visit. Once over the next stile, walk down to the

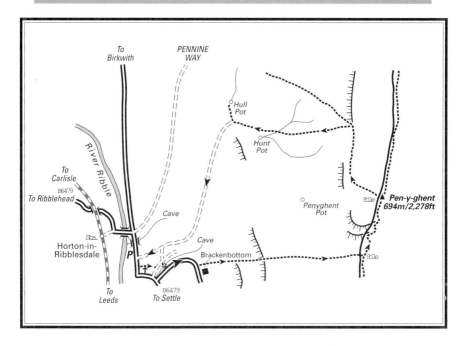

bottom of the small valley and turn right. In about two hundred yards, Hull Pot will be found quite suddenly and unexpectedly. Unlike Hunt Pot, Hull Pot is a huge amphitheatre 60ft (20m) deep with a fine waterfall at the back over which the water falls in wet weather before running across the floor and disappearing. The best view can be obtained from the left-hand side. In dry weather, the water sinks into the streambed a little further upstream.

Return to the track, and follow it down to Horton-in-Ribblesdale. When the road is reached, opposite a café, the car-park is only a short distance to the right.

Great Coum

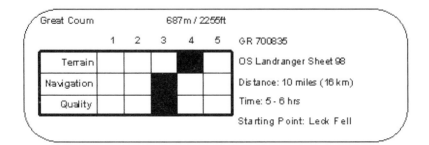

	1	2	3	4	5	
Terrain				■		OS Landranger Sheet 98
Navigation			■			Distance: 10 miles (16 km)
Quality			■			Time: 5 - 6 hrs

Great Coum 687m / 2255ft
GR 700835
Starting Point: Leck Fell

To the west of Whernside, a large block of ground rises around the head of Easegill, of which Great Coum is the highest point. The best route of ascent is from the Easegill side, making a circuit around the head of the valley before finishing by exploring the fine limestone formations and potholes in the valley itself.

Above the village of Leck, a single-track, dead-end road rises up to Leck Fell House and there is an area suitable for parking just before the road passes out onto the open moor. Although there is parking further up, the return is made to this point so there is nothing in it and parking here avoids a walk up the hard tarmac at the end of the day.

Start off, therefore, by continuing on up the road, passing through a gate on the right into a green lane when the road descends slightly to the house itself. The three men of Gragareth, the origin of which, like the Nine Standards of Nine Standards Rigg (Section 8), is unknown, can be seen above, and, in about 20 yards, a line up the steep hillside should be taken, thereby avoiding the worst of the rocky areas. Beyond the three men, the gradient eases and the hill becomes bleaker and damper, but continue on straight up the slope, perhaps finding some evidence of an intermittent path, to reach the trig point and the highest point in the county of Lancashire.

A much more distinct path leaves the trig point running north-east to meet the summit wall, then crossing it on a ladder stile. However, stay on the nearside of the wall and cross a conventional stile over a fence that descends into Easegill. The wallside is somewhat boggy in places but stepping stones by the wall help as the slow descent along the ridge

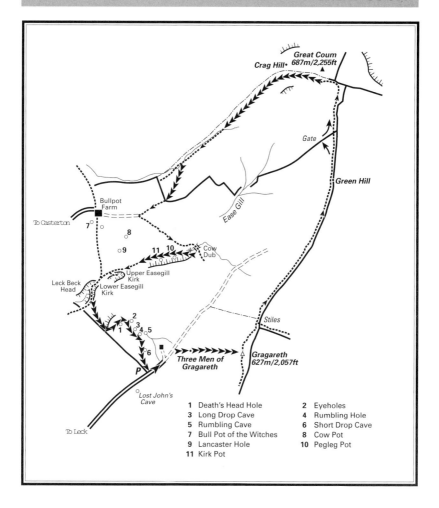

1	Death's Head Hole	2	Eyeholes
3	Long Drop Cave	4	Rumbling Hole
5	Rumbling Cave	6	Short Drop Cave
7	Bull Pot of the Witches	8	Cow Pot
9	Lancaster Hole	10	Pegleg Pot
11	Kirk Pot		

continues. However, after about two miles, the ridge rises sharply to the twin tops of Green Hill before descending very sharply to the col between it and Great Coum.

Leave the wall at this point and aim half left to reach a gate in a wall rising up from Easegill, returning back to the summit wall on the other side. The final slope is now reached and, surprisingly soon, the wall abuts onto another wall rising up steeply from Deepdale and continuing to the left. Follow it to the left to reach the summit, marked by a small cairn on the other side of the wall nearby, which is quite easily crossed. Although the Ordnance Survey suggest that the highest point is slightly earlier, where a wall descends into Dentdale, this cairn certainly does seem very slightly higher. However, back over the wall, which soon becomes a fence, the small path continues along past the trig point on Crag Hill and then slowly down the ridge separating Barbondale to the right and Easegill to the left. A heap of stones, named Richard Man, is passed on the left before the path enters some wetter ground near Aygill Head. The path cuts a line through the rushes and runs along by the infant stream and fence.

If the weather is clear, a transverse wall will be seen ahead and quite a large corner can be cut off by making a beeline half left for it, but if visibility is bad, continue along the fence until the two join, then go left. This transverse wall meets another descending the hillside further along to the left and it is possible to cross in the corner and pick up a path on the other side. In about a quarter of a mile, a path joins sharply from the left, marked by stakes, just before the track becomes a lane running down to Bullpot Farm.

The route was marked with stakes to help tired, wet and cold potholers returning, often in the dark, to Bullpot Farm, now the headquarters of the Red Rose Pot-Hole Club, from becoming lost and hypothermic. Today, the path is distinct but very boggy as it descends down, finally very steeply, to a bridge over Ease Gill. The main objective of the potholers is some distance upstream and is marked by a manhole cover. Named County Pot, this is the main access to the Easegill cave system, which is the biggest, and said to be the finest, in England. On the other side of the bridge, there is a sort of gate that gives access to the steep slope leading down to the beck below the waterfall of Cow Dub.

Hidden deep in a limestone gorge and guarded by a deep pool, the waterfall is difficult to see in its entirety without lying down on the ground and trying to peer around the corner under a piece of overhanging rock on the right. It is in this black pool that the beck sinks underground in normal weather conditions. The dry bed leads on and the going is easiest generally on the left (south) bank.

In about half a mile, at the base of a cliff, some leaning planks, supported by iron bars, cover the 80ft (25m) shaft of Pegleg Pot and just around the corner, between two ash trees, the even narrower shaft of Kirk Pot is discovered. Rising from this shaft, there is a strong draught at a constant temperature of 10ºC, refreshingly cool on warm summer days and warming in winter!

Before too long, a fence crosses the gill and prevents further access. Leave by a gate on the right bank and continue along above the wall and then fence to a stile. Cross it and traverse back along in the wood, into a gorge, to meet the streambed. Just up to the left is a large amphitheatre with some small caves in its walls and a dry waterfall at its head. Here again, the temperature is much cooler than it is elsewhere. However, return back over the stile but here do not follow the path up the hillside but drop down by the fence/wall to a ladder stile over which again is the dry streambed.

Another bigger gorge, Lower Easegill Kirk, opens up ahead and shortly after entering it, the path crosses to the left bank and gently ascends the steep grass on the left as the gorge level drops dramatically. It climbs up out of the gorge (note the cave entrance just below the path) and becomes more distinct as it runs through heather. If energy reserves are still high, it is well worth dropping back down to the river below the gorge and walking back up past the huge resurgence into the main gorge itself with several large cave entrances in its walls.

Soon, however, the main path crosses a wall running up the hillside on the left; follow it along its nearside a fair way until some fenced enclosures are seen on the left. Although the wall continues right up to the car, the diversion to the caves is well worth while. The first deep shaft is Death's Head Hole and this is followed by a few small holes, called the Eyeholes, and then Long Drop Cave.

However, another enclosure lies up ahead and this guards Rumbling Hole, so called because of a waterfall out of sight below its surface that can easily be heard. In total, Rumbling Hole descends a total of 390ft (120m), although not all at once. A very short distance further on, another fenced area contains a cave into which a sizeable stream disappears and it is this that is responsible for the rumbling in Rumbling Hole. The car lies roughly half right and is soon reached.

Anyone keen for some underground experience with waterproofs, torch and sturdy boots is recommended to cross the road and turn right above the wall to walk the short distance to Lost John's Cave. There is a stream entrance and a dry entrance and it is possible to enter one and emerge from the other as they converge after about 15 yards of safe but very rough and difficult travel. Do not be tempted to continue beyond the junction, though, as the system is very complex and intricate, with a total depth of 460ft (140m).

Great Knoutberry Hill

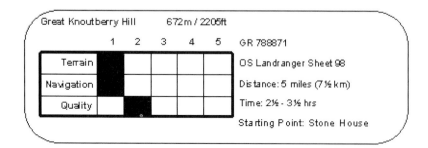

Great Knoutberry Hill is the high point at the south-eastern end of Widdale Fell and is best climbed from Stone House in Dentdale. Unfortunately, a circular route is not really possible, or interesting, given the bleak and featureless nature of the terrain.

Begin at Arten Gill, south-east of Dent on the Ribblehead road, just west of the youth hostel where the road crosses the river on a narrow stone bridge; there is parking for a few cars on the Dent side of the bridge. Walk east up a bridleway, tarmacked, signposted 'Arten Gill 1 mile' and past the houses. Continue up the bridleway, now rough and stony, under the railway viaduct and up the hill through a further two gates before it finally bends to the left, out of the valley.

Here, continue through a gate on a minor track running straight ahead which continues up to the watershed, affording fine views of Widdale ahead. Just before the wall on the left turns up the fell, cross a stile and follow a sketchy track up the fellside staying close to the wall. Many of the pits and depressions met alongside the path are remnants of the colliery which was once here and therefore are liable to collapse as some are blocked shafts or bell-pits. The wall leads directly to the triangulation pillar on the summit. From here, there are good views of the Three Peaks – Pen-y-ghent, Ingleborough and Whernside – and of part of the Lakeland Fells, but in other directions the view is quite bleak and uninspiring.

Return by the route of ascent, although, if transport can be arranged, some walkers may wish to continue to follow the wall/fence until it meets a track, upon which a right turn leads to the Dent to Wensleydale road above Dent Station, but there are no particular scenic advantages to this continuation.

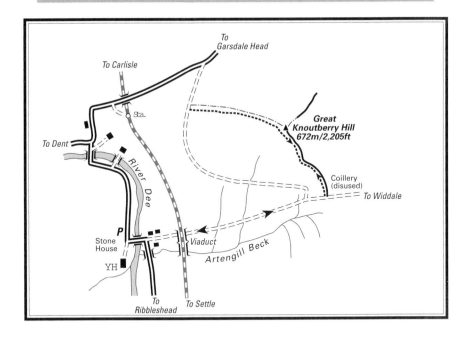

Dodd Fell Hill

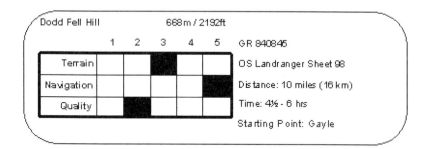

Dodd Fell Hill			668m / 2192ft			
	1	2	3	4	5	GR 840845
Terrain			■			OS Landranger Sheet 98
Navigation					■	Distance: 10 miles (16 km)
Quality		■				Time: 4¾ - 6 hrs
						Starting Point: Gayle

In the view from elsewhere, the average person could be completely forgiven for never having seen Dodd Fell Hill and indeed it is quite indistinguishable even when it is specifically looked for. It is, in fact, the tract of high ground bounded by Widdale, Wensleydale, Raydale and Wharfedale and as a viewpoint it excels. It is also one of the few places in England that is really a wilderness – a pathless waste, devoid of all landmarks; it is therefore best reserved for a clear day when the onwards route can be easily surveyed.

Park at Gayle about half a mile to the south of Hawes, reached up a road from the town past the Wensleydale Cheese Centre. There is parking on the right-hand verge on the Bainbridge road out of the village. The path leaves Gayle just after the first house on the right on that road and is signposted to Burtersett and Marsett. Follow it up through the first field in an almost straight line and then a diagonal line through the next few to cross a ladder stile, over which a signpost indicates a junction of footpaths. Continue straight ahead, signposted 'Marsett', to a ladder stile that is seen prominently ahead.

However, do not cross it but continue up the wallside to another less obvious slit stile at the head of the field, marked with yellow paint, just to the left of a barn. Straight across the next field and then up a slanting grass rake over the next. Cross over the one beyond, aiming for another slit stile just to the right of the wooded streambed, which has so far lain well to the left. Now follow the right-hand bank of the stream, crossing it above the first waterfall and then continue to a collapsed section of wall

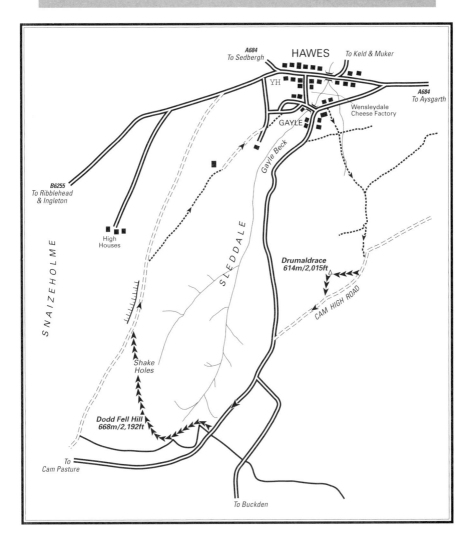

at the top of the field at the foot of a small gully in the steep slope beyond.

Once through the wall, a trod makes a rising traverse leftwards to reach the wall on the left-hand side of the field. Follow it up, passing through a gap, and diagonally up the next field to arrive at a collapsed section of wall in the top left-hand corner. Beyond, a small path through rushes leads to a track running left to a slit stile, which again is marked with yellow paint. Go through it, turn right and follow the wall up the short distance to reach the bridleway rising up from Burtersett. The bridleway crosses the next field to a gate and then bends around to the right; it then meanders slightly before making a second sharp right-hand turn at the beginning of a hairpin.

Here, follow a path half left that crosses the moor to reach the Cam High Road, the Roman Ingleton to Bainbridge road, through a blue gate. Turn right and follow the northern edge of Drumaldrace. At this point, there is no wall on the right-hand side but when you see one ahead beginning on the right, turn right and climb up to the small summit cairn on the Hewitt of Drumaldrace.

A small path leads onwards back down to the track, reaching it just before the wall begins. Continue along the track, which meets the tarmac road rising direct up from Gayle, and then continue along that also. When it forks, take the right fork, passing through a gate. At the second gate, leave the road and follow the wall up to the right on the nearside until it swings sharply left. A sheep track then begins to run half left through an area of deep shake holes before ending at the beginning of the rough ground.

However, the wall corner can be clearly seen ahead and it should be made for as best one can through the peat hags, following it along to the left when it is met. Some wet ground is found by the wall but in a few minutes a large black oozy patch is met. At this point turn right and climb up the hillside, which is not actually as rough as it looks, to the broad ridge and then right along that to the triangulation pillar on the summit, which is surrounded by fields of cotton grass in the summer months.

Aiming for the top of Great Shunner Fell, leave the summit in a northerly direction. After dropping over an edge, the Pennine Way is seen down to the left and a way should be made down to it before the slightly rising shoulder seen ahead. Follow the Pennine Way to the north, forking right at a cairn (signposted) and then keep on the clearly marked route down the hill to the road at the end of the drive to Gaudy House.

A short distance along the road to the right, a path leaves to the left across two meadows (still the Pennine Way) to a junction of paths. Here, leave the Pennine Way, which turns left, and, instead, follow the path half left towards the church steeple. This path ends on a small road at the back of Gayle through a kissing-gate and a right turn leads to a T-junction. Turn right and then right again at the next T-junction, which follows almost immediately, to cross a bridge, just over which the road forks. Take the left fork, which is the Bainbridge road, along which the car is only a short distance away.

Fountains Fell

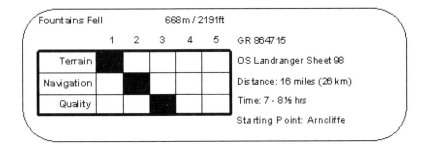

Fountains Fell poses a bit of a problem when it comes to making a shortish circular walk from valley level. It is quite easily climbed from the Malham Tarn area and Silverdale Head but a circle is out of the question. From valley level, it can be climbed either from Malham village or Littondale, both by circuitous routes. However, the best circle is made from Arncliffe in Littondale for even though the scenery around Malham is spectacular, it is best appreciated on a whole day rather than in a fleeting glimpse.

It is possible to park near the bridge on the Malham road in Arncliffe. Begin by walking up a lane to the right of the pub on the village green. This runs through a farmyard and turns into a rough lane but a stile on the right soon gives access onto a rising field path. This is the Monk's Road and it climbs out of the valley and runs along, crossing several stiles, high above the valley of the Cowside Beck above the impressive scars. After crossing the dry narrow valley of Dew Bottoms, where it opens out into an amphitheatre (note that there are some interesting remains of some settlements up on the left on the far side of the valley), the path turns away from the valley and crosses a neck in the hills to reach Middle House.

Continue straight on up a walled lane and then into a field. A cart track runs on, joins with another, and then drops down to a gate and ladder stile at the foot of the field. Over the stile, there is a fork. Take the right-hand branch, which drops down into a little valley to a stile in the fence near a line of telegraph poles. A faint path crosses to the telegraph poles and then climbs gently with them to the col ahead.

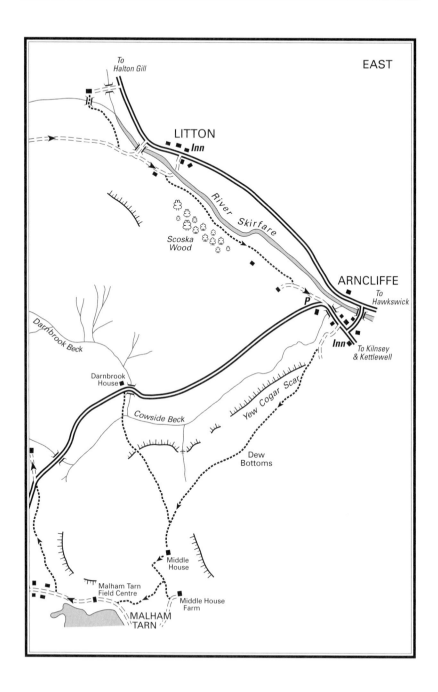

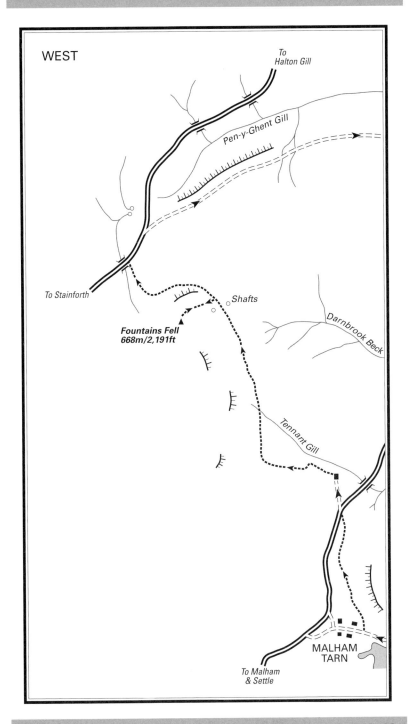

WEST

To
Halton Gill

Pen-y-Ghent Gill

To Stainforth

Shafts

Fountains Fell
668m/2,191ft

Darnbrook Beck

Tennant Gill

MALHAM
TARN

To Malham
& Settle

Before reaching the col, though, the path (now very faint) turns off to the right towards the fence, aiming for the lowest point on the skyline. So far unseen, the view ahead over Malham Tarn suddenly opens up as the path crosses over to a wall bounding a wood and then descends steeply to the track along the lake shore (also the Pennine Way).

Turn right and soon the road reaches Malham Tarn House, which is a field studies centre. The track runs around the back of the house and then onwards through a rocky cutting and along a terrace high above the tarn to emerge from the wood. Here, a path, signposted 'Pennine Way', crosses a stile, runs past some trees and then up a rocky valley, now back upon the limestone. This path maintains a fairly level course along the top of the inbye wall, before turning the corner and running across to the road, crossing another ladder stile in the process.

A farm road to Tennant Gill Farm soon turns off half left. Follow this almost into the farm but turn left just before the farmyard wall and follow this uphill instead, continuing straight on uphill to a ladder stile in the inbye wall. Now turn left initially and then turn right up the side of a broken wall, before following the well-defined track past shake holes and up onto the moor.

After what seems like an interminable climb, the two stone men come into view and, after passing a National Trust sign warning of open mine shafts and advising the passing walker not to deviate from the path, the summit wall is reached. Despite the National Trust's warning, a small path runs along the near side of the wall with not an open shaft in sight, only blocked bell-pits. Shortly, a well-built stone cairn and post come into a view to the left and another small path makes for them from the wall; this is the summit. A fine view of the Three Peaks opens up ahead, the sharp southern end of Pen-y-ghent being particularly impressive as is flat-topped Ingleborough.

Return to the main track by following the wallside but, before beginning the descent to the left, take time to look into the fenced shaft ahead. Unlike the others, this shaft has remained in excellent condition and its stone-lined walls can be seen descending into the depths. The best view is from the opposite side from the track and, a long way down, below the green moss, the coal seam will be spotted, appearing as a black deposit. However, descend down the track to the north, which is still the Pennine Way, and it eventually drops down to the road, turning down a wallside *en route*.

Shortly before it turns by the wall, a small pot-hole, only about 10ft deep, into which a little water trickles, opens up suddenly in the path.

Although of no massive depth, it is quite unexpected and a little dangerous. Turn right on the road and, after a short while, take a track on the right, signposted 'Bridle Road to Litton'. Follow this down the long slope into Littondale where it arrives at the river in the vicinity of a bridge. Do not cross the bridge but instead follow a track onwards through a gate and along until it forks near some ruined buildings. Take the right-hand fork, signposted 'Arncliffe', and continue along until just past some more farm buildings.

A gate on the right gives access into a field, signposted 'Arncliffe', and a path runs across it, turning left behind the next wall. It then passes through a small gate on the left and runs along the wooded riverbank before emerging once more into a field where the river curves around to the left. The path, always well signposted, crosses through several fields and the bottom end of the National Nature Reserve of Scoska Wood, the largest ash and rowan wood left in the Dales, before becoming a small lane and running along to the bridge in Arncliffe.

Potts Moor

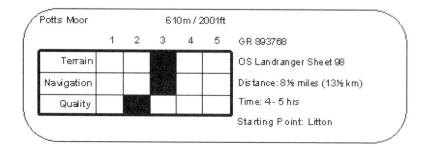

Potts Moor						610m / 2001ft
	1	2	3	4	5	GR 893768
Terrain			■			OS Landranger Sheet 98
Navigation			■			Distance: 8½ miles (13½ km)
Quality		■				Time: 4 - 5 hrs
						Starting Point: Litton

Birks Fell is the generic name given to the tract of high ground that separates Upper Wharfedale and Littondale. Depending upon which map is examined, its highest summit, Potts Moor, may or may not be just above 2,000ft, but it is included here just in case it is, or the Ordnance Survey find that it is another few feet higher, as they are adept at doing. If it is only 1,999ft, then so be it!

Potts Moor is also referred to as Horse Head Moor, which is actually another lower summit of Birks Fell a little further to the north-east, but marked much more prominently on Ordnance Survey maps. It is quite possible to climb to the summit from either Wharfedale or Littondale but the Littondale approach is described here because it is the shorter and there are no particular scenic merits to either route.

Park on the road in the vicinity of the Queen's Arms at Litton on the southern edge of the village. A track leaves the road slightly above the pub and this leads down through fields, turning through a right angle to meet another track coming down from the village. A left turn at this junction leads down to the river and then across the ford, which is normally dry in the summer. Turn right once over the ford and follow a track past some farm buildings, ignoring a path signposted to Arncliffe, which runs across the fields.

The track continues to run along above some conifers, before dropping down to the river at a bridge (which can be reached from Litton up the public road on the other side of the valley should the river be too full to cross at the ford). Do not cross the bridge but follow the

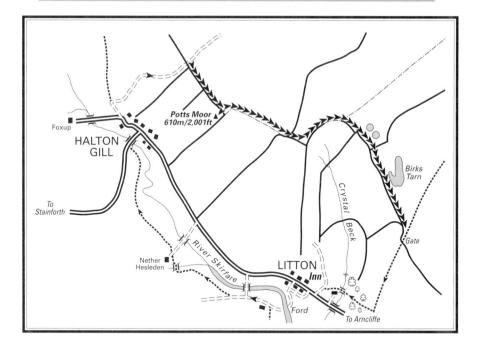

track, which gently ascends the left-hand slope. Soon a path (signposted) runs to the right across the field and continues all the way to the house at Nether Hesleden, which is reached over a bridge and through a gate.

This gate gives access to the foot of the garden in which a right turn should be made before immediately leaving through another gate at a higher level and onto the farm's access road. On the left, a sign marks the onward route but the authorities have overlooked providing a stile!

Luckily, the fence can be got over to cross a small paddock, two stiles at the other side of which give access into a larger field. A succession of ladder stiles, gates and ruined barns now follows along the signposted route to the bridge at Halton Gill. Note, however, the field system on the hill above the second field and the signs of a settlement in the field itself (the circular patches in which nettles grow).

Turn right at the bridge at Halton Gill and walk up the road as far as the village green, a left turn at which leads to the edge of the village on the Foxup road. Turn right through a gate just after the last habitation and follow the track up the hill. Ignore a signposted path on the left to Beckermonds and continue up to the gate in the summit wall. Behind the wall, turn right and walk along a small path through a profusion of clints and other small lumps. When the second wall runs downhill to the right and progress ahead is barred by a fence, the summit is close at hand. Climb the fence and then climb the wall corner to reach the elevated peaty summit with no cairn or other landmark to show its significance.

Cross back over the wall corner and fence and then follow the fence, initially to the north-east, but then to the south-east as it turns through a right angle. What lies ahead now is not inviting; a succession of peat gullies and other wet places beckon which are very reminiscent in some ways of the route to the true summit of Kinder Scout (Section 3). Negotiating the difficulties, continue on until a wall bars progress further. A gate (of sorts) is in the corner. Through it, continue following the wall, which turns up to the left and shortly becomes a fence. Another fence takes off half left with a gate through it and the wall leads onwards past some peaty tarns on the left. By this stage, the wall will either be a trusted companion or an object of hate due to the now interminable slog, but, like it or not, plenty more will be seen of it yet.

Another wall ahead bars progress and this one must be climbed but this is reasonably easy and a long, slow descent follows past the waters of Birks Tarn on the left. Eventually, a broken wall is reached, just beyond which lies the Litton to Buckden bridleway. Turn right and follow it steeply downhill, through a gate to a farm in the valley of Crystal Beck. Cross the stream or dry streambed on a small footbridge and continue along the lane ahead which climbs over a small hill before dropping down through a farmyard to the Queen's Arms at Litton.

Section 5 – Eastern Lakeland

Coast from Lancaster to Haverthwaite, River Leven, Lake Windermere, River Rothay, Thirlmere and St John's Beck to Threlkeld. A66 to Penrith, River Lowther to Shap and River Lune to Lancaster.

NAME	HEIGHT	IN SECTION	IN ENGLAND	IN BRITAIN
Helvellyn	950m/3,116ft	1 of 09	2 of 53	165 of 751
Fairfield	873m/2,863ft	2 of 09	7 of 53	279 of 751
St Sunday Crag	841m/2,760ft	3 of 09	10 of 53	324 of 751
High Street	828m/2,718ft	4 of 09	11 of 53	344 of 751
Red Screes	776m/2,547ft	5 of 09	18 of 53	433 of 751
Stony Cove Pike	763m/2,502ft	6 of 09	19 of 53	462 of 751
Seat Sandal	736m/2,415ft	7 of 09	25 of 53	509 of 751
Tarn Crag	664m/2,178ft	8 of 09	44 of 53	664 of 751
Place Fell	657m/2,154ft	9 of 09	46 of 53	682 of 751

The eastern part of Lakeland contains a mixture of well-known and popular landscapes with less-frequented and less dramatic areas. Helvellyn is perhaps the most climbed of any Lakeland mountain and its famous edges, Striding Edge and Swirral Edge, appear frequently in photographs and are used by walkers and scramblers virtually every day of the year. However, further east, the long valleys of Mardale, Kentmere and Longsleddale retain much of their original charm for here there are no honey pots like Glenridding and, when walking in areas like Longsleddale, even in the middle of summer, it is quite possible not to see another person for the whole day.

The section contains two main ridge systems. The Helvellyn and Fairfield ridge system is more popular than the High Street system due to the former's favourable position with popular places like Ambleside, Keswick, Grasmere and Patterdale nestling at the foot of its slopes. The separate mountains are largely to be found towards the southern end of both ridges as, to the north, both ridges become much flatter and bleaker.

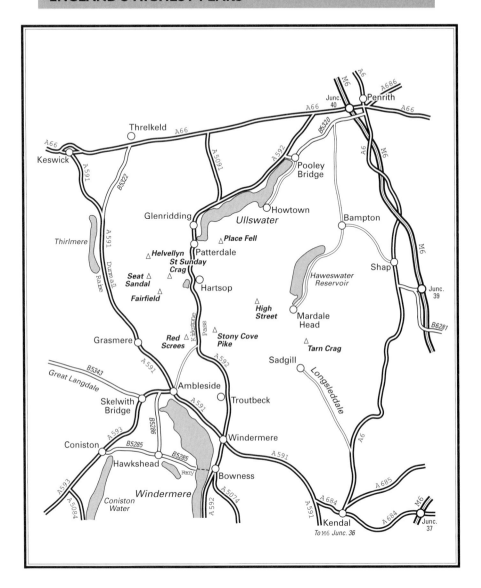

The Geology of Lakeland (Sections 5, 6 and 7)

It appears most appropriate to link the whole of the district together when discussing geology because, although there are many separate summits here, they are found in a quite compact area with the same basic rock formations.

The Lake District is formed from a massif of sedimentary and volcanic rocks deposited during the Ordovician and Silurian periods. The oldest rocks to be found are the Skiddaw Slates, formed from lower Ordovician sediments. However, the series is not completely formed from slates for, in amongst them, there are beds of flagstones and grits: one band in particular with a high quartz content has been termed the Skiddaw Grit. The rocks are highly cleaved and shaly which, unlike their counterparts in Snowdonia, renders them worthless to the construction industry. It also forms the typically smooth outline of the northern fells (Section 7) and the Newlands Fells, including Grasmoor (Section 6), for as the rock weathers, it breaks up into scree, which now covers the slopes and is seen to advantage on Skiddaw (Section 7). Occasional igneous intrusions are to be found amongst the other sediments high in the series, immediately prior to the overlying volcanic rocks. Where crags do form, such as on Grasmoor, they are formed from the bands of igneous rocks and grits, rather than the slates.

These volcanic rocks were deposited about 500 million years ago, in the upper Ordovician period, when Lakeland lay close to a tectonic plate boundary. At that boundary, a collision occurred between a section of dense oceanic crust that sank below the less-dense continental crust, into which it collided, supporting what is now Lakeland. This is termed a subduction zone and, as the oceanic crust sank into the Earth's mantel, it melted, causing a build-up of pressure. To relieve this, underwater volcanic vents became active and threw out magma and ash, forming a chain of islands, similar to the West Indies or the islands around the Pacific Rim today.

The magma that was thrown out can be divided into two forms: basic andesites, containing less than 50 per cent silica (silicon dioxide), and acid rhyolites, containing more than 50 per cent silica; the higher rocks of the Borrowdale series, as these Ordovician volcanics have been called, become increasingly rhyolitic in their composition. Being deposited underwater, bands of sediment, ranging from fine mudstones to coarse grits, which accumulated between eruptions, are to be found. Due to the heat and pressure, the mudstones underwent considerable metamorphosis, transforming them into true slates. However, not all the slates of the Borrowdale Series are formed from mudstones for amongst the layers of lava were also deposited large quantities of volcanic ash, which have since developed into green false slates, such as those quarried at Honister (Section 6). These layers of ash have often eroded much more than the lava-based rocks with which they are interleaved. This has led to a terracing effect on many hillsides, which is well seen on the Borrowdale slopes of Bleaberry Fell. These rocks, where now exposed on the surface, form the rugged, craggy hills and mountains for which Lakeland is best known.

In fact, the Borrowdale Series can be divided into several distinct groups. The earliest to be deposited was the Falcon Crag group, followed by the Ullswater basic andesitic group, the Sty Head garnetiferous group, the Scafell ash and breccia group, the Shap andesitic group and finally the Shap rhyolitic group. It is the Falcon Crag group that shows the lava and ash layers to their best and it is this rock that is exposed on the Borrowdale slopes of Bleaberry Fell. However, the Ullswater basic andesitic group differs little in its composition, but its well-cleaved ashes form the 'false slates' mentioned earlier at Honister Crag (Section 6). The Sty Head garnetiferous group is quite thin but is characterised by garnets, glassy red gemstones formed from silica, which are found in it. These garnets are thought to have been formed in the original volcanic activity and not as a result of the later intrusions that deposited so many other minerals.

The Scafell ash and breccia group contains very little lava but mainly pyroclastic material, ranging from coarse angular particles to the finest volcanic dusts; in the south, the ashes were compressed into slates, such as those found at Tilberthwaite, near Coniston (Section 6). The Shap andesitic and rhyolitic groups comprised the final volcanic activity, both being similar in structure to the rocks of the Falcon Crag group. At the same time, a small number of igneous intrusions were injected into the rocks of the Borrowdale Series and can be seen as sills and dykes, varying in composition from basic to rhyolitic. Some of these dykes contain less resistant rocks and these have weathered away completely; Mickledore, the col between Scafell and Scafell Pike (Section 6), is one such gap where the dyke has weathered. Some larger masses exist, including the Ennerdale and Buttermere granophyre, a pink rhyolitic rock consisting of feldspar (aluminosilicates of potassium and sodium), quartz (silicon dioxide) and chlorite (aluminium, iron and magnesium silicates), well seen on the Bleaberry Comb slopes of the Buttermere Red Pike (Section 6).

However, by the end of the Ordovician period, the intense volcanic activity had come to an end and, in the Silurian period, sedimentary rocks were once more being deposited; the first of these were the Coniston Limestones. Like in the upper beds of the Skiddaw slates, some rhyolitic lava flows are to be found amongst the Coniston Limestone group as the volcanic activity became less intense before dying out altogether. Limestones actually play a very small part in the series, which mainly consists of calcareous mudstones, often containing much fine volcanic dust, interstratified with limestones of varying degrees of purity. As such, where the Coniston Limestone appears on the surface, it supports much more lush vegetation than the surrounding acidic soils overlying the Borrowdale Series.

Other Silurian deposits followed, namely the Stockdale Shales, the Coniston Flags and Grits, the Bannisdale Shales and the Kirkby Moor Flags. These rocks are easily weathered and, as such, tend to form much less dramatic landscapes, characterised by low, rounded hills, extensive broadleaved woodlands and fertile farmlands with much deeper soils, than elsewhere in the district.

In the Devonian period, it would appear that no new rocks were deposited but, during this period, considerable earth movements occurred. Considerable lateral pressure was exerted on the rocks and this caused not only extensive doming and folding but also shattering of the rock, resulting in the formation of faults. With continuing pressure, blocks on either side of the fault slid independently from each other; this is a tear fault and these are well seen amongst the Coniston Limestones where the rock bands are, in places, displaced for over a mile. Along the line of these faults, fault-breccias (sections of broken rock fragments) came into being where the movement shattered the rock. These, where exposed, have since weathered; Windy Gap, the col between Great Gable and Green Gable (Section 6), is a good example of this, as is the gully descending from it into the upper reaches of Ennerdale.

Near horizontal faults appear to exist between the Skiddaw Slates and the Borrowdale volcanic rocks and between the Borrowdale Series and the Coniston Limestone as well as amongst the Borrowdale rocks and the Silurian beds; evidence for this is provided by the existence of fault-breccias. These earth movements uplifted the seabed, halting the deposition of sediment and forming dry land.

The other effect of the uplift was the development of the distinct cleavage in the Skiddaw Slates, mentioned above. Further uplift was caused by a granite intrusion, also of Devonian age, which is exposed near Shap (Section 5), on Carrock Fell (Section 7) and in and on the slopes of Eskdale, Miterdale and lower Wasdale (Section 6). The granite has been exposed here more due to erosion than any other factor but it did have effects on the existing rocks. The greatest was the penetration of hot mineralising solutions under pressure into cracks, developed as a result of the pressure earlier in Devonian times. As the solutions entered these cracks, the pressure was reduced and correspondingly they cooled, depositing their minerals in veins. In the past, these have been extensively mined; particularly notable are the copper-bearing veins above Coniston (Section 6), the iron mines of Eskdale (Section 6) and the lead and copper mines of the northern fells and Newlands (Sections 7 and 6 respectively).

By the Carboniferous period, the district had once more been submerged under a shallow sea but this time a warm tropical one. Tiny organisms and corals thrived on shelves and their bodies sank to the bottom to be compressed into limestone, similar to that seen in Sections 4, 8 and 9. Like in the Pennines, this limestone was then covered in the upper Carboniferous by layers of rocks of the Millstone Grit Facies (grits, shales and sandstones) and then Coal Measures as deltaic conditions and then tropical swamps became prevalent. Further uplifting followed but, unlike earlier, little folding took place and instead an elevated plateau developed. Semi-arid conditions now prevailed in the Permian and Triassic periods in which sandstones were deposited, including the Penrith Sandstone (Permian) and the St Bees and Kirklinton Sandstones (Triassic). These sandstones can also be seen on the Isle of Man (Section 11), which has a somewhat similar geological history. Mid-Cretaceous and Tertiary folding once more uplifted the district but these movements, along with the earlier ones, notably the granitic intrusion, began to allow the landscape to form into what can be seen today.

The movements had formed a domed plateau; the central dome existed somewhere in the Scafell Pike–Great End area (Section 6) but an axis runs eastwards from the dome, roughly through High Raise (Section 6), Red Screes (Section 5), Stony Cove Pike (Section 5) and Harter Fell (Mardale–Section 5). This initiated a rough radial drainage pattern. Around Scafell Pike (Section 6), it is truly radial, the valleys of Borrowdale (River Derwent), Buttermere, Ennerdale, Wasdale, Eskdale, Dunnerdale and Langdale radiating out like the spokes of a wheel. To the north of the east–west axis, Thirlmere, Ullswater, Mardale (Haweswater) and Swindale developed while to the south, there lies the Rothay (Grasmere), Troutbeck, Kentmere, Longsleddale and Borrowdale (Borrow Beck, near Tebay). These valleys began to erode the slopes of the dome, cutting straight valleys through the Triassic, Permian and Carboniferous deposits to hit the lower Paleozoic rocks. The exception to the rule of straight valleys is Ullswater, which has a bend in it; this is due to the fact that it runs along the line of a fault. Thirlmere is also a fault-valley.

As the valleys deepened, so the plateau surrounding them lowered also, the post-Paleozoic rocks being confined only to small patches on the summits of the highest hills and as concentric rings around the edges of the dome. Soon, all evidence of their existence in the centre of the dome had vanished. However, the northern fells (Section 7) interrupted the radial drainage pattern. This ground had formed a separate and indeed higher dome, which had initiated its own radial drainage; the erosion not only stripped it of its post-Paleozoic deposits but also much of its Silurian and Ordovician deposits, leaving only the lowest layer in the Paleozoic deposits, the Skiddaw Slates, exposed. Another dome existed on the Howgill Fells (Section 8) where today the Silurian deposits can be seen at heights well over 2,000ft (610m), whereas, in Lakeland they reach only lower elevations.

The rocks of the Lake District were now exposed in a more or less similar way to how they are today. Therefore, it seems appropriate to discuss their exposure on the surface before discussing the glacial and post-glacial alterations to the landscape. As already mentioned, the district at the end of the Tertiary period represented a large dome with other smaller ones surrounding it and minor anticlines and synclines within the various beds of rock. To recap, the formations began with the Skiddaw Slates (lower Ordovician and possibly earlier) and they were followed by the Borrowdale Volcanic Series (upper Ordovician), the soft Silurian sediments and finally the Carboniferous limestones and coals and Permian and Triassic sandstones. The easiest way to visualise the effect of the erosion upon the area is to imagine the top of the dome simply being cut off. In the north of the region, the Skiddaw Slates are to be found, north of a line drawn between Buttermere, Dale Head, Grange-in-Borrowdale and Penruddock (this is somewhat of an over-simplification as minor variations occur). Between this line and another, drawn between Millom, Coniston, Waterhead (Ambleside), Troutbeck, Kentmere and Sadgill (Longsleddale), lie the Borrowdale Volcanics. To the south of that line lie the Silurian rocks. Around the edge lies a surround of Carboniferous limestones (except on the west coast between Egremont and Millom) and Carboniferous coal measures lying on the Cumbrian coalfield around Whitehaven. Around these Carboniferous deposits, Permian and Triassic sediments are to be found in the Eden Valley and around Penrith but these are absent on the coast between Whitehaven and Maryport where the Carboniferous rocks form the shoreline. Again, the Permian and Triassic deposits are not to be found in the south-east where the Pennine Faults (see Sections 4 and 8) have elevated the land exposing the underlying Paleozoic rocks. Around Langdale, a syncline has exposed all of the rocks of the Borrowdale Series on the surface.

It is important to note that the Lake District that existed then had much fewer, if any, lakes, fewer crags and more rounded summits. It was the Ice Age that carved out the landforms seen today and it would have begun with a gradual build-up and compaction of snow into ice. This occurred first in valleys but as the quantities grew, it spread over connecting ridges, forming a huge ice sheet over the whole district. It is difficult to establish how much of the erosion caused by the Ice Age is attributable to this building-up phase of glaciation, as the huge power of the later ice sheet would have removed all its effects.

At the end of the period, the ice would have gradually diminished, exposing the ridges and summits and then eventually the valleys also; the last pockets would be in corries where little glaciers would survive for a short time. It was probably not quite this simple; minor fluctuations in temperature would have caused sporadic advances and retreats and possibly a major thaw followed by another subsequent build-up, removing the effects of the earlier period. What can be certain is that the ice was shed by the central east–west axis across the district mentioned above. It did breach this at two points, firstly at Kirkstone Pass and more dramatically at Dunmail Raise.

Northwards and westwards, the movement of the ice was inhibited by the Scottish ice, which was forced around the Lake District and to the east up the Eden Valley through the Stainmore Gap (Section 9). It was in the centre of the district, where the ice was able to move freely, where most erosion occurred, while to the north, in the Skiddaw group (Section 7) and to the west in the Howgill Fells (Section 8), where the Scottish ice inhibited the flow, glacial changes have been quite minor. Like present-day winds, the movement of the ice differed at separate altitudes: in the valleys it was constrained, being forced to move in the radial pattern mentioned earlier while, at higher altitudes, it is thought that it moved much more freely.

One example of the erosive action of the glaciers are rounded rocks known as roches moutonnées. These are exposures of rock that are smoothed and polished on the side that faces up the valley, while they are rough and irregular on the side facing down the valley. This is attributed to the scouring action of the ice as it passed over it and then a plucking action as it moved away. They occur often on all types of rocks and notable examples exist near Quay Foot Quarry in Borrowdale.

The glaciers had the effect of widening and deepening valleys. As there was more ice in the main dale than in tributary valleys, the main valley deepened much more leaving the tributary to emerge, once the ice had retreated, high on the valley side. These tributaries are known as hanging valleys, notable examples being the Watendlath valley on the eastern side of Borrowdale above Derwentwater, Gillercomb on the western side of Borrowdale at Seathwaite, and Bleaberry Comb opposite Buttermere. The latter is much shorter than the other two and has a corrie at its head. Another example seen on the High Raise route (Section 6) is Easedale where a hanging valley exists, ending at the Sour Milk Gill Waterfalls, and above the tarn exists a pair of upper corries.

Corries are formed mainly on the northern and eastern slopes of the fells where the snow collected most and small glaciers remained once the main ice sheet had retreated. These small glaciers plucked away at the depressions on the hillsides in which they formed, deepening their bases and steepening their walls. Notable examples are on the Buttermere side of the High Stile ridge (Section 6), on the eastern side of Helvellyn (Section 5), at the head of Mardale (Section 5) and above Coniston (Section 6). In some cases two corries can be found, as in the case of a small one to the north-east of The Old Man of Coniston (Section 6), which lies above Lever's Water, itself in a corrie.

Many corries have tarns in them, where the ice has deepened the floor, but in some cases they have silted up completely. At the mouths of other corries, moraines (collections of debris deposited by a retreating glacier) have formed a natural dam, deepening the tarn. The action of the ice in neighbouring corries has sometimes formed sharp arêtes between corries, Striding Edge and Swirral Edge on Helvellyn (Section 5) being prime examples. Corries, or combes as they are sometimes called, are similar to hanging valleys in that their outflow streams fall steeply down to valley level in a series of cascades, Sour Milk Gill near Buttermere (Section 6) being a prime example.

Valley glaciers were also irregular in their movement and, on occasions, deepened the valley at a particular point in which a lake may have subsequently formed. Many of the long ribbon lakes found in the Lake District are also dammed by moraines at their outflow. Another characteristic of glacial valleys is their U-shape in cross-section. This is a direct consequence of the widening, deepening and removal of interlocking spurs by the glacier. As the glaciers began to move more slowly or retreated, they deposited rock material in moraines which appear as small grassy hillocks often with damp, marshy ground in between them. An excellent example lies just above Black Sail Youth Hostel in Ennerdale (Section 6).

Other material has been deposited as boulder clay in valley floors and in some cases this has choked the valley so much that it has caused a diversion of the river. There are two good examples of this; the first is the Wythop Valley near Bassenthwaite Lake. This small valley, which supports only a small stream, begins high on the hillside on the eastern side of Bassenthwaite Lake near Beck Wythop. It then descends gradually down to Cockermouth, away from the lake, where it meets the present course of the River Derwent. Originally, this valley was the outflow of the River Derwent but because it became so clogged up by glacial drift (boulder clay), the river cut itself a new course and deepened its new valley. However, what has happened at the foot of Windermere is even more striking. At places such as Haverthwaite and Backbarrow, most would express surprise that such a big river as the Leven (Windermere's outflow) is flowing down such a narrow valley. The reason is that its original valley, a wide, almost dry dale, containing the village of Cartmel, became so clogged with glacial drift that the Leven broke over a low col into a neighbouring valley which supported only a small beck; the Leven has not had time yet to widen this valley sufficiently to satisfy its own requirements.

Where corries have not formed on the fellsides, many Lakeland ridges can easily be seen to be asymmetrical. Although not perfect due to corries, the Helvellyn range is a good example: on its western side it throws down quite dull convex slopes to Thirlmere, while it is much steeper and rockier on its eastern side. Great Rigg, a member of the Fairfield group, and Red Screes (both in Section 5) are prime examples, their north-western slopes being convex while their south-eastern slopes are distinctly concave. This is due to the fact that the strongest ice currents were to be found on the eastern sides of the valleys so it is here that they did most erosion, the original rounded outline remaining relatively undisturbed on the western slopes. Although most Lakeland ridges follow this pattern of convex slopes on the south or west and concave slopes on the north or east, Blencathra (Section 7) and Illgill Head (Wastwater Screes – Section 6) are exceptions to the rule, having steep slopes on the south and west and subdued relief to the north and west. In both places, there is evidence that there were exceptionally strong ice currents on these steepened slopes.

After the Ice Age, freeze-thaw weathering has produced scree slopes. Particularly notable are those on the southern side of Wastwater (Section

6). Also large quantities of peat have formed on the acid, wet hillsides from dead organic matter.

Access (Section 5 only)

The West Coast main line passes to the east of the district, with train services to Oxenholme and Penrith. A branch line between Oxenholme and Windermere has regular daily services in summer; in winter it still runs daily but the service is more limited. There are direct trains between Windermere, Manchester Piccadilly and Manchester Airport, again subject to the above restrictions. There are regular bus services linking Windermere with Ambleside, Grasmere and Keswick. The A591 links Kendal and Keswick via Ambleside and Grasmere (approachable from the south from Junction 36 of the M6). A weekend bus service runs between Penrith and the head of Haweswater. The A592 crosses Kirkstone Pass and runs between Windermere and Penrith via Patterdale (approachable from the north from Junction 40 of the M6).

Accommodation (Section 5 only)

There are plenty of bed and breakfast establishments and hotels in Ambleside and Windermere, with only a few around Patterdale and Glenridding. Either Ambleside or Grasmere is probably the best base; in Grasmere there are plenty of hotels but a few bed and breakfast establishments also, including a couple up the Easedale Road and a couple along the Red Bank Road. There are youth hostels at Thirlmere, Langdale (Red Bank), Grasmere (Butterlip How and Thorney How), Ambleside, Windermere, Patterdale and Helvellyn (actually above the village of Glenridding, at the foot of the mountain).

Helvellyn

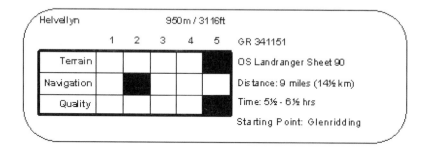

Helvellyn			950m / 3116ft			
	1	2	3	4	5	GR 341151
Terrain					■	OS Landranger Sheet 90
Navigation		■				Distance: 9 miles (14½ km)
Quality					■	Time: 5½ - 6½ hrs
						Starting Point: Glenridding

Helvellyn is without doubt the most popular mountain in England; thousands every year plod up to its summit in an unrelenting pilgrimage throughout the summer months. What's more, many of them would previously never have considered climbing a mountain. The ascent of Helvellyn by Striding Edge and descending by Swirral Edge is a Lakeland classic. Although Striding Edge is often revered, it is over hyped and it can easily be accomplished by using the traverse path, lowering the grade to a two, although the use of hands may be needed to keep balance.

In Glenridding, there is a pay and display car-park situated just off the road to the north of the small bridge in the village by the shops. The car-park is by the tourist information centre, which provides toilets and stocks Kendal mintcake, leaflets and books. Cross over the road bridge and walk up the other side of the beck on a lane that is unsurfaced after the village hall. The track continues up to a fork where the right-hand one should be taken to continue up the riverbank and past the campsite to reach Gillside Farm.

A left turn leads up the hill and past the farm to emerge onto the open hill at a ladder stile. Although Helvellyn is signposted ahead, turn left above the wall and follow a very distinct stony path that climbs steeply up alongside Mires Beck to reach the Grisedale–Glenridding watershed wall at a cairn. Here the track turns right and ascends, first straight up and then through hairpins, to rejoin the wall at the summit of Birkhouse Moor, a shoulder of Helvellyn. Ahead, the track maintains a fairly level course by the wall, crossing the Patterdale to Red Tarn track to join with

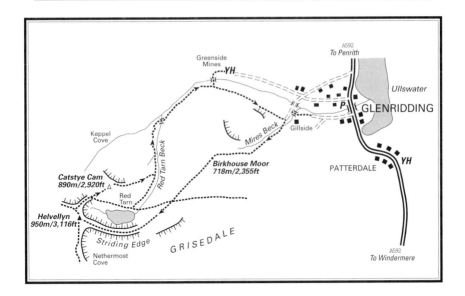

the Patterdale to Striding Edge path just beyond at the top of a small craglet.

Now unified, the approach continues along the northern side of the ridge before ascending to meet it at a small col marking the beginning of Striding Edge. A path, initially on the right, avoids all difficulties and keeps well below the crest but, in normal conditions and not in high winds, it is more exhilarating to adhere to the crest for the whole distance. There are no route-finding difficulties and the crest is delightful, narrow and easily walkable with only occasional use of hands in circumnavigating gendarmes (rocky pinnacles).

Eventually, the crest ends dramatically and a rocky chimney on the left should be used to descend to the traverse path just before this point. It is not difficult under normal conditions, although large rucksacks may be a bit of a hindrance. Beyond, the rock is more broken but can still be followed to the ridge, or alternatively one of the scree paths on either side. However, all routes reach the summit ridge close to or at a memorial to a Charles Gough, who fell off the ridge here to his death but was found three months later, still being guarded by his dog. The summit is marked by a large shelter and is only a short distance to the right; the trig point beyond is very slightly lower.

To descend, walk on past the trig point to reach a cairn on the right on the edge of the cliffs, about 200 yards in total from the shelter. This marks the start of Swirral Edge and this can be followed along its crest or avoided by using scree paths on either side to reach the col between Helvellyn and Catstycam (named Catstye Cam on Ordnance Survey maps). Continue up the broad stony track to Catstycam's sharp summit and cairn: an excellent viewpoint for the crags of Helvellyn and Striding Edge.

A smaller path descends eastwards along the top of the crags before turning grassy and reaching the track descending from Red Tarn. This leads down into the valley and along its southern flank, past Greenside lead mine on the opposite side of the valley (footbridge) and the youth hostel. However, keep straight on and after contouring along the hillside for some time, the path drops sharply down to join with the route of ascent where the open fell was reached earlier in the day. Return down the valley past the farm and campsite to the village centre.

Fairfield, St Sunday Crag and Seat Sandal

Fairfield	873m / 2863ft
St Sunday Crag	841m / 2760ft
Seat Sandal	736m / 2415ft

	1	2	3	4	5
Terrain		■			
Navigation		■			
Quality				■	

GR 358117, 369134, 343115

OS Landranger Sheet 90

Distance: 11½ miles (18 km)

Time: 7 - 8½ hrs

Starting Point: Grasmere

Fairfield forms a huge massif with many ridges radiating from it. A very common route is the so-called 'Fairfield Horseshoe' from Rydal, which is a circuit of Rydale (the unfrequented valley behind Rydal village). However, another very pleasant walk can be made by taking in St Sunday Crag and Seat Sandal, with ever-changing views and perspectives.

Park in Grasmere and leave the village on the old Keswick road to reach the bypass at the Swan Inn. Go straight across and up the lane to the right of the pub, then go second right up a small tarmacked lane, signposted to 'Stone Arthur and Greenhead Gill'. This lane leads to a gate onto the open fell, beyond which a left turn should be made on a path, signposted 'Stone Arthur', which rises steeply alongside the woods. When the top of the woods is reached, turn right and follow the main path that now makes a gently rising traverse of the valley's north-western slopes. Eventually, a ridge is met at which point the path turns left and ascends to the summit of Stone Arthur. Although so prominent from the valley, those hoping for a distinct sharp summit will be disappointed to find that it is simply the rocky end to a ridge, descending from Great Rigg beyond, to which the path continues.

Upon reaching Great Rigg, stunning views open up of Rydale beyond but also, less stunningly, of the path onwards up Fairfield. The path, which is broad and stony, leads without any deviation to the shelter on Fairfield's summit, perched on the edge of its northern precipices, overlooking the wild head of Deepdale. Leave the summit leftwards for a short distance before turning right down a steep, rough and stony path

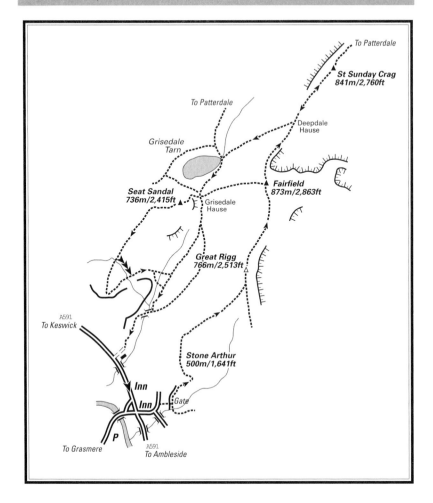

that leads down and then up to the sharp summit of Cofa Pike. Note that finding the correct route off Fairfield's summit in mist could be difficult and indeed dangerous. Beyond Cofa Pike, the path descends to Deepdale Hause and, just after a small cairn on the left (the position of which is worth noting for the descent), it begins to climb the long ridge of St Sunday Crag. After a long climb up a sharp ridge the summit cairns of St Sunday Crag are soon reached.

Return to the small cairn on Deepdale Hause and there turn right following a path that descends at first, before forking. Take the left fork, which runs along the base of a small crag, before descending down to Grisedale Tarn, meeting the Patterdale to Grasmere path close to the tarn's outflow. Turn left and walk along the lake shore before following the track up to Grisedale Hause. Here, turn right and follow a prominent path, climbing on scree, to the right of a crag to reach a grassy slope with an ascending stone wall that leads to the summit of Seat Sandal – a fine viewpoint for Grasmere.

To begin the descent, turn your back to the wall and walk forwards following the ridge to a cairn on the skyline, after which the ridge swings around to the left. There is evidence of a faint path and the route is marked by infrequent cairns. At about 1,500ft (460m), the ridge narrows to a small col and then immediately rises, for the first time. Here, leave the ridge and descend the tiny valley to the left, which leads down to a small path running above the fell wall. Turn left and follow the wall down to cross Little Tongue Gill and then meet the Patterdale to Grasmere path once again. If the ridge is followed, a stone wall is met through which there is no longer any access and then there is a long detour back up the valley to this point. However, having met the Patterdale to Grasmere path, turn right and follow the track down to the Grasmere to Keswick road at Mill Bridge. A short walk along the road to the left leads down past the Traveller's Rest to the Swan Inn and back to the end of the road leading down into Grasmere village.

High Street

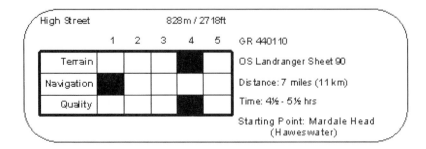

High Street						828m / 2718ft
	1	2	3	4	5	GR 440110
Terrain				■		OS Landranger Sheet 90
Navigation	■					Distance: 7 miles (11 km)
Quality				■		Time: 4½ - 5½ hrs
						Starting Point: Mardale Head (Haweswater)

Named after the Roman road between Ambleside and Brougham, High Street has a long and distinguished patronage. Otherwise known as Racecourse Hill, the summit is a long and quite flat grassy plateau on which the local shepherds and farmers met to feast and race their horses centuries ago. However, away from the summit, steep and precipitous slopes drop in almost all directions, appearing particularly impressive from Haweswater from where the mountain is best climbed.

A car-park at the head of the reservoir is the starting point and, as it is the only car-parking area to speak of in the valley, it fills up quickly during the summer. A track leads on through a gate at the end of the road and soon splits three ways. Turn right across the head of the valley and then back down the far side of the lake. The ascent follows the long ridge of Rough Crag and Long Stile between Riggindale and Blea Water. Although a steep and difficult short-cut climbs very steeply up the hillside, it is best to gain the foot of the ridge at the wooded peninsula of The Rigg.

A grassy path leads very sharply left, up through the bracken, circumnavigating the worst of the crags by keeping mainly to the left-hand side of the ridge, before passing over Rough Crag with impressive retrospective views of Haweswater and descending very slightly to the small tarn at Caspel Gate, from where there are fine views of Blea Water and the crag behind it. On the crags to the right above Riggindale are to be found the only nesting pair of eagles in England and, if you are lucky, you may see them soaring high above the surrounding valleys.

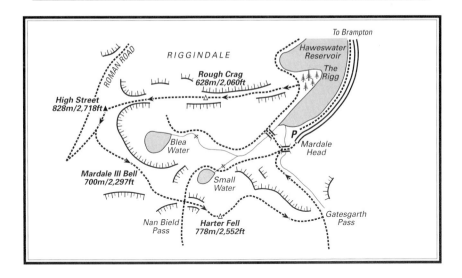

Beyond the depression, the ridge rises sharply up to the summit plateau and again the path keeps mainly to the left-hand side of the ridge. It finishes at a cairn on the top and a grassy track leads off half left past a few small cairns to meet the summit wall just to the right of the trig point. The Roman Road lies a short distance down the hill beyond the trig point, but if it is visited, a return should be made back to the summit. There are fine views in all directions; the highest point of the Pennines, Cross Fell, is clearly in view across the Eden valley as is Ingleborough's flat top to the south-east. All the major Lakeland peaks are visible, including those out to the west, Great Gable and the Scafell group and even the other Harter Fell above Eskdale.

Continue on by the wallside until a track takes off to the left at a cairn and gradually descends down south-eastwards to a small depression before climbing slightly to the rocky summit of Mardale Ill Bell. Onwards, the track now descends sharply down to Nan Bield Pass, the main route between Mardale (Haweswater) and Kentmere. However, keep straight on and steeply up to the summit of Harter Fell. Unfortunately, Harter Fell is thought to miss out very slightly on separate mountain status, although Wainwright believed it to have exactly 500ft of ascent from the pass, but all are recommended to climb it, firstly for its fine views and also because a traverse of its summit is a fitting end to the walk.

At the summit cairn, adorned with remnants of an old fence, long since disappeared, a new fence is met and this should be followed to the left where there is a path which soon becomes much more distinct and continues along the fence before leaving it to drop down to the summit of Gatesgarth Pass, the route between Mardale and Longsleddale. A left turn leads down a series of hairpins on a stony track close to the Gatesgarth Beck and into the inbye to meet the valley track at the junction just above the car-park, mentioned at the beginning.

It is very easy today to see Mardale as an empty valley and imagine that it has always been so but once, before the invasion of Manchester Corporation, there was a populated valley and thriving community. There always was a lake but much smaller and much more graceful. The new Haweswater, as reservoirs go, is very beautiful and looks almost natural – the dam is rarely seen. The name Mardale Head lives on in the name of the car-park but gone is the village, its ruins only exposed in extremely dry summers. Below the car-park in longer dry spells, two walls can be seen emerging from the water which once enclosed the lane that ran out onto the hill. In this light, it is easy to see why the passes of Nan Bield and Gatesgarth are so large and distinct, being important routes to the valleys of Longsleddale and Kentmere to the south. The site of the new hotel is unfavourable from a walker's point of view, two miles from the head of the valley, and is not a replacement for the lost Dun Bull inn in the old village of Mardale Head. The main relic of the settlement today is the Old Corpse Road that links Mardale and neighbouring Swindale, in a similar style to the one between Eskdale and Wasdale in western Lakeland.

Red Screes

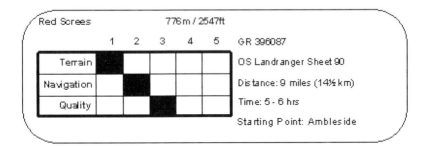

Red Screes is a very separate mountain from its neighbours. To the east and west there are the large troughs of Kirkstone and Scandale passes. Its summit sits at the top of two gradually descending ridges to the south and the north, which help to give the peak a real mountain feel. In many ways, it is very similar to its slightly lower neighbour, Stony Cove Pike, on the other side of Kirkstone Pass. However, they differ in one way: unlike Stony Cove Pike, Red Screes throws down an array of cliffs, crags and red scree, from which it takes its name, down to the Kirkstone Pass Inn and road far below.

The most pleasing circuit on the mountain can be made from Ambleside. Although the route does not climb the craggy slopes above Kirkstone, it is none the worse for that as the rock is too poor to give a good scrambling route and the scree slopes are steep and loose enough to make progress purgatory. It is possible currently to park very close to the start of the route in Ellerigg, a small part of Ambleside. Take the Kirkstone Pass road at the northern end of the town and take the second turning on the left, Sweden Bridge Road. This slowly climbs a little uphill before forking; take the right fork and continue to its top.

There is parking on the right above some self-catering accommodation, which, unlike the other properties in the street, has off-road parking so nobody's access is blocked. Start by walking up a rough road running west that cuts through to the lane leading up on the left from the fork. Follow it up to the right, where, in a few yards, the tarmac ends and a rough track leads on beyond a gate through some

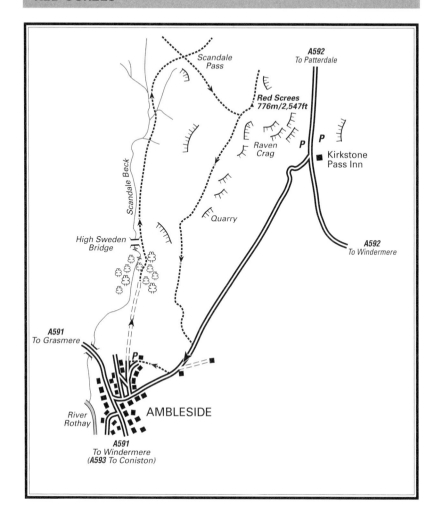

woods above the rushing stream to High Sweden Bridge. Do not cross the bridge but stay on the track, which soon becomes a walled lane, before emerging onto the open fell and, with no variation possible, continues up to the summit of Scandale Pass where a fine view of Brothers Water opens up ahead.

Turn right at the top of the pass and follow a path by the wall, which runs very steeply up the slope before becoming very indistinct on the summit plateau, by which time the wall has ended. In clear weather, the summit cairn and trig point can be seen away to the left and a beeline should be made for them avoiding a few tarns *en route*. In mist, continue straight on to reach the track running up the south ridge from Ambleside and follow that to the left. The summit is in quite a spectacular position, perched on the edge of a near vertical drop down to the road on the Patterdale side of the pass far below. The views are extensive, Windermere can be seen almost in its entirety, but, unfortunately, only a small part of Ullswater is visible, though all the major peaks are in view.

The descent is a blessing for tired feet, a stroll down the gently graded, mainly grassy south ridge with fine views down the length of Windermere always ahead. The track is very clear and, initially, runs along the edge of the crags giving a view down to the Kirkstone Pass Inn. Danger signs mark the presence of Pets Quarry on the left, just beyond which the path turns right along the top of a wall before crossing it on a stile. The route from here onwards lies mainly down a grassy lane, which, at times, is wide enough to be called a field, but it is not continuous in the middle, the path running straight ahead along the edge of a field.

It reaches the Kirkstone Pass road above Ambleside at a peculiar arrangement of gates, first a pair of narrow iron gates and then a wooden gate out onto the road itself. Turn right and in a few hundred yards, the Rowanfield Country Guest House will be passed on the left, where the road curves first to the right and then to the left. On the left-hand bend, a track, signposted to Ellerigg, leads straight ahead, through a gate and along the bottom of a wood. Where it enters a field, it turns sharply uphill but a 'No Footpath' notice makes it clear that the onwards route lies along the path at the bottom, which, after passing through another field, crosses into the driveway of a house and then leads out through a pair of gates to the starting point.

Stony Cove Pike

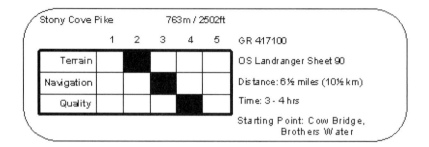

Stony Cove Pike						763m / 2502ft
	1	2	3	4	5	GR 417100
Terrain		■				OS Landranger Sheet 90
Navigation			■			Distance: 6½ miles (10½ km)
Quality				■		Time: 3 - 4 hrs
						Starting Point: Cow Bridge, Brothers Water

Stony Cove Pike is in many ways a twin to Red Screes on the other side of Kirkstone Pass; they are virtually the same height and they are both very separate bearing no subsidiary summits. However, in one way, Stony Cove Pike is different – it is much quieter. It is often noted that the fells to the east of Kirkstone Pass are much less visited and this is borne out in the absence of large paths and the presence of wildlife, for this mountain is the only place on which I have seen a wild red deer outside of Scotland.

To the north, Stony Cove Pike throws down several fine ridges while to the south it displays a much more boring face. Therefore, it is best climbed from the north and the best place to park is at Cow Bridge at the northern end of Brothers Water where there is a small car-park. Leave the car-park and walk up the road towards Kirkstone Pass before shortly taking a small road on the left, signposted to Hartsop. Continue up this road until the tarmac ceases and then pass through another small car-park before turning right and crossing the river, signposted 'Pasture Bottom'.

Cross a ladder stile into a field where the track turns left. Ignore this and continue up the wallside to a stile at the top of the field and then, staying by the wall, continue up to where the ridge is met and the wall turns down to Brothers Water. The path now steeply ascends the ridge until it levels off close to the summit of Hartsop Dodd, where a wall is met. The retrospective views over Patterdale during this ascent are quite lovely. Now follow a path on the right-hand side of the wall past the

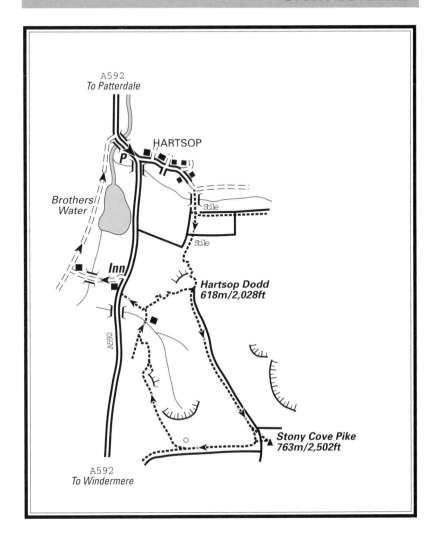

summit cairn on Hartsop Dodd and then up the long gentle hill onto the top of Caudale Moor. Shortly after a wall joins from the left, cross the wall and aim across a small wet depression to the summit cairn and enjoy the fine views.

Return to the wall and cross it, before keeping straight on across a depression, containing a few tarns, aiming for the right-hand cairn on the skyline. Turn half right and aim for another cairn beyond, from which the route is apparent, following a narrow ridge above Kirkstone on the left and Caudale on the right. After passing some quarry workings below on the right, the faint path descends down the ridge more steeply to meet the old quarry road running in a groove. Although the groove splits later on, all join up again and hairpin down to cross the Caudale Beck and continue on down to the main road just above the Brotherswater Inn. Walk down the road to it and through its car-park, before turning left on a track that crosses over the campsite and runs across the valley to Hartsop Hall. Turn right behind the hall and follow a wide track along the shores of the lake to arrive back at the car-park.

Tarn Crag

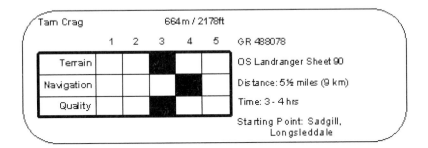

Tarn Crag		664 m / 2178ft			
	1	2	3	4	5
Terrain				■	
Navigation					■
Quality			■		

GR 488078

OS Landranger Sheet 90

Distance: 5½ miles (9 km)

Time: 3 - 4 hrs

Starting Point: Sadgill, Longsleddale

The valley of Longsleddale is the most easterly Lakeland valley, in that it is a U-shaped glacial trough. Further east the landscape of the Shap fells is much more reminiscent of that of the Pennines. Tarn Crag is certainly the outlier of this group, but nevertheless is a very interesting climb.

On the A6, a few miles north of Kendal, a little, unknown road, signposted 'Longsleddale 4½', runs up through the small hamlet of Garnett Bridge, past another settlement with a chapel, to the end of the public road at Sadgill Farm. Beyond, a quarry track continues up the valley for a further 1½ miles. There is parking on the verge at the entrance to this track, although it should not be blocked as it is still used by the farmer.

To begin with, follow this track for a short distance and pass through the first gate on the right into a field. Turn left and pass through another gate, into another, larger field, where a vague path follows the wall steeply uphill. If for some reason it is impossible to pass through these gates, it is possible to climb the wall a few yards beyond the gate with the use of a well-placed throughstone.

Some signs of booted passers-by will be found by the wall, but it is a very steep start for first thing in the day! Once the wall has made a right-angled bend, things do not get much better although the angle does relent slightly. There is now also bracken; if it is tall, a good route can be found where a stream descends the fell a little further to the right. The target is a small gully to the right of the prominent buttress ahead. This gully contains no scree and leads up onto a sheep track rising to a wall

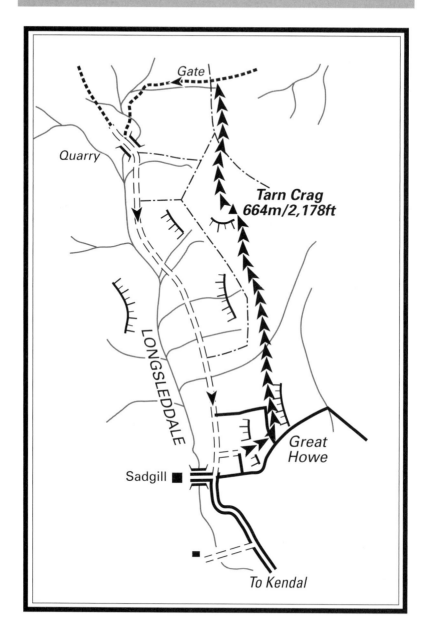

below a crag with a small tree growing on it. Slightly to the right, the wall has collapsed a little and is quite easily crossed.

Once over the wall, traverse the fellside on another sheep track, which stays quite close to the line of the wall. When the wall turns downhill, a near level traverse of the fellside leads to a fence, which rises from the valley, and runs roughly along the same line as the wall did. Soon, a fence takes off to the right, which needs to be climbed. Those with long legs will manage to do it with both feet astride the fence on the ground. Those with shorter legs need not despair, as it is easy to climb the pig netting on either side.

Continue along above the fence until over the first boggy area; here take off half right aiming for the prominent feature of the Haweswater Aqueduct survey post (18°). Another boggy depression will need to be crossed before the final climb up, on grass, through the small craglets can begin. The survey post does not grace the highest point; instead this is marked by a small cairn half right.

The route onwards is not clear. Walk in a northerly direction to where a junction of fences will be found. Climb the fence on the right – this will pose no problems – and keep going north, following the fence down to the depression at the head of Mosedale. Before the footpath is reached running from Mosedale to Longsleddale, a bog has to be crossed; this is best done not next to the fence but a little to the right of it. Once over it, an indistinct path will be found running from right to left. Turn left, through a gate, and follow it through the bog and down into the upper valley.

On the opposite slopes, a quarry can be clearly seen with its obvious faces of bare rock and spoil heaps, remaining as relics to the industrial past of this, the most tranquil of Lakeland's valleys. When the river has been crossed, the quarry road is met and a left turn leads down out of the hanging valley into the glacial strath about one mile along the quarry road above Sadgill.

Place Fell

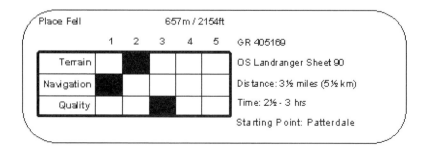

Place Fell					657m / 2154ft	
	1	2	3	4	5	GR 405169
Terrain			■			OS Landranger Sheet 90
Navigation	■					Distance: 3½ miles (5½ km)
Quality			■			Time: 2½ - 3 hrs
						Starting Point: Patterdale

Place Fell is very dominant when viewed from Patterdale, and indeed from most places along the shore of Ullswater. It rises steeply from the lakeside through slopes clothed with juniper, gorse, bracken and heather and riddled with grey crags. Place Fell can be climbed from either Patterdale or Howtown, and would make a nice walk if the steamer were taken from Glenridding to Howtown and the return made over Place Fell. However, a delightful walk can be made from Patterdale, especially nice on a warm summer's afternoon when the view is best appreciated.

Patterdale is not filled with opportunities for car-parking, in fact there are only a few places here, unlike at Glenridding. From Kirkstone Pass, there is a small lay-by on the left with space for three or four cars just before the White Lion; from Glenridding it is on the right just after the White Lion and the Post Office. This lay-by should not be confused with the White Lion car-park. The route begins by walking up the road towards Kirkstone for about ten yards, before turning down a tarmac lane on the left. This crosses the river and leads up to some houses on the other side of the valley, where it forks. Take the left fork, which is a bridleway, signposted to Boredale Hause, shortly passing through a gate on the right (signposted).

After one hairpin, leave the path running up the hillside for a grassy path ascending on the left. After passing through a disused quarry, a path forks left (downhill); ignore this and instead follow the grass path straight ahead, which traverses the hillside. Soon an interesting cave is passed on the right and an ornate iron bench (though hopefully you won't require use of it yet!). The path continues its mainly level traverse until it splits

The south ridge of Black Hill (Section 2)

Ribblehead Viaduct (Section 4) from Gatekirk

Pen-y-ghent (Section 4) from Sulber Nick

The summit of Ingleborough (Section 4)

Gaping Gill (Section 4)

Red Screes (Section 5) as seen from Stony Cove Pike

The summit of Stony Cove Pike (Section 5)

Looking towards Helvellyn (Section 5) from Catstycam

The summit of High Raise (Section 6)

Pillar (Section 6) from Gamlin End on High Crag

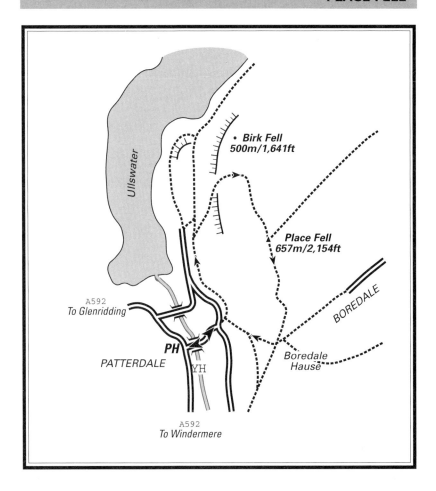

above a smooth grey rocky knoll on the left with a line of larches at the bottom. Take the rising right-hand path, instead of the descending left-hand path.

This path rises up the fell with spectacular views of Ullswater through delightful thickets of juniper. At 1,500ft (460m), the juniper is left behind and the path runs up a small grassy gully with some smooth rocky outcrops on either side. Before the ridge is met, the path again forks; here go right and follow this path, which crosses two bogs and ascends around the top of Grey Crag, before finally reaching the ridge south of The Knight. Now the triangulation pillar on Place Fell's summit comes into view. Cross the bleak depression ahead and ascend to the summit, which is situated on a little rocky knoll.

To descend, follow a wide and eroded path running south over Round How, which descends to the ruined sheepfold on Boredale Hause. Turn right here and follow a path that joins with many others, but all end up at the gateway through which access to the open fell was first gained earlier in the day.

Section 6 – Western Lakeland

The River Derwent from Workington to Keswick, the River Greta, St John's Beck, Thirlmere, River Rothay, Windermere and the River Leven to Haverthwaite. The coast from there to Workington.

NAME	HEIGHT	IN SECTION	IN ENGLAND	IN BRITAIN
Scafell Pike	978m/3,210ft	1 of 14	1 of 53	138 of 751
Great Gable	899m/2,949ft	2 of 14	4 of 53	237 of 751
Pillar	892m/2,927ft	3 of 14	6 of 53	249 of 751
Grasmoor	852m/2,795ft	4 of 14	9 of 53	313 of 751
High Stile	807m/2,648ft	5 of 14	13 of 53	376 of 751
The Old Man of Coniston	803m/2,635ft	6 of 14	14 of 53	385 of 751
Kirk Fell	802m/2,631ft	7 of 14	15 of 53	388 of 751
Grisedale Pike	791m/2,595ft	8 of 14	16 of 53	408 of 751
High Raise	762m/2,500ft	9 of 14	20 of 53	464 of 751
Dale Head	753m/2,470ft	10 of 14	21 of 53	475 of 751
Robinson	737m/2,417ft	11 of 14	23 of 53	507 of 751
Pike of Blisco	705m/2,313ft	12 of 14	30 of 53	575 of 751
Seatallan	692m/2,270ft	13 of 14	35 of 53	604 of 751
Harter Fell	653m/2,143ft	14 of 14	47 of 53	686 of 751
Bow Fell[1]	902m/2,959ft	–	–	–

[1] Bow Fell has very slightly less than 500ft (150m) of ascent all around but it only misses out by a few feet. It is certainly a great distance from its parent mountain, Scafell Pike, though it is such a well-known and dominating summit that no book of England's mountains would be complete without it.

Western Lakeland contains some of the most dramatic and most remote country in England. Impressive crags and corries abound with other noteworthy features, such as the Wastwater Screes and Wastwater itself,

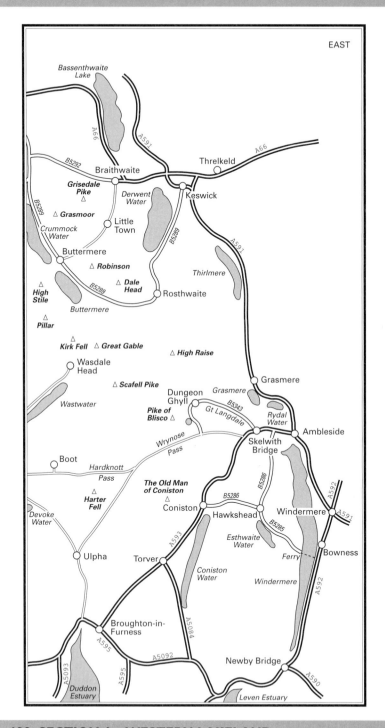

EAST

Bassenthwaite Lake

A66

A591

A66

Threlkeld

B5292

Braithwaite

Keswick

Grisedale Pike △

Derwent Water

B5289

Grasmoor △

Little Town

Crummock Water

B5289

Buttermere

△ Robinson

A591

Thirlmere

High Stile △

B5289

△ Dale Head

Rosthwaite

Buttermere

△ Pillar

Kirk Fell △   △ Great Gable

△ High Raise

Wasdale Head

△ Scafell Pike

Grasmere

Grasmere

Dungeon Ghyll

B5343

Wastwater

Pike of Blisco △

Gt Langdale

Rydal Water

Ambleside

Wrynose Pass

Skelwith Bridge

Boot

Hardknott Pass

△ Harter Fell

The Old Man of Coniston △

Coniston

B5286

B5286

Windermere

A592

A591

Devoke Water

Hawkshead

B5285

Ulpha

A593

Esthwaite Water

Ferry

Bowness

Torver

Coniston Water

Windermere

A592

Broughton-in-Furness

A5084

A595

A5093

A5092

Newby Bridge

A590

A595

Duddon Estuary

Leven Estuary

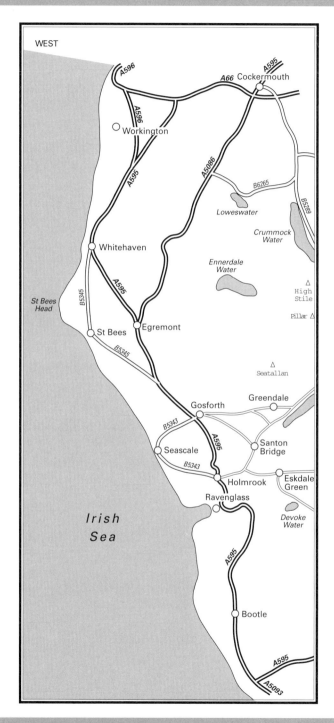

WEST

A596

A595

A66 Cockermouth

A596

Workington

A5086

B6265

B5289

Loweswater

Crummock
Water

A595

Whitehaven

Ennerdale
Water

△
High
Stile

Pillar △

St Bees
Head

B5345

A595

St Bees

Egremont

B5345

△
Seatallan

Greendale

Gosforth

B5343

A595

Santon
Bridge

Seascale

B5343

Holmrook

Eskdale
Green

Ravenglass

Devoke
Water

Irish
Sea

A595

Bootle

A595

A5093

the deepest lake in England. The ridges radiate out from the highest point in England, Scafell Pike, and most of the ground here lies consistently above 2,000ft (610m). As the geology of the Lake District is very similar, it is discussed wholly within Section 5 on page 99.

Access

There is a rail service to the coastal towns, stations of use to walkers being at Ulverston (bus to Coniston and Ambleside), Ravenglass (from where there is a narrow gauge steam railway up Eskdale to Boot), Drigg, Seascale, Sellafield, St Bees and Workington (bus to Cockermouth and infrequent summer service from there to Buttermere). There is a frequent daily train service between Manchester Airport, Preston, Lancaster, Ulverston and Barrow-in-Furness. There are regular Monday to Saturday trains between Barrow-in-Furness and Carlisle, servicing the western part of the district and a limited Sunday service between Carlisle, Workington and Whitehaven only. A branch line from Oxenholme, on the West Coast main line, runs to Windermere and there are regular daily services in summer, but in winter, although it still runs daily, the service is more limited; there are direct trains between Windermere, Manchester Piccadilly and Manchester Airport subject to the above restrictions. A bus service connects Windermere, Ambleside, Grasmere and Keswick with a summer service between Ambleside and Old Dungeon Ghyll (Great Langdale).

By car, it is more difficult to reach the western side of the district than the east. The A590, A5092 and A595 together run around the coast, linking Junction 36 of the M6 with Ravenglass, Workington and Carlisle. The A591 leaves the A590 at Kendal and goes through Ambleside and Grasmere on its way to Keswick, and the A66 links Junction 40 of the M6 with Keswick, Cockermouth and Workington. Coniston can be reached along the A593 from the A590 to the south and Ambleside to the north. The only other way from east to west is across the mountain passes of Wrynose and Hardknott. This route has severe gradients (up to 1:3) and countless very sharp, acutely angled hairpin bends; it links Little Langdale (normally reached over Blea Tarn Pass from Great Langdale), Dunnerdale and the head of Eskdale.

Accommodation

On the eastern side, there is accommodation in Ambleside and Grasmere (see Section 5) but for many of the hills it will be necessary to be in the west. There are several inns and a hotel in Eskdale as well as a few bed and breakfast establishments around Eskdale Green. At Wasdale Head there is a hotel, while there are quite a few places around Buttermere (very busy in summer). Accommodation is plentiful in Coniston and Keswick. There are youth hostels at Keswick, Derwentwater, Borrowdale (Longthwaite), Honister Hause, Buttermere, Ennerdale (Low Gillerthwaite), Black Sail (upper Ennerdale), Wastwater, Eskdale, Coniston (Holly How and Coniston Coppermines), Hawkshead, Elterwater, Langdale (Red Bank), Grasmere (Butterlip How and Thorney How), Ambleside and Windermere.

Scafell Pike

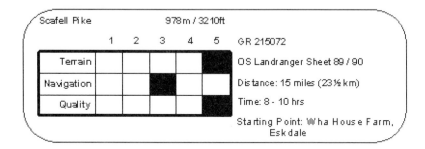

Scafell Pike						978m / 3210ft
	1	2	3	4	5	GR 215072
Terrain					■	OS Landranger Sheet 89 / 90
Navigation			■			Distance: 15 miles (23½ km)
Quality					■	Time: 8 - 10 hrs
						Starting Point: Wha House Farm, Eskdale

Scafell Pike is a grand mountain when viewed from afar, but upon close acquaintance it is stony and bouldery. Its finest appearance is from Eskdale and this provides the most pleasing approach. The walk also includes the summit of Scafell, which narrowly does not fit the criterion of a descent of 500ft on all sides, but it is certainly a dominant 3,000ft peak of England. However, because of the relative remoteness of these two peaks and the difficult crossing between Scafell Pike and Scafell (overall the route involving 4,000ft of ascent) it does make for a very long day.

From the car-park (which is to be found half a mile up the valley beyond the youth hostel) walk up the road for 100 yards (east), and take the farm road on the left. Shortly, before Taw House Farm is reached and, as the road bends right to it, a gate on the left gives access to a path running above the wall. This path eventually leaves the inbye just before the bridge over the Cowcove Beck. On the other side of it, the valley path should be left for the Cowcove zigzags, which start in about a hundred yards. At the top of the hairpins, the path enters a maze of hanging valleys but, despite crossing several low cols, it keeps on the right, southern side of the main beck and, after a while, crosses a tributary, Damas Dubs.

Immediately after the ford, a path (indistinct at first) branches right and this should be taken (in preference to the path straight ahead). This path keeps out of the peaty ground in the valley and runs over a low pass into Upper Eskdale, above Esk Falls. A sheepfold is shortly reached.

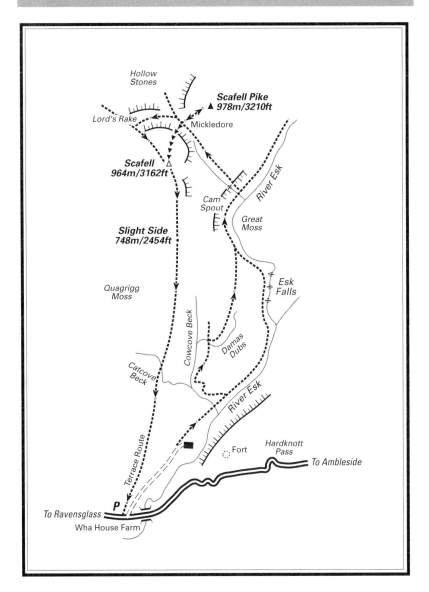

The view onwards up one of England's wildest valleys is impressive, but there is still much ground to cover. Continue up the north side of the valley to the fine waterfall of Cam Spout, opposite the huge morass of Great Moss on the other side of the river. This is where the climbing starts in earnest. On the right-hand side of the waterfall, the path climbs up through rock. Some scrambling is necessary; however, there is no exposure and the easiest line is never technically difficult. Scramblers will be interested to note that harder variations are possible closer to the stream.

Once above the waterfall, follow the path up to the col at the head of the valley, known as Mickledore. From here, turn right up a clear path that climbs the last 500ft through stony terrain to the highest ground in England. Once the extensive view has been savoured, reverse the route of ascent to Mickledore.

From Mickledore, Scafell's crags rear up dauntingly skyward. Although so close, Scafell's summit is not obtainable from here, except by the experienced scrambler tackling Broad Stand (see section on scrambling alternatives on page 244). Instead, look down on the Wasdale side of Mickledore to the prominent narrow gully known as Lord's Rake, cutting across Scafell's crags about 100ft below the pass. When at the bottom, the steep scree is uninviting, but the rise to the first col is the worst. In the upper reaches of the first ascent, the best footing is to be found on the right. When on the first col, the Rake can be seen crossing an amphitheatre below crags to another col. Beyond that, after another short descent, the final ascent leads to the west ridge of Scafell; three ascents, two descents in total. After the nasty beginning, the rake ends all too soon. A walk on scree leads to Scafell's summit bringing to an end a difficult but enjoyable ridge walk.

From Scafell's summit there is still a long way to go. A pleasant ridge, soon becoming grass (a blessing for tired feet), leads south to the rocky bump of Slight Side from where it is well worth studying the route onwards. The first part is largely pathless and it is essential for later to locate the path that leads safely onwards through the complex terrain of crags and small, boggy hanging valleys.

What should be noted is a line of cairns running down the ridge that eventually ends. From here on, keep left of the huge bog on the Burnmoor Tarn side (Quagrigg Moss), but do not descend too far into the valley of the Cowcove Beck. About half-way in between the moss and the stream, a sketchy path will be seen; aim for this. This path keeps above the rounded turret of Cat Crag and on into the valley of the Catcove Beck. Keeping up on the hillside, the path runs along the northern side of Eskdale, earning it the name of the Terrace Route, before leading straight back into the top of the car-park at Wha House Farm.

Great Gable and Kirk Fell

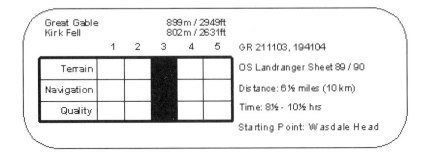

Great Gable			899m / 2949ft		
Kirk Fell			802m / 2631ft		
	1	2	3	4	5
Terrain					
Navigation					
Quality					

GR 211103, 194104

OS Landranger Sheet 89 / 90

Distance: 6½ miles (10 km)

Time: 8½ - 10½ hrs

Starting Point: Wasdale Head

Although many great Lakeland peaks – Scafell Pike, Scafell, Gable and Pillar – surround Wasdale Head, it is Great Gable that dominates the scene. Its lower neighbour, Kirk Fell, is hardly noticed by many as anything other than a steep, rounded, stony hill. However, when viewed from Ennerdale, the mountain reveals itself in quite a different light, as a peak defended by the huge crags of Boat How. On this route Kirk Fell is visited first because, majestic as it is, it cannot rival Great Gable for mountain scenery.

At Wasdale Head, car-parking is to be found on the right a few hundred yards below the inn on a large grassy area. From here, continue up the road, past the inn, turning immediately left down the far side of it. Behind the inn, turn right and, after passing through a gate, the path runs alongside the river past Row Head Farm. Resist the temptation to cross the packhorse bridge, the track beyond leading into fields. The path soon begins to climb steeply and, once through a gate, turn left up Mosedale. The path runs virtually level until it splits at a large cairn; here take the right-hand path, which passes through a gate, then over a stream and climbs up a number of hairpins into the hanging valley of the Gatherstone Beck. Continue climbing to reach the ridge at Black Sail Pass, revealing fine views of Ennerdale ahead.

At the top of the pass, turn right and follow an obvious track up to the base of the crags. Here there is a divergence; the best route continues straight up the crag, following the line of metal fence posts quite closely (essential in mist). This path weaves an intricate way up the crag, requiring a little scrambling, but with no problems whatsoever. The

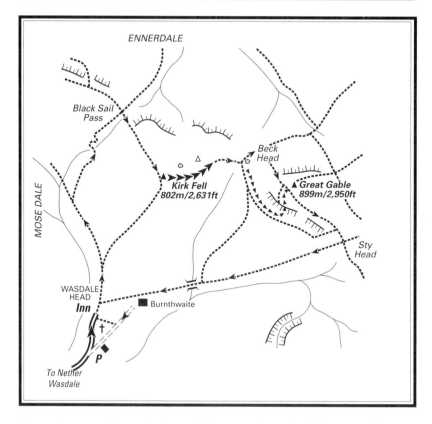

alternative route from the base of the crags is on the left, proceeding up a rather smooth and slippery gully to the top. At the top of the crag, follow the line of fence posts over the bleak but nevertheless quite pleasant summit plateau. Although this section is largely pathless, in mist the fence should serve as quite a reasonable guide. However, in very thick mist (i.e. visibility of less than ten yards) a few missing fence posts could pose a slight problem. The fence leads directly to the summit cairn and small shelter.

At the summit, the fence turns through a right angle and its direction is not especially clear but, if followed, it leads down to the depression at Kirkfell Tarn (in mist it is essential to locate the fence which runs in a north-easterly direction from the summit). Beyond is the east summit, which can be avoided by crossing below the south side of Kirkfell Tarn and making a gently rising traverse before turning inwards to find the fence posts before the sharp and craggy drop down to Beck Head. For purists, the fence posts running over the east summit may be followed to reach the same point but with a little more ascent. In mist, do not leave the fence posts, as the area is pathless and confusing. A short sharp descent then leads down Rib End to the tarns at Beck Head, where it is advisable to deviate from the fence as it runs through the middle of one of them! At this point, scramblers may wish to deviate and undertake the scramble described towards the back of the book around the Great Napes.

Walkers, however, should follow a prominent path ahead, which climbs steeply up Gable's screes to the right of Gable Crag, to reach the flat summit plateau and cairn. To descend to Sty Head, follow the line of cairns running west. This soon develops into an improved footpath descending the steep slopes; no navigational problems will be encountered. Sty Head Pass is marked by the mountain rescue team stretcher box. From here, the descent to Wasdale Head can be made by following the clear main path south, which soon turns west and then south-west. When the descent is finished there is a long walk through farmland, the path leading over the Gable Beck on a footbridge and then through the farmyard at Burnthwaite. From here, the farm's access road runs down past the chapel and back to the car-park. For those wishing to visit the inn or hamlet, a path runs across the fields from just before the chapel.

Pillar

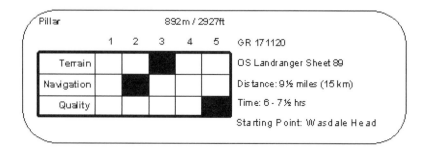

Pillar is the highest point on the long ridge separating Wasdale and Ennerdale to the west of Kirk Fell and, like the latter, it is not dominant in the view from Wasdale Head, instead standing back at the head of Mosedale.

At Wasdale Head, car-parking is to be found on the right a few hundred yards below the inn on a large grassy area. From here, continue up the road and then turn left down the far side of the inn. Behind the inn, turn right, and after passing through a gate, the path runs alongside the river past Row Head Farm. Resist the temptation to cross the packhorse bridge but keep straight up the path, which climbs steeply through a gate, beyond which the main path should be followed to the left up Mosedale. The path runs virtually level until it splits at a large cairn; here take the right-hand path, which passes through a gate, then over a stream and climbs up a number of hairpins into the hanging valley of the Gatherstone Beck. Once in the upper valley, turn left following a path that climbs up the left-hand flank and then makes a rising traverse to meet the ridge well to the left of Black Sail Pass.

Here, turn left and follow the main path, which contours around the slopes of Looking Stead, before suddenly giving spectacular views down into Ennerdale on the right. The path now rises and, at the top of this first rise, at a cairn, a small path takes off to the right, descending initially. Follow this route, Robinson's Traverse, which makes a traverse of the steep and precipitous slopes above Ennerdale, rising and falling, giving new vistas and surprises, to Robinson's Cairn where Pillar Rock

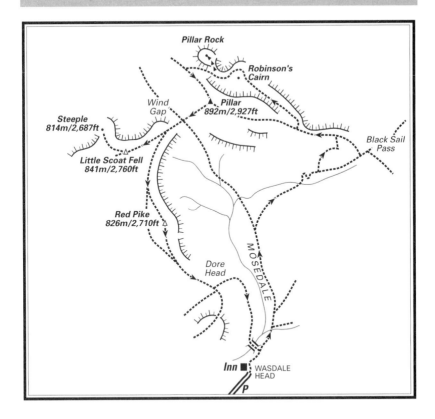

comes into view ahead. The path now descends into the delightful Pillar Cove and then turns left, climbing steeply uphill on scree, before turning right and running along the Shamrock Traverse above the large crag, after which it is named, to arrive at the neck between Pillar Rock and the mountain.

From here, it is well worth undertaking the simple scramble to the right onto Pisgah – the lowest summit of Pillar Rock, as the ascent of the Rock itself is a dangerous and exposed scramble even by its easiest route, not to be undertaken unroped or without adequate experience. Those who are experienced enough to undertake the ascent should see the section on alternative scrambling routes on page 247.

After visiting Pisgah, follow a path on the steep scree straight up the slope to the summit of Pillar itself. Leave the summit in a south-westerly direction, making a steep and loose descent to Wind Gap before following the ridge to the summit of Scoat Fell, ignoring a path contouring around the slope to the left. From here, it is well worth making the short journey out to the sharp summit of Steeple, which provides an excellent view back to the crags of Mirk and Mirklin Coves.

Returning to the summit of Scoat Fell, descend the pathless south slopes to the col between it and Red Pike, meeting the path direct from Pillar *en route*. The summit of Red Pike, perched on the edge of crags overlooking Mosedale, is then only a short, easy walk away. Continue following the south ridge over the rocky prominence known as 'The Chair' and on down to Dore Head, at which point, a left turn leads down a scree run into Mosedale to meet a path in the valley. Turn right on this path, which leads back through fields and over the packhorse bridge behind Row Head Farm to rejoin the outward route.

Grasmoor and Grisedale Pike

Grasmoor			852m / 2795ft			
Grisedale Pike			791m / 2595ft			
	1	2	3	4	5	GR 174203, 198225
Terrain		■				OS Landranger Sheet 89 / 90
Navigation		■				Distance: 10½ miles (17 km)
Quality			■			Time: 6½ - 8 hrs
						Starting Point: Braithwaite

This route makes a fine high-level walk around Coledale. Although the mile-age and time may seem long, surprisingly little effort is needed. The scenery is varied, with spectacular views of Coledale, Newlands and Buttermere.

Braithwaite is a lovely but somewhat confusing village. If approaching from Whinlatter Pass, the car-park is just before the village centre across a little bridge on the right. If approaching from Keswick, follow the Whinlatter Road and cross a bridge on the left, which gives access to the same car-park. This bridge is signposted to 'Youth Centre and Coledale'; the car-park is on the right just past the Methodist church.

From the car-park entrance, an unsurfaced track climbs a small bank to meet a higher lane by a pub. Walk left around the front of the pub and then turn right on a surfaced lane that climbs the hill to High Coledale Farm. This lane should not to be confused with the mine road up Coledale itself, which leaves the Whinlatter Road a little further out of Braithwaite. When the road turns right to the farm, take a path that continues to rise up onto the open fellside. The initial ridge is not the ridge of Sail and Grasmoor, but simply a subsidiary ridge that must be crossed first. When the path forks shortly, take the right-hand branch, which leads to the right-hand dip in the skyline between Stile End and Outerside. Here, the path turns half right, contouring along the breast of the fell, to join the mine road (unsurfaced) coming up from Stair; ahead now is Sail. The road continues up, becoming, less substantial to pass the mine and reach the ridge at the Sail–Scar Crags col; a right-hand turn and a stiff climb lead up to Sail's summit pastures. The summit cairn of Sail lies just off the path to the right.

Returning to the path, continue on down to the small depression,

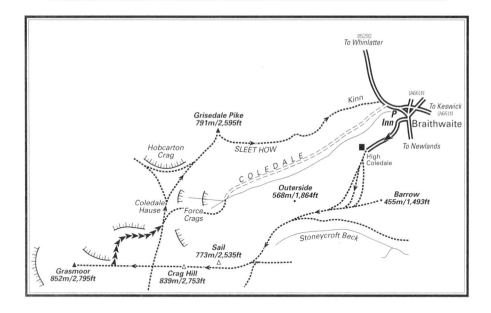

before ascending the narrowing, rocky ridge to the summit of Crag Hill (otherwise known as Eel Crag) with its triangulation pillar. The objective is now clear: the rounded hill ahead, which is Grasmoor. Follow the path down to the wet depression and then follow the track, becoming increasingly stony, to the cairn on Grasmoor's summit. A short walk westwards leads to Grasmoor End, where the ground falls vertically away down to Crummock Water, providing an excellent viewpoint.

To descend from Grasmoor, return to the col between Grasmoor and Crag Hill and turn left following the path down to Coledale Hause. However, if it is a clear day, interest can be added by descending east-north-east from the summit and following a faint path around the rim of Dove Crags to reach the above-mentioned path. Cross straight over the hause, and follow a path, indistinct at first, which ascends past some fenced shafts to the ridge at the col above Hobcarton Crag. Turn right and follow the broken wall over a minor knoll and then up to the main summit of Grisedale Pike.

The route back to Braithwaite lies down the east ridge. Follow a steep and difficult path, on rough scree, until the ridge begins to level off and grass appears underfoot. Before too long, the path leaves the ridge and descends its southern, Coledale flank to arrive on the grassy plateau of Kinn. The route continues on a path through bracken to reach the Whinlatter Pass road a short distance above the car-park.

High Stile

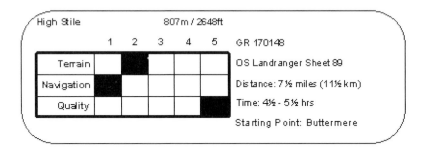

High Stile						807 m / 2648ft
	1	2	3	4	5	GR 170148
Terrain		■				OS Landranger Sheet 89
Navigation	■					Distance: 7½ miles (11½ km)
Quality					■	Time: 4½ - 5½ hrs
						Starting Point: Buttermere

To the south-west of Buttermere, there lies a long high ridge of which the highest point is High Stile. To the south of the ridge, steep but generally uninteresting slopes fall down to the conifer plantations of Ennerdale but, to the north, the flank erupts into crags which fall down into three fine corries high above Buttermere.

The best way to visit the summit is to traverse the ridge between High Crag to the east and Red Pike to the west, crossing High Stile in the middle, the walk being best accomplished from Buttermere, where there is parking down a lane by the Bridge Inn for the sum of three pounds. Alternatively, there is limited free parking in a lay-by up the Newlands Road. The ridge may be walked in either direction but the stretch along the lakeshore is perhaps best done in the morning while it is still quite quiet and the legs are fresh.

The lane by the Bridge Inn forks in front of the Fish Hotel; the parking is to the right but the track on the left runs down to the lake and is the start of the walk. However, before reaching the lake it runs through fields, first turning left and then to the right; ignore another track through a gate on the right that leads to Scale Force. When the pasture by the lake is reached, turn right down a track by the hedge, to reach a footbridge over Buttermere Dubs. Once over the bridge, turn left, pass through a gate and then avoid all paths leading uphill, instead following the lakeside track. Scramblers wishing to undertake the route on Grey Crag (see section on scrambling alternatives towards on page 249) should leave the walking route here.

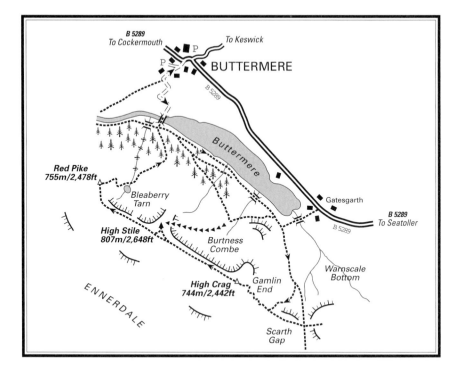

However, walkers should keep by the lakeside all the way through the wood and afterwards until, once over the first beck, Comb Beck and, when underneath, Low Crag, fork to the right up a rising path amongst bracken. Ignore any paths to the left or right and follow it to a fence, where there is a stile, and then on, high above the valley, to a gap in a wall. Here, the main path leads ahead to the notch in the skyline which is Scarth Gap but, on the nearside of the wall, a path, over scree at first but then grass, leads uphill, before crossing the wall at a collapsed section, just before it swings around to the right. Now running back above the wall, the path is quite distinct and runs up to the ridge below Gamlin End where especially fine views of Pillar and Pillar Rock open up ahead.

A recently improved path climbs up the very steep slopes of Gamlin End to the right to reach the small summit of High Crag, from where there are fine views of the length of Ennerdale, the fells at its head and the fells around Wasdale Head. A somewhat narrow ridge, with a path above the crags on its eastern flank above Burtness Comb, now leads onwards to High Stile, the path becoming slightly lost on its summit plateau. There are three cairns of roughly equal altitude on the summit but the highest point is on the northern ridge, although not at the largest cairn, instead at a smaller one about 30 yards further north. Return to the large cairn and then continue around to the right, above the crags, to another cairn above a drop down to the connecting ridge to Red Pike. To avoid this steep drop, aim around to the left and then along a path on a grassy ridge that rises up to Red Pike, the summit of which, like High Stile's, is out along its northern ridge to the right.

From the summit, a steep path leads north down to Bleaberry Tarn but ignore any deviations to the summit of the grassy knoll of Dodd, running along the ridge to the left, about half-way between the summit and the tarn. From the outlet of the tarn, follow a path on the right bank of the stream discharging from it, until a wall is found running away to the right. Although a small path runs ahead very steeply down by Sour Milk Gill, it is steep, arduous, awkward, difficult and not recommended. Instead, a cairned path runs along the hillside to the right before turning down the hill and then back left, descending more gradually through the wood and back to the lake shore at the foot of the lake where the outwards route is rejoined.

The Old Man of Coniston

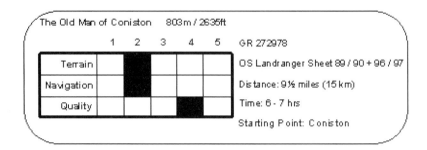

The Old Man of Coniston   803m / 2635ft

	1	2	3	4	5
Terrain		■			
Navigation		■			
Quality				■	

GR 272978

OS Landranger Sheet 89 / 90 + 96 / 97

Distance: 9½ miles (15 km)

Time: 6 - 7 hrs

Starting Point: Coniston

Many visitors to Coniston glance up at its 'Old Man', even if they don't climb it. Many, particularly in summer, make a pilgrimage to its summit up the wide and well-trodden track out of the back of Coniston. However, relatively few venture out northwards into the rest of the Coniston Fells. North of the Old Man, there is a long ridge with no significant drops in it until after Swirl How, where its east ridge drops down almost far enough to give an outlier, Wetherlam, its separateness, but not quite far enough!

Park in the centre of Coniston, either in the pay and display car-park by the toilets on the Hawkshead road or, out of season, on one of the town's back streets. Leave the village by the road running up the hill to the Black Bull pub from the opposite side of the main road bridge over Church Beck; this road is signposted to the 'Sun Hotel'. Walk up the road to the inn and, immediately after it, turn right through a farmyard on a path, initially signposted 'Old Man & Lever's Water 2½' and later, in the farmyard, 'YHA'. This path runs up the side of Church Beck, past some fine waterfalls, to a bridge over it, known as Miner's Bridge. Once over the bridge, turn left and shortly turn right on a track rising up the right-hand hillside, which soon enters some slaty spoil from the mine workings. When the track hairpins right to Tilberthwaite, continue straight on, following a gently rising grassy path along the hillside. From the path, there is a good aerial view of the Lower Coppermines Valley.

The hills behind Coniston hold a secret not revealed to those that do not venture into them. Here, in this valley, and the corries surrounding

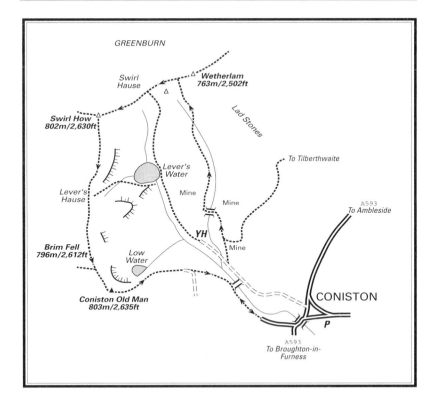

it, were three separate copper mines and a quarry, of which many relics can be seen today and indeed the valleys themselves are well worth exploring on a day when weather rules out the higher fells. However, many of the more remote shafts are unfenced and care should be exercised. The warning not to explore too close must again be repeated when it comes to adits or levels (horizontal passages running into the hillside) as these often open out into vertical shafts. Children and pets should be kept under close control and sheep should not be surprised close to vertical drops, as they will run directly away from their possible attackers, even if this is into a shaft.

The track leads into the upper valley of Red Dell, past a smelting mill and a large opening to a level on the right in a cutting (known as Cobbler Hole), before crossing the beck. Ahead is a large area of fenced shafts, some of which can be seen from outside the fence. On the hillside above, there is a raised tramway running up to some levels below Keppel crag. This walk, however, keeps up the valley on the left-hand side of the stream (be careful not to confuse the indistinct path with an old leat running to the mine) and up to the foot of the cascades above. Follow a sketchy path on the left of the stream into the upper corrie where it crosses to the right bank of the stream and climbs up to the ridge at the top. A short walk to the right leads to Wetherlam's summit.

Return to the point where the ridge was first reached and continue straight on, following a path slightly on the Greenburn side of the ridge to the next col, named Swirl Hause. Continuing up the path ahead ascending Prison Band, the summit of Swirl How is reached. Leave its summit by walking south to Lever's Hause, from where the track climbs the long gentle slope to Brim Fell and on the short distance to the summit of the Old Man himself.

From the Old Man, follow the tourist track down from the summit (initially south-east, then east). This path leads down with no description needed past Low Water and an old quarry with an adit, short section of railway and an aerial ropeway. Continue on down the quarry road until it bends sharp right and starts to contour along to the Walna Scar Road. Here, follow the second path on the left. The first (which should be ignored) runs back left almost level, whereas the second descends initially and then runs down to Miner's Bridge, from where the outward route can be reversed back to the village.

High Raise

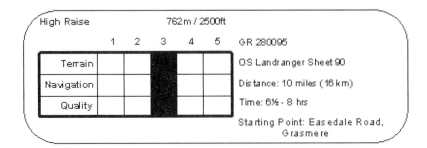

High Raise					762m / 2500ft	
	1	2	3	4	5	GR 280095
Terrain			■			OS Landranger Sheet 90
Navigation			■			Distance: 10 miles (16 km)
Quality			■			Time: 6½ - 8 hrs
						Starting Point: Easedale Road, Grasmere

High Raise is the highest point of the long, flat, featureless ridge running from Watendlath to the north and ending spectacularly in the Langdale Pikes to the south. A lack of clear and reassuring landmarks close to its summit, however, make this a walk for a day with good visibility. An alternative route for both walkers and scramblers is given in the section on scrambling routes towards the back of the book, the route beginning at Dungeon Ghyll in Langdale and including the fine rock scenery of the Langdale Pikes and Pavey Ark.

However, the best walking route begins behind Grasmere, up the valley of Easedale which runs down into the back of the village; a small road leads up the valley from the Red Lion. After about half a mile there is a small car-park on the right (pay and display) and this is where cars should be left. Walk up the road for about 300 yards, ignoring a road to the right, until a path leaves it on the left, going through a small copse and crossing the river (signposted 'Easedale Tarn'). This path runs through the inbye and up the left-hand side of the prominent waterfalls of Sour Milk Gill on the left-hand side of the valley.

At the top of the waterfalls, the hanging valley of Easedale unfolds. The path on the left-hand side of the now slightly rising valley shortly leads to Easedale Tarn. Keeping on the left side of the tarn, the path follows the left bank of the stream and climbs steeply up into the upper corrie with some mild scrambling *en route*. The 'Matterhorn' of Belles Knott is very prominent during the climb above Easedale Tarn and can easily be incorporated by crossing the stream and walking up its back

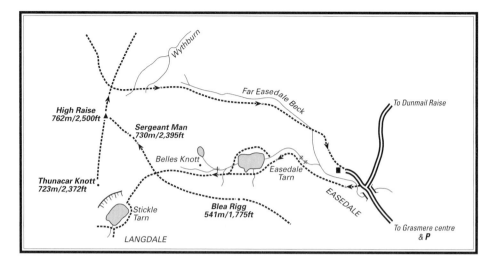

face. However, the main path begins a rising traverse of the southern side of the corrie, eventually turning south up into some shallow gullies to arrive at the ridge separating Easedale and Langdale. At this point, Stickle Tarn comes into view ahead.

Turning right (north-west) climb the ridge, bearing left to the shapely summit of Sergeant Man. From here, the view onwards should now be surveyed. The crags and rock of Easedale are now behind and ahead is a large, dreary plateau. High Raise is the 'lump' north-west from here and a faint path is noticeable. Follow your chosen route, although avoiding wet ground altogether is virtually impossible. The summit is reached unexpectedly but is a welcome sight.

High Raise is graced with a triangulation pillar and several stones and has excellent views all around. However, the view along the Thirlmere–Borrowdale ridge is rather bleak but Langstrath looks very impressive.

When the view has been enjoyed, begin a northwards then north-east descent to Greenup Edge. Being the major pass between Grasmere and Rosthwaite, it is graced with an excellent path. Descending right, eastwards, the path traverses the head of the waterlogged Wythburn valley. Only at the next pass does the descent into Far Easedale begin. In mist, it is important to remember to descend only after the second pass; otherwise the destination will be Wythburn (Thirlmere), several miles north of Grasmere.

The path descends quickly into Far Easedale, eventually crossing to the northern bank at the end of the hanging valley. After another descent, the path runs down past Brimmer Head Farm and out to the end of the Easedale Road about half a mile from the day's starting point.

Dale Head and Robinson

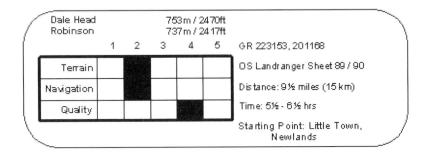

Dale Head			753m / 2470ft			
Robinson			737m / 2417ft			
	1	2	3	4	5	GR 223153, 201168

	1	2	3	4	5	
Terrain		■				OS Landranger Sheet 89 / 90
Navigation		■				Distance: 9½ miles (15 km)
Quality				■		Time: 5½ - 6½ hrs

Starting Point: Little Town, Newlands

Dale Head certainly dominates the head of Newlands with its interesting and craggy north face, which is in complete contrast to the grassy shoulder it throws down to Honister Hause. Robinson, reputedly named after a previous owner, presents the walker with an unusual feature on its summit – a pair of parallel rock walls with a gravelled 'roadway' in between.

The walk begins from the quiet hamlet of Little Town. Car parking is available to the south of the hamlet on both sides of Chapel Bridge; however, this is the only parking in the vicinity and therefore fills up quite quickly.

Begin by walking up the road from the parking place towards Little Town but turning back sharp right over a stile which gives access to a path running up to the old mine road. Follow this track up the valley past the remnants of Goldscope Mine on the right and up to the workings of Castlenook Mine below the obvious crag, butting out into the valley on the left about half-way up. Beyond here, ignore a path on the left and instead follow the track (now on grass) down to the river, crossing it on some stepping stones and continuing steeply up the fellside on a path, which, although visible from afar, is indistinct to start with. This rises up, crosses Far Tongue Gill, and then hairpins up into the upper corrie to the old mine workings of Dale Head Mine. Follow the path, which, after an initial rise, traverses back to the left on a grassy shelf to meet the east ridge of Dale Head quite close to the summit. Turn right and follow the ridge to the fine cairn.

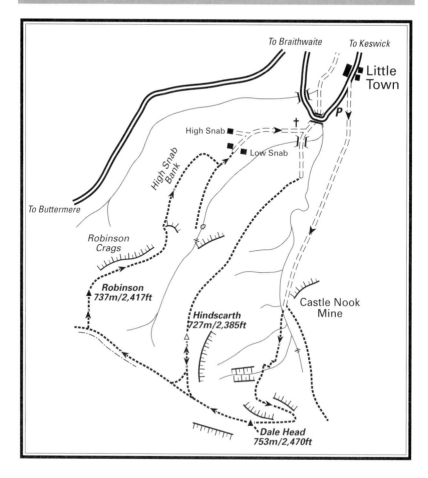

Continue on down the west ridge, which narrows and passes over some small rocky turrets before dropping down to Hindscarth Edge. If Hindscarth is to be visited, turn right and follow the gently rising track to its summit, before returning down the ridge to meet the main Dale Head to Robinson path (included in the time). Follow the path onwards over Littledale Edge and up onto Robinson at which point a fence appears. When a large cairn is reached at the top of the slope, turn right and follow the path for a short distance to the distinctive summit.

The descent begins by walking north-east from the summit, picking up some cairns and then a path. This path leads down the north-east ridge in a dramatic position by the edge of Robinson Crags before it drops sharply down four large rock steps that are very slippery in the wet. Climb the short distance out of the col and continue following the narrow grassy ridge of High Snab Bank. Towards the far end, leave the ridge for a gently descending grass path on the eastern side, which soon joins onto the main downwards path. Turn right and follow this extremely steep path down past a group of pine trees to the farm road below. Here, turn left and, after passing through three gates, it becomes tarmacked and leads down uneventfully to Newland's Church. Turn left beyond the church to join the road in the vicinity of Chapel Bridge.

Pike of Blisco

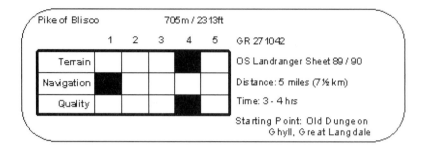

Pike of Blisco						705m / 2313ft

	1	2	3	4	5	GR 271042
Terrain				■		OS Landranger Sheet 89 / 90
Navigation	■			■		Distance: 5 miles (7½ km)
Quality				■		Time: 3 - 4 hrs

Starting Point: Old Dungeon
Ghyll, Great Langdale

Pike O'Blisco, as it is more often known, is clearly in view from Langdale, if over-topped by its surrounding neighbours – Crinkle Crags, Langdale Pikes and Bowfell. It does, however, have many special qualities and is certainly a good excursion, best saved for a fine day.

Begin by walking up the road towards Blea Tarn from Dungeon Ghyll, where there is a pay and display car-park, free to National Trust members. After passing the buildings at Wall End, continue up the road around the first few hairpins. When an obvious path leaves to the right, making a level traverse of the fellside, follow it across a few streams and up to the head of the valley. The track then continues over a small depression after which some scrambling is required up a small rock band. Shortly afterwards, there is a fork in the paths; both lead to the summit. The left-hand path leads to the summit without much more scrambling. The path running half right runs straight up to the summit cairn with some scrambling. If the more sporting finish is desired, follow the right-hand fork, which involves two easy climbs up small craglets. When the summit is reached, there are two cairns on small rocky knolls; the further (north-western) summit is slightly higher.

To begin the descent, follow a path, running in a southerly direction initially, which leads eventually down to the pass at Red Tarn. Here, after passing a small fenced enclosure on the left, turn right down the path into Oxendale. When at the bottom, cross the bridge and turn right along the valley track. This leads to the farm at Stool End and on through the yard, before continuing down its tarmacked drive, back to the road by the entrance to the Old Dungeon Ghyll Hotel.

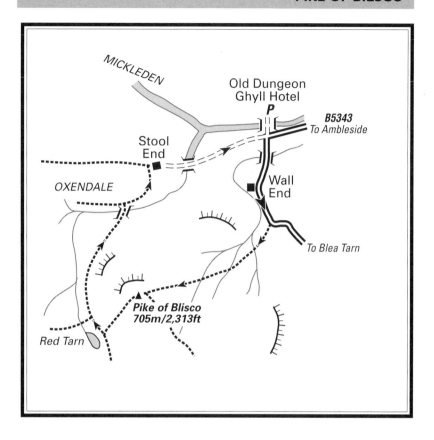

Seatallan

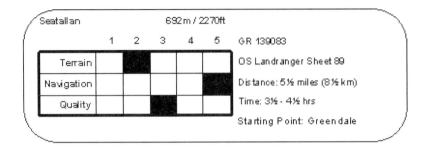

	1	2	3	4	5	
Seatallan						692m / 2270ft
						GR 139083
Terrain		■				OS Landranger Sheet 89
Navigation					■	Distance: 5½ miles (8½ km)
Quality			■			Time: 3½ - 4½ hrs
						Starting Point: Greendale

Seatallan is probably one of the very best examples of a separate mountain. Unlike others, which are simply the highest point of a long chain or ridge, Seatallan rises abruptly from its surroundings with no subsidiary heights whatsoever. On two sides, its grass slopes rise almost vertically but only the south ridge ascends to its summit with ease as a long, grassy incline. Seatallan has no crags or scree worthy of any mention; however, its two shoulders, Middle Fell and Buckbarrow, do boast some significant crags, particularly the latter. Eager scramblers are well advised to fulfil their passion by climbing the good route on Pike Crag (part of Buckbarrow's south face) up to its summit cairn (see section on scrambling alternatives on page 256).

The walk begins and ends at Greendale where there are a few holiday cottages. The hamlet can be reached either from Gosforth or Wasdale Head but less easily from Nether Wasdale. There is a good hard parking surface to the east (Wasdale Head side) of the cottages but please note that the parking opposite the cottages is strictly private.

Begin by walking west on the road and crossing the river before turning right and following a grassy strip between a wall on the left and some gorse bushes on the right. This gives access to the fell and a path runs up onto a shoulder where it becomes less distinct. However a larger path running left to right will be found by climbing straight up the fellside a short distance. Follow this path to the right and, after crossing two streams and passing a sheepfold, the track bears steeply uphill. Once out of the valley, it is well worth walking left to Buckbarrow's summit for the fine view it has of the lake, which is lost completely in the view from Seatallan.

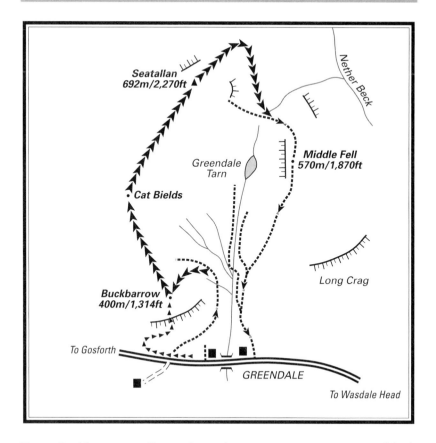

From Buckbarrow, walk north-north-west over a succession of little hillocks to the fine cairn on Glade How and then, skirting a slight hollow, aim up onto Seatallan's south ridge. A small path does lead from Buckbarrow all the way to Seatallan's summit, although it is difficult to find; this section of the walk is very difficult in misty conditions. Once Seatallan's south ridge has been gained, follow it up at quite a gentle gradient to its summit overlooking Blengdale. The large cairn on the summit is reputed to have been built by the prehistoric peoples who lived on Stockdale Moor on the other side of Blengdale. Those with an interest in archaeology will be amply rewarded by an excursion to Stockdale Moor, which harbours many tumuli, cairns and ancient enclosures.

To avoid the extremely steep eastern face and the worst of the peat hags at Greendale Head, walk north, past a small cairn and then down quite a steep, narrow ridge. Some way down, rocks start to appear again and, a little below a prominent steeple-shaped rock and some more extensive big boulders, bear right down towards the escarpment above Nether Beck. It is worth noting, especially in mist, that Seatallan is extremely bleak and featureless, but that is not its only trap. The valley to the east of its summit is Nether Beck and not Greendale which lies further to the south, and a mistake here would mean about three miles extra walking at valley level. It is interesting to note that the head of the lake is visible from this point, which shows the differences in the aspects of the valleys. However, cross the peat hags at Greendale Head where the driest ground is to be found near the edge of the escarpment above Nether Beck and start to ascend Middle Fell ahead between Nether Beck and Greendale.

By contouring to the right above Greendale Head, a path will be picked up which has crossed over the middle of the bog, which, if followed to the left will lead to Middle Fell's summit cairn (another good viewpoint for Wastwater). Another path will be found, indistinct at first, leading south and this leads down the fellside to join with the path coming down Greendale and then leading straight back to the car by the cottages. It is worth noting the excellent view of the gorges and slender waterfalls of Tongue Gills seen from the lower reaches of the south-west ridge of Middle Fell.

Harter Fell

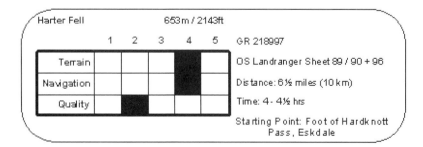

Harter Fell						653m / 2143ft
	1	2	3	4	5	GR 218997
Terrain				■		OS Landranger Sheet 89 / 90 + 96
Navigation				■		Distance: 6½ miles (10 km)
Quality		■				Time: 4 - 4½ hrs
						Starting Point: Foot of Hardknott Pass, Eskdale

Harter Fell is clearly seen from Eskdale and the walker is amply rewarded by its delightful summit, which rises to a rocky cone standing proud of everything else. It certainly has an aura of a mountain twice its height.

Begin by parking in Eskdale at the foot of Hardknott Pass at a small layby by Jubilee Bridge. Begin by crossing the gill on the old packhorse bridge and follow the path slanting up the fellside. Shortly after crossing a stream, it crosses back into the inbye and then out of it again at a higher level. Once back on the open fellside, follow the path uphill, leaving it soon for an initially less obvious path slanting off half left, marked by a few cairns. Follow this path, which is initially almost level and then steepens. After a long climb through craggy terrain, it turns back left to the highest outcrops.

The cairn and trig point do not actually grace the highest point; this is the next outcrop to the north-east, which can be climbed reasonably easily, albeit with one initial large awkward step, on the side facing the trig point.

From the summit, follow a path running in a north-easterly direction, which soon splits. The left-hand path runs eventually to Hardknott Pass and the right branch down into Dunnerdale. Following the left-hand path, descend down to a boggy plateau, where the path stays slightly on the Dunnerdale side of the ridge. Follow it down, crossing a stream, to a stile in a fence just by a forestry plantation. Cross the stile and follow the path above the plantation, crossing another stile (but do not enter the forest); immediately before the stile, there is another stile and gate on the

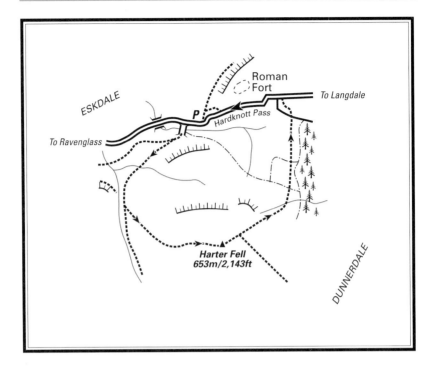

right, which should be ignored. Continue on until a broken-down wall is reached. After crossing the wall, follow it to the left to reach the motor road near the top of Hardknott Pass.

Here, turn left and, soon, above the first hairpin, follow a track leading straight on (as the road bends to the left), marked by a sign reading 'Public Footpath'. Follow this down until it meets the road again lower down. Now carry on down the road to the small car-park by the Roman fort. It is well worth at this point making the small detour to the right to see the remains before returning to the road. Keep following the road down and, on the top of another hairpin, follow another footpath off to the right, which, after passing through a V-shaped gap in the wall, descends back down to rejoin the road just above the car-park at the foot of the pass.

Bow Fell

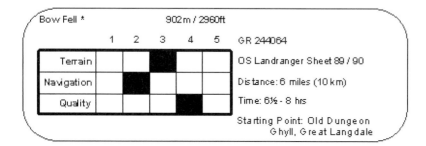

	1	2	3	4	5
Terrain			■		
Navigation		■			
Quality				■	

Bow Fell * 902m / 2960ft

GR 244064

OS Landranger Sheet 89 / 90

Distance: 6 miles (10 km)

Time: 6½ - 8 hrs

Starting Point: Old Dungeon Ghyll, Great Langdale

Bow Fell, as spelt by the Ordnance Survey, otherwise known as Bowfell, is a fine mountain. Although more photographs are probably taken of the Langdale Pikes (tops of High Raise), Bowfell dominates the scene at the head of the valley. The normal route of ascent by the Band and Three Tarns reveals little of the mountain's fine crags, but the variation described here makes a fine day's excursion.

From the pay-and-display National Trust car-park at Old Dungeon Ghyll (free to NT members with their membership card), walk back out to the tarmac road and turn right. After a few yards, the road bends left; here take the tarmacked farm road running across the fields to Stool End Farm. Once at the farm, continue though the farmyard and onto the open fell. The path soon splits; take the right-hand branch (signposted 'The Band'). After a long climb, the path levels off around the 1,800ft (550m) contour; here look for a path branching right, following around the edge of the Mickleden escarpment. At another small junction, bear half right along another small path below the crags. This is called the Climber's Traverse but at no point requires scrambling ability; there are stunning views down into Mickleden. After about one third of a mile, the path comes under Cambridge Crag to a large spring.

At this point, there is a prominent rising flat slab on the left. There is a scree slope to the right of it and this provides the non-scrambling route. However, much easier and much more enjoyable progress can be made by walking up the angled slab itself. Once at the top, the summit is in view half right. From here there are lovely views of Eskdale and the Scafell Group.

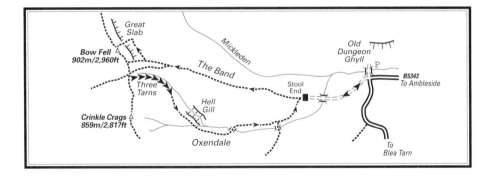

When ready to leave, go back to the main path crossed above the slab on the ascent and turn right (south), following the stony descent to Three Tarns. When at the pass, turn east down the Langdale Path. However, when this begins to contour to the left to join the Climber's Traverse, follow the small valley straight down on its right-hand side; there is a visible route denoted by a change in grass colour. This gives a speedy and much more pleasant descent to the stony Band. In mist, though, the clear path on the Band should be taken. Assuming the initially pathless route is taken, a more defined and terribly improved path materialises, running along the edge of Hell Gill. This continues down past Whorneyside Force to meet the path coming down on the right from Red Tarn, which crosses the Oxendale Beck. Although down at valley level, there is still a mile to Stool End and then another mile back to Old Dungeon Ghyll from there.

Section 7 – Northern Lakeland

The River Derwent from Workington to Keswick then A66 to Penrith. River Eamont and then River Eden from there to Rockcliffe and the coast to Workington.

NAME	HEIGHT	IN SECTION	IN ENGLAND	IN BRITAIN
Skiddaw	931m/3,054ft	1 of 3	3 of 53	189 of 751
Blencathra	868m/2,847ft	2 of 3	8 of 53	286 of 75
Knott	710m/2,329ft	3 of 3	28 of 53	564 of 751

The northern fells are much smoother than their more southern counterparts, with the exception of the southern face of Blencathra. Indeed, the northern parts of this section are unseen by most visitors to Lakeland and many would not know that they even existed. From the grassy summit of Knott to the rocky dome of Skiddaw, the third highest mountain in England, and the crags and edges of Blencathra, this region supports a great diversity of mountain scenery. The geology of this section, along with that of Sections 5 and 6, is discussed entirely within Section 5 (see page 99).

Access

The A66 dual carriageway links Junction 40 of the M6 with Keswick and the A591 Keswick with Carlisle. There are West Coast Main Line services to Penrith from where there is a connecting bus service to Keswick.

Accommodation

While accommodation is plentiful in Keswick, it is sparse elsewhere. There are a few bed and breakfast establishments in Threlkeld and in some other villages but, nevertheless, Keswick would provide the most versatile base. There are youth hostels at Carlisle, Carrock Fell, Skiddaw House and Keswick.

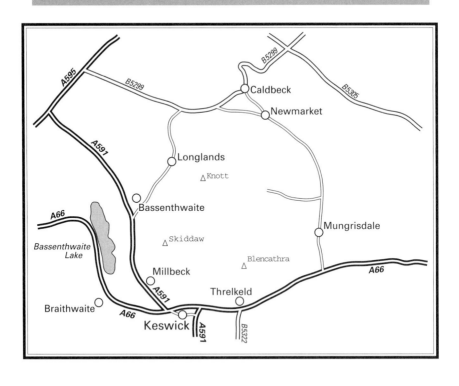

Skiddaw

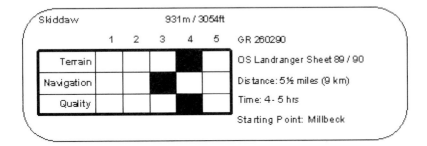

Skiddaw						931m / 3054ft
	1	2	3	4	5	GR 260290
Terrain				■		OS Landranger Sheet 89 / 90
Navigation			■			Distance: 5½ miles (9 km)
Quality				■		Time: 4 - 5 hrs
						Starting Point: Millbeck

Unlike any of the other major Lakeland fells, Skiddaw supports no crags but is no less majestic for that. It stands proudly at the centre of a huge massif, its summit lying on a ridge that lies continuously above 3,000ft for two thirds of a mile. Apart from a few fleeting glimpses, the stony cone of the High Man himself is not seen from the edge of the massif, the grassy foothills hiding the higher ground behind.

Many of Skiddaw's visitors follow the well-known track from Keswick that begins behind the old railway station and curves around Latrigg before meeting the end of a small road rising up from Appletreethwaite at Underskiddaw, where there is also parking at a higher altitude. Beyond, the track climbs around the slopes of the Little Man and over Jenkin Hill before making the final ascent up to the South Top and on to the middle top, before reaching the actual summit and trig point. The track is so wide that cars have been driven up, although this is no longer possible, as the gates are now too small. There are no steep gradients and the path is safe in the thickest of mists or the blackest of nights but is nevertheless a long drag: 17½ km/11 miles, 5½–6½ hrs from Keswick; 12 km/7½ miles, 5–5½ hrs from the road end at Underskiddaw.

The route described here begins at one of those places with a glimpse into the interior of the massif – Millbeck. Park on the Dancing Gate road out of the village, which goes on to meet the Keswick and Carlisle road to the north-west. There is parking opposite and beyond the entrance to a track that runs obliquely back to the right when approaching from the village and is marked by a wooden board in the hedge, reading 'Skiddaw

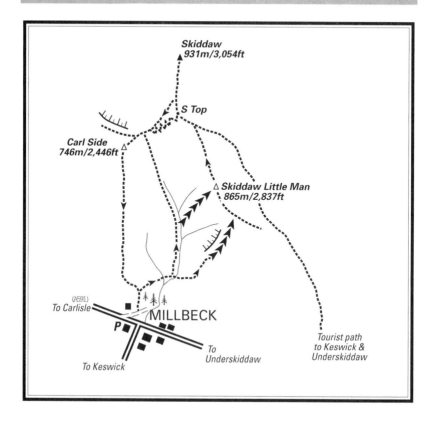

Footpath'. Up the track, a gate on the left (signposted) gives access to a path running under some trees to emerge through another gate onto the fellside. It soon forks; take the right-hand fork, which gently ascends to a gate and stile and then contours along to meet the stream at the site of an old weir. It is here that decisions should be made.

It is possible to take the 'easy' route, which is to cross the stream and follow the path beyond which curves around to the left and begins to climb the slopes of the Little Man before ending at the edge of the heather. The most interesting line then keeps close to the top of the small crags to the left and leads up to reach a diversion path from the 'tourist' track up Skiddaw at the small summit cairn of Lesser Man; the summit of Skiddaw Little Man is just a short distance to the left.

The other more testing, strenuous and interesting alternative is to ascend the south-west arête of the Little Man at an average angle of about 1:0.5 or 200 per cent. To do this, stay on the left bank of the stream following a small path, initially through bracken, to find a larch tree opposite the first main tributary stream on the right. Note that this larch is not the first one seen on the ascent from the weir. Here, cross the beck and follow the tributary up to the right, the best footing to be found on the right initially. It is necessary to crisscross the stream and to use heather and bilberries as hand holds, as it gets steeper higher up. Leave the stream and climb leftwards to ascend to the lower outcrops of rock, which soon merge to form a more distinguishable ridge.

Some evidence of a path will be found on the right, proving that others have passed this way before. The arête itself is jagged and sharp but a little disappointing as it rises no more than a few feet above the grass on either side. It soon merges into the slopes above and a final haul upwards leads unerringly straight to the summit of Little Man.

A path leads north-eastwards from Little Man, picking up a fenceline that leads up to the tourist track. A final climb leads to the south cairn and then onwards along a level ridge to another cairn (the middle summit) and then down and up to the trig point and main summit. A fine view including southern Scotland, the Isle of Man, Borrowdale, Derwentwater and Bassenthwaite Lake awaits, but although the jagged peaks of the Coniston, Scafell and Wasdale groups catch the eye, they are best seen from the south summit from where the descent commences.

Although a loose track leaves from the middle summit, it is better to follow a smaller, more pleasant path, leaving a few yards before the cairn on the south summit and descending the steep and stony west-facing slope to Carlside col, where there is a small tarn. From here, a path leads down into the valley on the left but keep straight on, the path soon forking. Take the left fork which climbs to the summit cairn on Carl Side before dropping quite steeply at times down its south ridge, passing a quartzite knoll *en route* to reach the kissing-gate through which access to the fell was first gained.

Blencathra

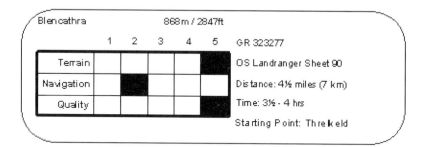

Blencathra						868m / 2847ft
	1	2	3	4	5	GR 323277
Terrain					■	OS Landranger Sheet 90
Navigation		■				Distance: 4½ miles (7 km)
Quality					■	Time: 3½ - 4 hrs
						Starting Point: Threlkeld

Whenever Blencathra is in view, it commands attention, certainly so from close quarters. It rises steeply from the small village of Threlkeld in rocky, stony, barren slopes, which are impressive to say the least and cannot fail to inspire adventure. An equally impressive ridge, all of which are sharp and some true arêtes, matches each deep, ravine-like valley. This route ascends perhaps the best ridge of all, Hall's Fell Ridge, traverses along the top of the crags and then descends by the grassy, pleasant slopes of Blease Fell.

There is space for car-parking in Threlkeld up the road to the Blencathra Centre on the right, situated where the road bends to the left. Follow a path, which begins by the car-park, up the left-hand side of the wooded Blease Gill, crossing a footbridge, to emerge through a gate onto the open fellside. Follow the wall on the right and then turn right as it does to join a footpath running above it. This path runs across the breast of Gategill Fell to the valley of Gategill. Here, ignore a path running up the valley to the left, which leads to an old mine, but instead take another path, half left, which hairpins up the broad face of Hall Fell through heather.

Soon the ridge sharpens and the route begins to take on a real mountaineering feel. As in other places, a walker's traverse path avoids most of the difficulties but in a few places, the crest of the ridge is unavoidable; the views into the depths of Doddick Gill and Gate Gill are quite fantastic. However, rather than following the traverse path, it is much better to adhere to the crest of the ridge, giving an exhilarating scramble throughout. The ridge leads directly up to Blencathra's summit.

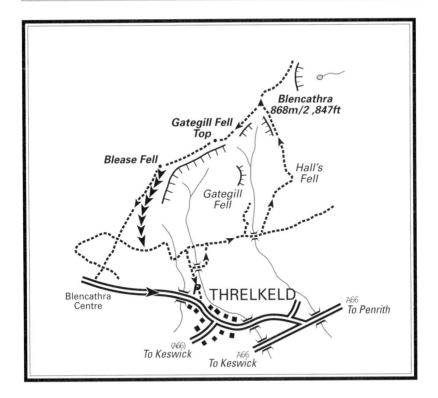

Those who were expecting a sharp summit, in keeping with the Threlkeld face, will now be disappointed to find that the back of the fell is the absolute opposite to the front. Sheep pastures and upland meadows fall gently away down to Roughten Gill.

However, the southwards view is quite tremendous, as is the view down to Threlkeld, which seems very far below. To begin the descent, walk west along the rim of the crags, passing over the summit of Gategill Fell, to arrive on Blease Fell, from where a recently improved path drops down to the road near the Blencathra Centre but, in practice, it is quite safe to descend the grassy hillside in any place, interest being added by keeping close to the edge of Knowe Crags with views over them into the depths of Blease Gill. Wherever the slope is descended, a road or contour path will be met. Either way will lead to the Blease Gill area, the route of ascent being joined, if not on the road, just above the footbridge over Blease Gill, from where a path leads to the road.

Knott

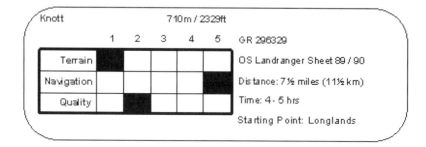

Knott is the highest eminence of the Uldale or Caldbeck Fells. This group forms a bleak block of moorland with no large drops, giving only one separate summit; this is Knott. The slopes of Knott have been extensively mined in two different areas, these being Carrock Mine in the Caldew Valley and Roughton Gill Mine. Carrock Mine is certainly a place to avoid but Roughton Gill is less dangerous. For lovers of wild scenery, this is an excellent place, but lovers of bare rock will be disappointed.

The hamlet of Longlands is remote from main roads; it is easily approached from Caldbeck and Uldale but narrow lanes abound when approaching from the Keswick area. There is parking in a lay-by and on the surrounding verges for about seven cars by the small bridge. Begin by climbing a stile by a gate on the right just after the bridge on the Uldale side. Once over the stile, turn right, fording a small stream and walking up a slowly ascending path just above the wall. There is a great temptation to climb higher up the fellside but this should be ignored. The path runs up and past a small wooden hut on the right before entering very innocuously into the Ellen valley.

Ignoring a fork in the track to the left, keep relatively level and ford several streams before climbing up to the prominent gash in the fellside ahead, named Trusmadoor. When going through the pass, ignore paths to the left and right and descend straight down the small distance to the ford over the Burntod Gill. On the other side of the gill, a path, obvious from Trusmadoor, hairpins up the fellside ahead before petering out around the 1,800ft (550m) contour.

Keep below the line of the peat on the right and contour along to the

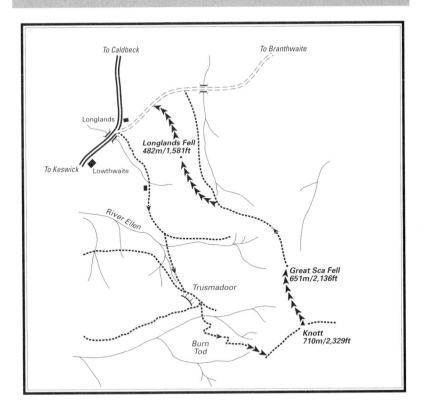

headwaters of the gill. The position of the summit is not quite so near as may be imagined, and the route to it is certainly not obvious in clear weather, let alone mist (in which the whole area is best avoided). Climb right, crossing an obvious escarpment in the peat, to rise up onto the ridge beyond. Here, turn left and a path will be picked up which passes a small cairn *en route* before leading straight up to the surprisingly large summit cairn.

To return to Longlands, walk north-west over rough ground to the col between Knott and Great Sca Fell. A track should be picked up here that leads past the cairns on Great and Little Sca Fells. After the latter, the track initially runs right but then sweeps back left to run down the ridge towards Lowthwaite Fell. When it shows signs of leaving the ridge to descend into the valley on the right, leave it and continue up an indistinct track onto Lowthwaite Fell and beyond onto Longlands Fell. From Longlands Fell, continue on the track until the steepness of the ground on the left eases and then descend to the old road, crossing the base of the fell (this also avoids a large bog near the gate at Longlands). Turn left on the old road to finish the descent back to the day's starting point.

Section 8 – North Yorkshire Dales and the Howgill Fells

River Ure from Mylton-on-Swale to Garsdale Head and the Clough River to Killington. River Lune to Shap, River Lowther to Penrith, Rivers Eamont and Eden to Brough, the A66 and A1 to Catterick and then the River Swale to Mylton-on-Swale.

NAME	HEIGHT	IN SECTION	IN ENGLAND	IN BRITAIN
Great Shunner Fell	716m/2,349ft	1 of 8	27 of 53	552 of 751
Wild Boar Fell	708m/2,324ft	2 of 8	29 of 53	570 of 751
Tarn Rigg Hill	678m/2,224ft	3 of 8	37 of 53	627 of 751
The Calf	676m/2,219ft	4 of 8	38 of 53	637 of 751
Lovely Seat	675m/2,215ft	5 of 8	39 of 53	640 of 751
Rogan's Seat	672m/2,205ft	6 of 8	40 of 53	644 of 751
Nine Standards Rigg	662m/2,171ft	7 of 8	45 of 53	671 of 751
Yarlside	639m/2,096ft	8 of 8	48 of 53	703 of 751

Wensleydale and Swaledale, the two northernmost of the Yorkshire Dales, are surrounded by bleaker mountains that do lack some of the grandeur of the southern area (Section 4). However, the scenery is still very interesting and the valleys themselves are, some would say, the best in the whole of the Yorkshire Dales National Park. Out to the west, the hills of Mallerstang follow a similar trend, but beyond them, the Howgills are completely different in both their geology and their scenery.

In the Ordovician and Silurian period, sediments were deposited here which, along with earth movements along the Pennine boundary faults, resulted in a raised area of land, known as the Askrigg Block (see Section 4). The rocks underlying Wensleydale and Swaledale are similar to those exposed at Ingleton, Malham and in Ribblesdale but here they do not appear on the surface. Indeed, as in Section 4, the rocks that form the valleys and hills (excluding the Howgills) were deposited in the Carboniferous period, about 345 million years ago, and are sedimentary in nature.

In the lower Carboniferous period, the area was covered by a warm, shallow shelf-sea in which limestone was deposited. However, a delta began to encroach upon the sea from the north, which brought about different conditions and resulted in the formation of different rocks. The rocks deposited lie in the Yoredale Beds, named after Wensleydale ('Uredale'). The beds consist of a cyclical series of limestones, deposited in the shallow shelf-sea; clastic sediments which in turn can be broken down into fossilliferous shales, deposited underwater as the delta encroached, unfossilliferous shales and siltstones, deposited on the delta slope, and flagstones and sandstones, deposited on the delta platform.

Terrigenous sediments form the highest part of each cyclothem and can in turn be subdivided into thin fireclay, which underlies thin coal seams, both being deposited in the tropical swamps which existed on the delta top. These coal seams were mined, as seen on Great Shunner Fell. The Yoredale Beds are more extensive here than in Section 4 as deltaic conditions, spreading from the north, reached here first whilst limestones of the Great Scar Group were still being deposited around Ingleborough.

In total, there are eight cyclothems in the Yoredale Series in this area, each beginning with a band of limestone, namely from the Great Scar Limestone upwards, Hawes Limestone, Gayle Limestone, Hardraw Scar Limestone, Simonstone Limestone, Middle Limestone, Five Yard Limestone, Three Yard Limestone, Undersett Limestone and Main Limestone. As can be seen from the southern end of Pen-y-ghent (Section 4), the upper cyclothems from the Yoredales are present but, below the Middle Limestone, they are missing, the lower ones being replaced by Great Scar Limestones. It can be seen from the first cyclothem, beginning with the Hawes Limestone, that the transition to deltaic conditions was slow as most of the deposits are of limestone. The depth of the Yoredale deposits, around 1,000ft (300m), shows that there was not a change as such in sea levels but rather a continuous subsidence of the sea floor over the entire region, as the beds extend a large lateral distance with little vertical change, except where affected by faulting.

The individual cyclothems themselves were caused by the lateral movements of channels within the delta, causing erosion of sediments, as deposition would have stopped, or possibly sudden subsidence of the seabed. Either of these would cause that area of the delta to be once more covered by a shallow sea, in which limestone could be deposited. As the

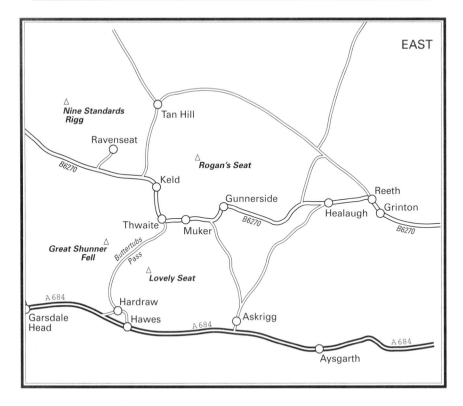

delta again encroached, different conditions existed at different stages.

Shales would be deposited in the initial stages but, as the distributaries advanced, conditions would be suitable for the sandstones to be deposited before a sandbar enclosed a lagoon, which would eventually silt up and then become a swamp, resulting in the deposition of fireclays and coal seams. As the area once more subsided or as the delta channels moved laterally, the sea would invade once more and another cyclothem would begin. However, it should not be assumed that each layer in a particular cyclothem was built up in the same amount of time. Sandstones and siltstones can build up relatively quickly in times of flood, whereas the deposition of limestone, which consists of the crushed remains of dead sea creatures, would take much longer.

In the upper Carboniferous period, deltaic conditions became more constant and therefore the rocks become more regular. Firstly, rocks of the Millstone Grit Facies (grits, shales and sandstones) were deposited and above that the Coal Measures. Much of these layers have been subsequently eroded but a protective coating of Millstone Grit still

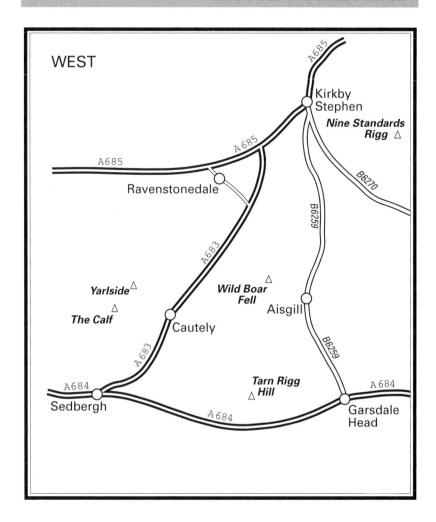

remains on the tops of the hills. However, although all the rocks were deposited by the end of the Carboniferous period, the landscape at that time would have been unfamiliar.

Apart from erosion, the subsidence of the North Sea Basin in Tertiary times pushed the western Pennines upwards which lead to a north-east dipping strata. This, apart from earlier deposition of rocks of the Yoredale Facies, also accounts for why the Great Scar Limestone, seen in Aysgarth Falls, is so very far down in the valley bottoms, appearing around 600ft (180m) and below, in direct contrast to the Great Scar Limestones of Ingleborough (Section 4). During the Ice Age, the landscape was finally moulded into what is seen today, the centre of the ice sheet being over the Mallerstang area and Great Shunner Fell.

As the limestone layers in the Yoredale Beds are so thin, the pot-holes seen in abundance in Section 4 are largely absent here, the exception, of course, being the Buttertubs and other shallow cave systems, such as those of Baugh Fell and the Angerholme Pots. What do exist, however, in both valleys, particularly in Wensleydale, are long scars and terraced slopes.

Due to the fact that the Yoredale limestones were deposited on a fairly level lateral plane, they maintain a very level course along valley sides and across the valleys as well. The terracing effect results from the difference in erosion rates between the harder shales, which protect the softer limestones below. There are cascades on valley sides as tributaries fall over the scars and small, wide waterfalls on the main valley rivers, such as Aysgarth Falls (Wensleydale) and Catrake Force and Wain Wath Force (Swaledale).

The most famous waterfall of all is Hardraw Force near Hawes. Here, the water falls over the hard shale and forms a plunge pool. The limestone below the shale is then eroded, undercutting the shale, until it eventually collapses and the waterfall recedes. Most of the main tributaries have similar gorges headed by waterfalls at one or, in some cases, at several points along their length.

The area to the north of Swaledale has been extensively mined for lead, which occurs in veins, occupying fissures in the rock. These fissures occur in zones of weakness and such zones are found here, but also near Alston (Section 9), Grassington Moor and Hebden Gill (Section 4) and on Greenhow Hill near Pateley Bridge. A more detailed discussion of the formation of the Pennine lead veins and how they were mined is given in Section 9.

Out to the west, the Howgill Fells are substantially different, their rocks being more akin to those present in the south and far east of the Lake District. They are formed mainly from Silurian sediments, lying on older Ordovician deposits, and are bounded on the northern side by a band of Bannisdale Slates. However, the summits themselves and the Lune Gorge and Whinfell Ridge to the west are all formed from Coniston Grits. The grits were the first to be deposited and that deposition appears to have taken place relatively quickly in quite shallow water. This is because the sedimentary particles that form the rock are quite coarse, implying that there was not sufficient time for them to be weathered into smaller particles by abrasion, which would have resulted in the formation of a finer grained rock, such as a siltstone.

However, in the middle of the Coniston Grits, there is a band of mudstones. These mudstones are bedded and break along that bedding so they are often termed flaggy mudstones. These would have appeared to have been deposited much more slowly, perhaps due to stronger currents, as they have a much finer texture. However, in the Coniston Grits of the Sedbergh area, there is a band of calcareous grit, which has been termed the Crook and Winder Grit. This layer is not replicated in the Coniston Grits of the Lake District.

The Bannisdale Slates are sandy mudstones but they are interleaved with hard sandstones, lying in thin bands, and beds of grit, which occur only occasionally. The alternation between mudstones and gritstones is very rapid and there are many shallow beds that give the rock a striped appearance. Unlike in Lakeland, the Bannisdale Slates of the Howgills have yielded many fossils, mainly graptolites, which are not found in the Lake District.

In the Triassic period, the subsidence of the North Sea Basin caused huge earth-movements along the Pennine boundary faults. It was these movements that caused the rocks of the Howgills to be thrown into juxtaposition with the Carboniferous sediments of the Dales. Between the Kendal–Carnforth Fault and the Dent Fault, which follows roughly the line of Barbondale (Section 4) and the Rawthey Valley as far as the Cross Keys (Cautely) before continuing to the Stainmore Gap (see Section 9), the ground was uplifted.

This had the result of bringing the basement rocks that underlie the Dales (see above and Section 4) to the same level as the overlying Carboniferous sediments. To the west of the Kendal–Carnforth Fault lie Carboniferous limestones, seen in Whitbarrow Scar where there are also caves and resurgences and, of course, to the east of the Dent Fault where the Yoredale Beds of the late part of the Dinantian (Lower Carboniferous) period are found.

The change is striking between Cautely and Ravenstonedale between which points the fault roughly follows the line of the A683. To the east of the road lie Stennerskeugh Clouds formed in the Yoredale Limestones, above which lie the rocks of the Millstone Grit Facies formed in the Upper Carboniferous period and well seen in the Mallerstang-facing crags of Wild Boar Fell and High Seat, producing wet waterlogged ground. In contrast, to the west of the road lie the Howgills, with the grits there forming thin soils which support grassland but which are well drained and dry underfoot.

The Howgills were affected little by the Ice Age although they did support an ice sheet of their own. Glaciation made only very minor changes, although it did have the effect of diverting the eastwards progression of the Lake District Ice northwards through Stainmore Gap and southwards to Morecambe Bay.

The Settle–Carlisle Railway

It is probably fair to say that had the Settle–Carlisle line been anywhere else then it would probably have been closed long ago. It was built by the Midland Railway Company, which was desperate to reach the Scottish border. They had reached Leeds and then expanded via Skipton and Settle to Ingleton where, at the time, a large amount of coal mining was taking place (see Section 4). The London and North Western Railway Company also had a station at Ingleton and Midland passengers who wished to continue their journey north were expected to change there. However, due to the rivalry and hostility between the companies, connections were not good and those that did exist were often purposefully missed.

Therefore, between 1869 and 1876, the Midland Railway Company realised that with the West and East Coast routes occupied, they would have to take their line straight through the heart of the Pennines and then up the Eden Valley to Carlisle. The route included ten tunnels and a few other minor ones with seven large viaducts. Dent Station (Section 4) is the highest main line station in Britain at 1,145ft (350m) and the summit of the line at Aisgill (Mallerstang) is at 1,165ft (355m). In its early days, the line was a great success, bringing tourists into the Dales when there were few cars around. However, like many lines, a steady decline set in after the war and when, in 1983, British Rail announced that it intended to axe the line between Ribblehead and Appelby-in-Westmorland, it could hardly have been a surprise. However, in 1989, the government refused permission for the line to be closed and the line has recently been given Conservation Area status. The necessary repairs were started in 1990 and a new service between Leeds and Carlisle was launched with six trains a day.

Recent plans by the government to increase rail freight haulage and reduce road haulage seem to have secured the line's future. With the East and West Coast main lines already overcrowded, the Midland main line and the Settle–Carlisle line have been named as a new freight route to the Scottish border to increase capacity.

Access

There are stations on the Settle–Carlisle line at Garsdale Head, from where there is a bus service to Hawes, and at Kirkby Stephen but no stations in Mallerstang itself. Currently there is a frequent Monday to Sunday service with trains departing Leeds and Carlisle. A Sunday special between Preston (sometimes Blackpool North) and Carlisle runs along the route from Hellifield northwards and then returns. It is possible to connect with this service from Manchester Victoria by changing at Clitheroe. As far as vehicle access goes, the B6270 runs between Richmond (reachable from either Scotch Corner or Catterick on the A1) and Kirkby Stephen along the length of Swaledale, although it is narrow and bendy in places. The A684 between Junction 37 of the M6 runs through Sedbergh, Garsdale Head, Hawes and then down the length of Wensleydale to Leeming Bar on the A1. Buttertubs Pass links Hawes and Thwaite (Swaledale).

Accommodation

There is plentiful accommodation of all types in Hawes and this would provide a good base for Wensleydale and Swaledale as well as for parts of Section 4. However, Sedbergh is the best base for the Howgills and Mallerstang Fells, the accommodation being more limited than that in Hawes but, as well as the town centre establishments, there are a few out of town along the Garsdale (Hawes) road. Apart from Hawes, there are many bed and breakfast establishments in Askrigg and Aysgarth. In Swaledale, options are a little more limited in the upper valley but there is plenty of accommodation in Reeth and Richmond and 'over the top' in Kirkby Stephen. There are youth hostels at Hawes, Aysgarth, Kirkby Stephen, Keld and Grinton (near Reeth).

Great Shunner Fell and Lovely Seat

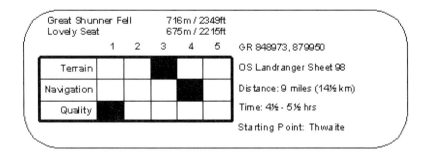

		1	2	3	4	5	
Great Shunner Fell							716m / 2349ft
Lovely Seat							675m / 2215ft
Terrain				■			GR 848973, 879950
Navigation					■		OS Landranger Sheet 98
Quality	■						Distance: 9 miles (14½ km)
							Time: 4½ - 5½ hrs
							Starting Point: Thwaite

These two hills sitting on either side of the Buttertubs Pass do little to attract attention, throwing down rough, bleak slopes to the road, particularly from Great Shunner. Indeed, Lovely Seat is by far the more interesting of the two. A circular walk on both individually is impossible but they can be linked conveniently into a rough moorland walk from Thwaite in Swaledale, but are best left to a clear summer's day due to navigational difficulties and the large peat morass found on the descent from Lovely Seat.

There is limited parking in the Thwaite area in a lay-by on the Muker road, just before the junction with the Hawes road descending from Buttertubs Pass. Walk down into and through the village, following the road up the hill on the other side. Shortly, a signpost on the left marks the point at which the Pennine Way turns to the left up a rough track. Follow this track up through the inbye and out onto the open moor by some sheep pens. The path, although unimproved to begin with, has had a lot of work done on it in the last few years. Almost all the way to the summit, large slabs have been laid down across the black mire that covers most of this slope and the erosion control work has improved the going considerably. The path continues very clearly with no deviations over a subsidiary top and then up to a stile in a fence, at which point the summit shelter is only a few yards further on. The trig point, which is marked on the map, does exist but it is quite excusable to walk around for a bit and not find it. It is in fact built in to the end wall of the shelter that faces out to the path used in the ascent.

The descent from here to Buttertubs is pathless but not difficult.

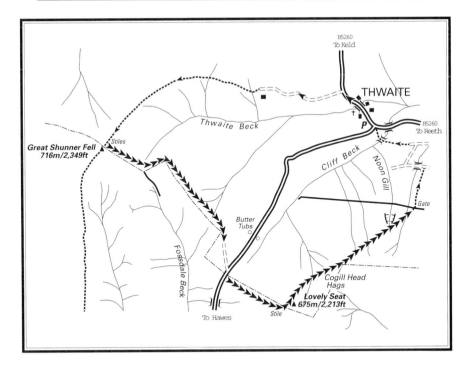

Return to the fence but, instead of crossing the stile, follow the nearside down for a while until another stile is reached, which should be crossed. Despite the rather roundabout route, the fence is a good guide across the rather wet stretch of moorland and follows the ridge perfectly. A vehicle track of some description will be picked up when the fence starts to descend steeply off Little Shunner Fell and at the end of this descent, when the fence turns a right angle to the right, if the day is clear, the track may be followed onwards to the summit of Buttertubs Pass, passing a coal pit *en route*. This coal pit is part of the remains of the coal industry which thrived on the seams of coal found in Great Shunner's Yoredale Beds prior to the coming of the railway to Hawes.

If it is misty, however, simply follow the fence to the road. From the cattle grid on the top of the pass, walk up the far side of the fence, where a small path will be found. This runs close to the fence across one small levelling and then steeply up to the summit plateau. Some stones help in crossing back over the fence at the other side of which a small path leads up the final few yards to the tall summit pillar cairn. Just beyond the cairn and with its back to it, there is a stone seat for two facing out over Swaledale.

If the day is at all misty, return to the fence but do not cross back over it; instead, follow the nearside around and across some very black peat hags, which are very nasty and oozy in the summer and should be left alone in winter. However, if the weather is clear, it is possible to cut a corner off by not following the fence and avoiding the worst of the peat hags. Walk initially on a bearing of 64° to Lovely Seat's north-eastern top and then pause to survey the scene ahead. The fence line should be made out crossing the bog and then turning sharply to the right just beyond. It is possible to find a route through the hags that avoids as little peat walking as possible but it is imperative to reach the fence just where it emerges from the hags but before it turns right.

At this point, do not follow the fence around to the right but continue along the line in which it has been travelling (58°) to the top of the small hill beyond. Readers looking at the OS Outdoor Leisure map should note that the fence is not shown and that it does not follow exactly the line of the parish boundary, which is shown. This means that you are in fact standing on point 631m at GR 888957 and not point 621m nearby, as you might expect. If the day is clear, locate a pair of barns on the middle slopes of Kisdon (opposite) towards the right-hand side, near a house, at about the 1,245ft (380m) contour. If it is misty then just try to follow the line along which you have been walking. Three peat gullies will be crossed: the first is quite wide and, depending upon just what line you are on, it may count as two or even three but they are very close together.

A way further on, a second is crossed, this one narrow and deep and then further on a third. The line should then lead to a deep, rocky gully, quite close to its head. Walk around its head and follow along the back of a small hill with a liberal scattering of white limestone rock. A small, shallow valley descends the short distance to the wall, where a gate close to some sheep pens gives access to a bridleway leading down through the inbye. Follow it down through the top field to meet a small lane. Here, turn left and cross a small bridge, immediately over which another lane drops down the hill to a barn. Turn left through a gate and follow this track along, sometimes at the bottom of the field, sometimes as a walled line until it emerges at the top of a field, where it becomes a bit lost.

However, stay close to the top wall and a gated slit stile will be seen to the right of a field gate giving access into a wooded gill. A bridge crosses the gill just below a small waterfall and passes out through another slit stile onto a track. Ignore a slit stile on the right into a field but follow the track down to the road, along which the car is only a short distance to the left.

Wild Boar Fell

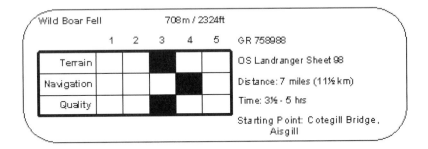

Wild Boar Fell	708m / 2324ft				
	1	2	3	4	5
Terrain			■		
Navigation				■	
Quality			■		

GR 758988

OS Landranger Sheet 98

Distance: 7 miles (11½ km)

Time: 3½ - 5 hrs

Starting Point: Cotegill Bridge, Aisgill

Rising gradually from Stennerskeugh and Ravenstonedale, Wild Boar Fell erupts on its eastern flank into crags and scree as it drops down into Mallerstang and it is from this side that it is best approached. It is reputed that it was here that the last wild boar in England was shot.

Mallerstang is a peculiar place, one long glacial trough that does have a low pass in it, which, although mostly unnoticed, is the main watershed of northern England; to the south flows the Ure and to the north the Eden. Park just to the south of Aisgill where the road crosses the railway on a bridge where there is a lay-by and an old quarry over which the Cote Gill discharges. Begin by walking down the road and over the bridge to reach the farm, where a gate on the left gives access to a track that runs up the hillside and under the arches of the railway viaduct. Note the flowstone formations on the underside of the arch that are unusually thick and made of the same rock found in caves but formed there much more slowly.

A gate under the arch gives passage onto the open hillside and the track splits. Keep straight on along the track that soon peters out in some damp ground. Ahead, the beck flows out from a gorge, known as Aisgill Kirk, into which it is possible to walk and, if the stream is not in spate, continue to the waterfall at the end along the rocky streambed. Return back out of the front of the gorge and contour to the left across the hillside to reach the inbye wall, which rises up from the railway line.

A faint path, which soon becomes clearer, runs along the uphill side of the wall to reach the green and verdant limestone pastures, where the

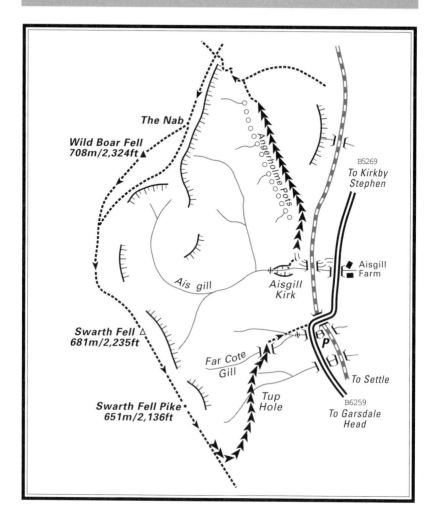

The Nab

Wild Boar Fell
708m/2,324ft ▲

Angerholme Pots

B5269
To Kirkby
Stephen

Aisgill
Farm

Ais gill

Aisgill
Kirk

Swarth Fell △
681m/2,235ft

Far Cote
Gill

P

To Settle

Swarth Fell Pike •
651m/2,136ft

Tup
Hole

B6259
To Garsdale
Head

wall turns downhill. Now leave the wall and keep along the edge of the limestone sward, not encroaching upon the wetter ground to the left. Eventually, a wide spur of tussocky grass, slightly raised, penetrates into the limestone, but cross over it on a small and wet path. To the left, since the wall was left behind, have been a series of shake holes some of which contain pot-holes. These are the Angerholme Pots. Here, by the path, there is a cluster, one of which is open and deep, into which a small stream pours.

After careful inspection, continue along the path back onto the limestone and then aim half left up towards a path that can be seen rising across the steep escarpment. Reach its bottom and then proceed up it to reach the ridge at a wall corner. A path runs back left along the edge of the scarp all the way up to a cairn on The Nab where the summit plateau begins. The path along the scarp edge continues but leave it for another path running southwest which leads to the trig point, surrounded by a shelter cairn.

Leave the summit on a bearing of 226°, passing a small shelter and then picking up a faint path that leads down to a fence, which should shortly be crossed on a stile. The path continues down the far side, in due course picking up the path that has run along the escarpment, before descending down sharply to a wall at the col between Wild Boar Fell and Swarth Fell. After the wet depression, the path continues by the wall until it bends to the right, at which point the path keeps straight on up to the summit cairn. It leads on south-south-east and then drops down to another depression and then up again onto Swarth Fell Pike at which point the fence is rejoined (the path has been running roughly parallel to it for some time). Do not cross the stile but instead continue along the nearside down a first steep drop in the ridge and then down a second at which point strike off left on a bearing of 112° initially before curving around back to the left just before the ground begins to descend more steeply.

A small valley, Tup Hole, will be seen ahead and this should be reached, the easiest going to be found on the drier, right-hand side. Cross the main stream into which this tributary flows and then, when the stream enters a small 'gorge', cross it to the left over a small col into first a tributary valley with its own 'gorge' and then over again to another gill. However, do not descend into it but stay on the hillside until the slope leads down to stream level where some old railway sleepers make a makeshift bridge. A faint path on the far bank leads down to the quarry and the barbed wire fence, which can be crossed by passing through a gate a short distance to the left.

Tarn Rigg Hill

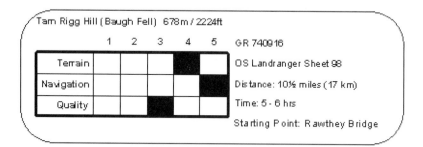

	1	2	3	4	5	
Terrain				■		OS Landranger Sheet 98
Navigation					■	Distance: 10½ miles (17 km)
Quality		■				Time: 5 - 6 hrs

Tarn Rigg Hill (Baugh Fell) 678m / 2224ft
GR 740916
Starting Point: Rawthey Bridge

The northern aspect of Baugh Fell is wild and untamed; indeed, the whole fell does not support a path of any size and this route should be left alone in mist and prolonged wet periods as the ground is quite boggy. Having said that, however, the route of ascent, by the River Rawthey, is best when heavy overnight rain has cleared to sunshine, swelling the river so that its cascades turn into roaring cataracts.

Park on the A683 Sedbergh to Kirkby Stephen road where it crosses the river, north of the Cross Keys. If approaching from Sedbergh, note that it is not the first car-park but the second, about 80 yards down from the bridge. Set off by walking towards the bridge before passing through a ramshackle gate on the right onto the open fell. A track beyond (the old road) leads onwards for a short distance before turning sharply to the right.

At this point, continue more or less straight on through some rushy ground before following the inbye fence, which becomes a wall up the slope. When it turns left, continue straight ahead and, in about 20 yards, a gently rising traverse path will be met running right to left. Follow it high above the Rawthey until another wall rises up from the valley with a house and conifers beyond. Here aim right for about 30 yards to meet another track (the old quarry road) running across the hillside. Now, follow it to the left as it traverses along to meet the river in the vicinity of a conifer wood. At the far end of this, it descends to the water's edge and there is a bridge from which the waterfalls in the woods can be seen.

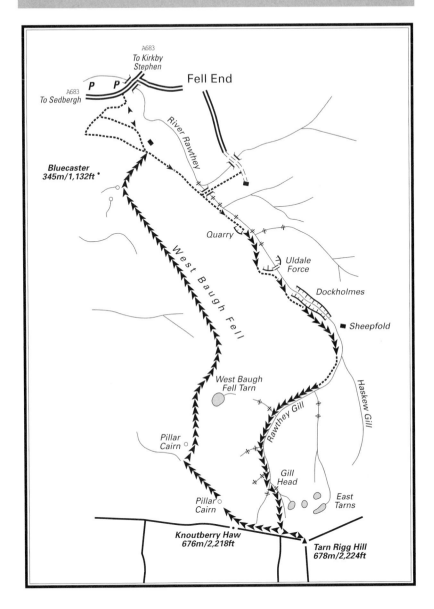

However, do not cross the bridge but continue up the right-hand bank past some lovely falls, one of which is quite impressive. Eventually, a small slippage brings the track to an end and a route must be picked across the rocks either at the water's edge or higher up to connect with the path which leads up to the quarry spoil. The path continues up the spoil at the far end to some ruined buildings and then onwards up the riverbank.

Ahead, a large falls bars progress but this really only whets the appetite for what is yet to come. Escape in good time on a small sheep track ascending the right-hand slope to run along the top of the cliffs. However, before the corner is rounded, a dull roar will be heard and this signals what is to come. The path, now just above the river, rounds the bend and soon a huge, wide, 80ft (25m) high force will be seen. Named Uldale Force and relatively unknown, when the river is in spate, it is, in my opinion, certainly one of the best waterfalls in England, perhaps even the very best given its secluded position. However, cliffs and steep grass should deter too close an inspection but, if the grass is very dry, it may be possible to approach a little closer. However, the escape route is on the right just before the cliffs start and once again a small path runs along the top to reach the river above.

Soon, the limestone gorge of Dockholmes will be seen ahead and this is also impassable so escape up the hillside in good time to find another path running above it, which ends rather abruptly on a very steep grass slope above the gorge. It is best here to climb higher and then descend back to the river above the gorge as the steep grass is difficult to walk on as well as dangerous for obvious reasons.

The river is still quite large and the valley continues until a fork in the streams just after the wall on the left side of the valley has climbed away up the hillside. The Rawthey continues as the right fork in confined surroundings. Again it is necessary to climb a little up the steep grass sides to circumnavigate small cliffs, which the beck is in the process of enlarging. In no time, the stream forks again; continue up the right-hand fork by the chattering and tumbling water. Were the setting not so beautiful, the going could almost be described as purgatory but soon the excitement reappears with another waterfall passed by a small scramble on the right.

The valley continues until a fork in the stream, above which both tributaries fall steeply down into the confines of the gill. Follow the left fork up onto the moorland above, until the Rawthey finally becomes no more amidst a peat bog. However, by walking due south, the summit wall will be reached either just before or just after a wall running down into Garsdale. The highest point is up to the left just where the next wall drops down into Garsdale at a small kink in the summit wall. The summit itself is unmarked and the exact position is very difficult to distinguish.

To begin the return, follow the wall back west across the depression and up onto the slightly lower summit of Knoutberry Haw with its trig point. Here, the walk becomes even more difficult and rough; strike out on a bearing of 348°, which should lead to a pillar cairn in about half a mile. Here bear half right around the head of a small valley to two prominent pillar cairns (a third smaller one is found on arrival). A bearing of 20° leads down to West Baugh Fell Tarn, missing it only by a hundred yards or so.

In about another quarter of a mile, the ridge turns to the north and then to the north-west as it descends to the col before the small hill of Bluecaster, becoming increasingly wet all the time, especially so in the rushes just before the col where there are a number of shake holes, some of which are very large. Leave the ridge here and follow the line of shake holes down a small dry valley to the right to reach the quarry track where it was met earlier in the day, just above the ruined house. Return along the last stretch to the car by the route of ascent.

The Calf and Yarlside

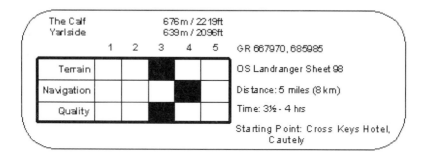

	The Calf			676m / 2219ft			
	Yarlside			639m / 2096ft			

	1	2	3	4	5	GR 667970, 685985
Terrain			■	■		OS Landranger Sheet 98
Navigation				■		Distance: 5 miles (8 km)
Quality			■			Time: 3½ - 4 hrs

Starting Point: Cross Keys Hotel, Cautely

These two summits in the Howgill Fells are completely different. Yarlside rises from the surrounding landscape as a huge, separate, steep-sided, grass dome, while The Calf is simply the highest point of a huge undulating moor when viewed from the east, but the centre of a huge ridge system when viewed from other directions.

Although one popular route for the ascent of The Calf begins at Sedbergh, the two hills can be linked together into a very enjoyable excursion from the Cross Keys Temperance Hotel, 4½ miles north of Sedbergh on the Kirkby Stephen road; a lay-by beyond the hotel allows parking for five or six cars. From the lay-by, a path descends down steps to cross a footbridge over the River Rawthey. Ignore the paths running left and right, and start straight up the ridge rearing ahead, which is called Ben End. Continue upwards until there is a slight levelling and, here, a stonewall should be seen to the right. Cross over to the wall and follow its gradually rising traverse of the slopes of Yarlside.

Shortly, it reaches its highest point and falls away into the valley of Westerdale, so here take the left-hand rising path. This, although indistinct in places, leads to the saddle between Kensgriff and Yarlside. At this point, the direct ascent on the left up the frightfully steep slope of Yarlside is not a very nice prospect. However, hairpinning to the right to the vicinity of a stony gully and back again leads eventually to the summit ridge. Thankfully, the summit is not far away along a small path and it is graced with a small, but interesting, cairn.

With the height gained on Yarlside, the descent to Bowderdale Head

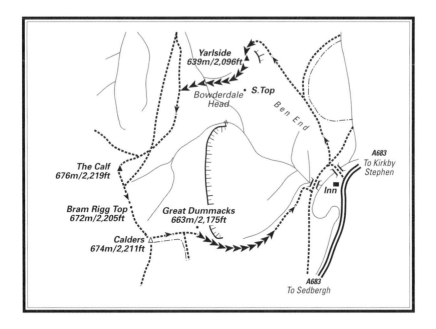

is not a welcome prospect. However, it is not as bad as it may seem. Begin by continuing along Yarlside's ridge to the col between the north and lower south summits. Descend into the gully on the right, which fairly painlessly runs down to the col at Bowderdale Head. Aim slightly right here, to reach a path climbing up the right bank of a gill, on the opposite side of the pass (this path is clearly visible during the descent of Yarlside). When the path disappears, aim up the hillside to meet a large and distinct path making a rising traverse to the left from lower down in Bowderdale on the right. Turning left, the path makes a gradual ascent to the summit plateau of The Calf. After passing a tarn on the right, follow a path left to the triangulation pillar in about half a mile.

To descend, follow the Sedbergh path running south-south-east over Bram Rigg Top and onto Calders. Here, backtrack from the cairn for a few feet and follow a wire fence running east, branching right at the first fork and leaving the fence to go left at the second fork. This path runs over the featureless top of Great Dummacks to the top of Cautley Crag.

Here, turn right along the crag's edge and begin a descent when at a bearing of 60° or less with the Cross Keys Hotel. A very steep descent leads down to the headwaters of Pickering Gill and an obvious green path running down a beautiful narrow alpine-style ridge. The path makes a steep descent at the end of this to cross the gill shortly before a double confluence. It now keeps down the gillside crossing onto the right bank and then back to the left shortly before a waterfall graced with a reasonably large tree. Here, further progress would seem to be barred, but the track makes an unlikely narrow traverse of a broken crag ahead to descend gently above the beck. A hairpin bend eventually leads the path across the stream once more, just above the inbye wall, and then it runs along the breast of the fell to join with the valley path. Turn left here, cross over the footbridge over the Cautley Holme Beck and continue up the valley to cross over the River Rawthey once more on the Cross Keys footbridge.

Rogan's Seat

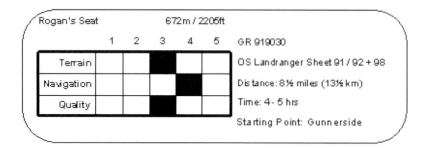

Rogan's Seat						672m / 2205ft
	1	2	3	4	5	GR 919030
Terrain			■			OS Landranger Sheet 91 / 92 + 98
Navigation				■		Distance: 8½ miles (13½ km)
Quality			■			Time: 4 - 5 hrs
						Starting Point: Gunnerside

Rogan's Seat has come in for a lot of criticism as being boring and bleak, adjectives that perfectly describe some of the routes of ascent. However, I would suggest that those who utter such derogatory statements have plodded up the long, hard moorland track from Gunnerside or Keld and would perhaps find different adjectives if they followed the route described here.

Park in Gunnerside near the bridge in the centre of the village where there is room for about ten vehicles. On the opposite side of the small bridge from the car-park and opposite the pub (open all day), a track leads up the bank of the beck, signposted on the wall to 'Gunnerside Gill'. In a few hundred yards a white gate is reached in front of a large house. Turn right in front of it and climb some steps on the right to follow the path around the rear of the property. The path then leads up by the gill through woodland; at one point a signpost clarifies the issue by saying 'Gunnerside Gill–Woodland Route', although the alternative route is not obvious. Climbing high above the stream in the ash woodland, it eventually emerges at the top of the wood at the beckside once more. Beyond, the track climbs up the hillside and then contours along to reach the main area of mine workings. The buildings to the left of the path were part of the Bunton lead mine and were the place where the ore was washed, crushed and then stored in the bunkers nearby ready for smelting elsewhere. Several gullies are to be found around the workings; these mammoth, natural-looking excavations are called hushes. They are formed when water is dammed up

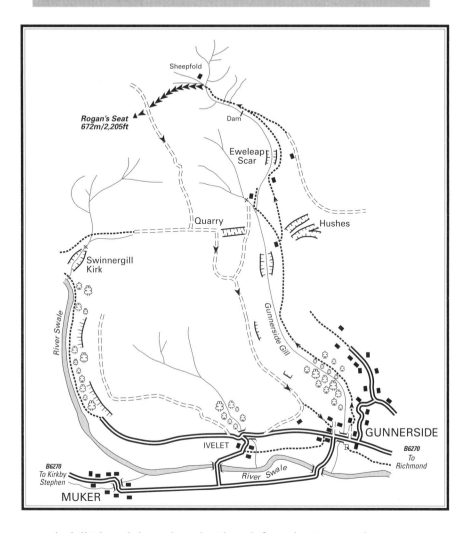

on the hillside and then released with such force that it carves these massive gullies that exposed the mineral veins. However, many have open shafts in their bottoms combined with loose scree, making for a lethal combination so intimate exploration is not advised.

At the far side of the workings, two main paths are seen on the hillside, one lower one descending to the valley floor and a higher one, rising up the fellside. Aim up to the higher one, following several small branching paths *en route* and passing two well-preserved adits, one above and one under the path – again, explorations should not be too intimate.

The track seen rising up the hillside continues along, dropping slightly back to the rising beck, another ruined building and level platform between it and the river. At the other end of this level area, a much smaller path continues along above the stream, rising and falling, passing high above the narrow, rocky confines of Eweleap Scar, through which the beck tumbles below. The path eventually joins a higher level track contouring along the hillside just short of an old breached dam, constructed to hold water for use at the Blakethwaite Smelt Mill, the ruins of which are to be found at the junction of Gunnerside Gill and Blind Gill but not seen on this route.

Continue along the grassy track, past a fine cascade, to another, higher dam beyond which lies a peaty, wet quagmire. Walk to the right along the dam to a small notice that informs visitors that the bridleway ends here. However, a sheep track leads on, indistinct at first through the rushes but becoming much more visible as it runs through the heather past more rocky confines at beck level to reach a well-built sheepfold, on the opposite bank, which would serve superbly as a shelter on a rough day.

It is here that the rough walking begins; turn left, aiming up towards a 'gash' in the skyline. This turns out to be a small, eroded streambed in the peat and, following it onwards, gives much better progress than on the heathery grouse moor to either side. When it does end, keep on the same line through the heather to arrive on the well-engineered track close to the summit, which is marked by a largish cairn constructed on top of a big peat hag.

To return to Gunnerside, walk down the track, passing a shooting hut on the right until it swings around to the left, joining with another track coming in from the right. Ahead lies a medium-sized reservoir, Moss Dam, which was constructed to fulfil the same purpose as those seen earlier in Gunnerside Gill. The track then runs towards the valley but turns to the right after descending only slightly.

It then continues along the hillside, joining with another rising up from the mines and yet another rising track further along. When finally it swings to the right around the hill above the village, a small cairn on the left marks the start of a descending grassy path to the village. It is quite clear, at one point following a sunken pathway, and reaches a gated slit stile at the back of some houses. Through the stile, turn left along the wall and then descend down to the road opposite the post office, only a few yards above the car-parking area.

Nine Standards Rigg

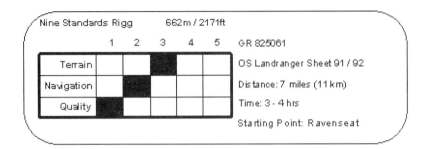

Nine Standards Rigg			662m / 2171ft			
	1	2	3	4	5	GR 825061
Terrain			■			OS Landranger Sheet 91 / 92
Navigation		■				Distance: 7 miles (11 km)
Quality	■					Time: 3 - 4 hrs
						Starting Point: Ravenseat

Above Keld, the green valley pastures give way to rough, bleak moorland and all signs of human comfort are left behind. Nine Standards is the fell to the right of the Swaledale–Kirkby Stephen pass when approaching from Keld and the bleak slopes viewed from here are replicated on all other sides. The best approach is from Swaledale and a high start is guaranteed. An ascent from Keld involves a long walk up the valley for little real gain in height as Keld itself is at 1,020ft (310m). It is recommended to start near Ravenseat Farm in Whitsundale, a little known minor tributary of the Swale above Keld, which is only a few hundred feet higher. If, however, Keld is the desired starting point then a pleasant path runs along the top of Cotterby Scar and up to Ravenseat; this forms part of the Coast-to-Coast route.

Ravenseat is reached up a small road (signposted), which leaves the Kirkby Stephen road on the right about two miles above Keld. There is no parking at Ravenseat itself but there is room for about four cars at the beginning of a footpath on the right, signposted to Hoggarth Bridge. Continue, on foot, along the tarmac towards Ravenseat and then follow a footpath along the wallside on the left before a cattle grid. This path stays close to the wall and follows it around, meeting a path coming up through the farmland from Ravenseat direct, which will be used if ascending from Keld. The path continues, crossing a small stream, to where the wall turns to the right and a noticeboard is found.

This noticeboard is directed towards Coast-to-Coast walkers and asks them to use certain routes to ascend Nine Standards Rigg at particular times of year, in theory to allow the footpath to regenerate. Between December and April, they wish them to walk along a route which does not actually reach the summit, while through the summer the route described here in descent is permitted between May and July while the route of ascent is permitted between August and November. This would mean that by following these regulations, it is impossible to make a circular route.

It is for you to decide whether you wish to follow these instructions or whether you decide that, as you are presumably not a Coast-to-Coast walker, the regulations do not apply to you and therefore you may go where you wish. The circular route described here assumes that you decide to follow the latter option although it is quite possible to use either the ascent or descent descriptions in reverse should you wish to follow the first option.

Turn right and walk steeply uphill behind the notice to a stile. Over this, stay by the wall and descend the short distance to the valley below. The path then leads up through what is, in places, wet ground, by the river and high above it to reach two sheepfolds. The first is fairly ruinous but the second is well built and would provide good shelter on a rough day. The path continues up the valley for a short distance further before turning up the hillside. All up the valley, and now up the hillside, the route is marked with stakes, painted blue at the top apart from the odd one which is painted yellow. The hill is long and tedious but, apart from just at the beginning, it is not steep. After crossing several very wet peat gullies, a path is met running left to right and a right turn leads up to the trig point. This is actually the highest point although the viewfinder on the next bump appears to be higher from this angle. Walk on towards the viewfinder and then on to the piles of stones from which the hill takes its name.

The purpose or builders of the stones are unknown although they are shown on maps as old as those of the eighteenth century. There are many possible suggestions for why they were constructed, ranging from trying to give attacking Scots the impression that there was a fort on the hilltop to suggestions that there was no real reason for their construction but that it was simply something to do!

After developing your own theories, return to the trig point and descend to the junction of paths just beyond. Continue along the ridge through some very difficult wet, peaty ground to a second cairn. Here the path turns left, crosses a small bridge (another illogical structure given the much wetter ground already crossed) and then turns back to the right to reach the track running across the moor from the motor road to the shooting hut at Ney Gill. Follow it to the left to its end at the shooting hut and then take a path onwards down the valley to rejoin the route of ascent by the notice board.

Section 9 – The North Pennines

Rivers Eden and Irthing from the Solway Firth to Gilsland. Hadrian's Wall from there to Holmhead and then the Tipalt Burn, River South Tyne and River Tyne to Tynemouth. The east coast from there to Middlesbrough and the River Tees to Barnard Castle and then A66 to Brough. The River Eden from there to the Solway Firth.

NAME	HEIGHT	IN SECTION	IN ENGLAND	IN BRITAIN
Cross Fell	893m/2,930ft	1 of 4	5 of 53	247 of 751
Mickle Fell	788m/2,585ft	2 of 4	17 of 53	412 of 751
Burnhope Seat	747m/2,450ft	3 of 4	22 of 53	486 of 751
Cold Fell	621m/2,037ft	4 of 4	51 of 53	725 of 751

Unlike further south, there are very few incisions in the ridges of the North Pennines. This gives rise to a landscape of very high ground but with surprisingly few separate summits. The two main eastward-flowing valleys, Teesdale and Weardale, carry large amounts of water and gradually slope upwards, staying quite large at high altitudes. The geology, however, is very similar to that of the rest of the Pennines, the rocks here being deposited in the Carboniferous period, about 345 million years ago, in deltaic conditions.

The basement rocks are Ordovician and Silurian sediments, being gritstones and mudstones, similar to those seen in the Howgill Fells (Section 8) and at Ingleton (Section 4). However, due to a granite intrusion in the Devonian period, these rocks were pushed up in the Pennine areas causing the development of boundary faults. To the west, there is the Pennine Fault and to the north, in the Tyne Gap, there is the Stubblick Fault. Thus, in the Carboniferous period, when warm shallow seas encroached upon the land, this area of high ground, known as the Alston Block, escaped the early stages of lower Carboniferous deposition. Indeed, it was soon covered by a delta spreading southwards from the north which brought about the deposition of a group of rocks, common in the Pennines, known as the Yoredale Beds, named after Wensleydale

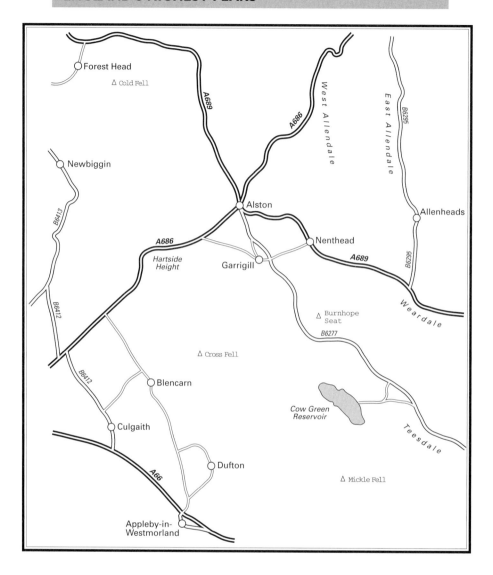

('Uredale') (Section 8). The beds consist of a cyclical succession of limestones, shales, sandstones, fireclays and thin coal seams (see Section 8 for more detail). As the delta reached here before regions further south, there are eleven cyclothems of the Yoredale Series in the North Pennines as opposed to eight around Wensleydale and even less further south around Ingleton (Section 4).

However, as deltaic conditions became more firmly established in the upper Carboniferous period, rocks of the Millstone Grit Facies (grits, shales and sandstones) and then Coal Measures were deposited. All of the coal measures have since been eroded and much of the Millstone Grit Facies although the hills and ridges still have a protective capping of millstone grit. However, in the Carboniferous period, a volcanic intrusion, known as the Whin Sill, deposited molten magma which cooled and solidified to form quartz dolerite. As it cooled underground, it cooled much more slowly than it would have had it been on the surface, so therefore it formed larger crystals and that resulted in a medium-grained rock. The intrusion stretches from Upper Teesdale through Cross Fell, where it can be seen in crags on its western escarpment, along Hadrian's Wall to the Farne Islands off the Northumberland coast.

It is best seen in the crags immediately to the north of Hadrian's Wall, where, like in many other places where it is exposed on the surface, it forms small cliffs of between 50ft (15m) to 100ft (30m) in height. Other good examples of the Whin Sill are at Cauldron Snout, where the River Tees falls off its edge, at Maizebeck Force nearby (both waterfalls are seen on the Mickle Fell route), Falcon Clints and Cronkley Scar. However, where it touched limestone bands in the Yoredale Beds, the intense heat melted the limestone. It then recrystallized into a crystalline sugar-like marble which weathers to form sandy soils low in phosphorus and high in lime. The only two places in Britain which have this rock, Widdybank Fell and Cronkley Fell, are both at the head of Teesdale and are part of the Upper Teesdale National Nature Reserve, renowned for its wide variety of rare lime-loving plants known as the Teesdale Assemblage.

However, the Whin Sill was not the first volcanic intrusion in these parts. As already mentioned, in the Devonian period, about 362 million years ago, a mass of molten granite intruded into the Askrigg (Sections 4 and 8) and Alston Blocks as a result of the Caledonian earth movements, pushing the Askrigg and Alston Blocks up and establishing the Pennine boundary faults. Boreholes in Weardale and Raydale (a tributary on the southern side of the Ure, Section 4) have proved the existence of the granite below the Carboniferous sediments at a depth of 2,000ft (600m) and 1,650ft (500m) respectively.

As granite cools, it develops a network of joints and cracks through which solutions can flow. In the later stages of cooling, in the early Permian period, hot saline solutions, originating from a lower part of the granite that was still cooling, were forced, under pressure, through these joints and into cracks in the limestone (tension faults). In the limestone cracks, the pressure reduced and consequently the solution cooled, allowing many minerals contained in it to be deposited in veins. These minerals included galena (PbS – lead sulphide), fluorspar (CaF_2 – calcium fluoride), barite ($BaSO_4$ – barium sulphate), dolomite ($CaMg[CO_3]_2$ – calcium magnesium carbonate), calcite ($CaCO_3$ – calcium carbonate), witherite ($BaCO_3$ – barium carbonate), pyromorphite ($Pb_5[PO_4]_3Cl$ – lead chloro-phosphate), quartz (SiO_2 – silicon dioxide), pyrite (FeS_2 – iron sulphide) and sphalerite (ZnS – zinc sulphide), some formed by metasomatism – reaction of the solutions with limestone.

Certain areas, zones of weakness, possessed many tension faults and these zones became the principal mining areas. The most productive veins occur below the Grassington Grit (a rock of the Millstone Grit Facies) and around the Main Limestone (a limestone band in the Yoredale Beds – see Section 8), both of which acted as stratigraphic traps. These veins vary in size but are generally quite narrow (a few inches to a few feet), quite deep (hundreds of feet) and great distances in length (anywhere between a few hundred yards and a few miles). Other deposits, known as lenticles, occur between limestone beds as lateral precipitates.

The mines, mainly for lead extraction, began as small, open-cast affairs, where gangs of men were leased a length of vein by the landowner and would then quarry that vein on the surface. However, in the eighteenth century, shaft mining began as companies began operations. It was customary to sink a shaft on or close to the vein and then take off levels to the side at 60ft (20m) intervals. The mining took place on the roofs of these levels, the floor being gradually raised by wooden planking, which has now rotted and is treacherous. Adits that appear on the surface are either horizontal entrances to shafts or drainage channels to remove water from the sump or pool that existed at the bottom of the mine.

Another method of extracting lead was one that used water to create a hush. A turf dam was constructed on the moor and then the water released, tearing away the surface vegetation, rock and some lead. This process was repeated several times, creating massive ravines in the hillsides. Sometimes, hushes were combined with shaft mining – having removed the surface vegetation and rock, shafts were sunk in the hush to exploit the ore in the vein at greater depth. This is why it is very dangerous to walk in the bottom of a hush with which you are unfamiliar. Some of the best examples of hushes are those in Gunnerside Gill (Section 8).

The lead that came out of the mine or hush was in the form of galena (lead sulphide) but mixed with other minerals (listed above) and rock; a profitable vein would contain over 5 per cent galena, a rich one over 10 per cent and some outstanding ones up to 25 per cent. The ore then had to be dressed before it could be smelted. The material would first be washed in a nearby stream to carry away the lighter material and then what was left was finally sorted by hand before the pieces of galena were broken up into a uniform size. They were finally crushed, originally using a heavy iron plate known as a bucker. Later, iron hammers and rollers were introduced, powered by water wheels that were fed by leats often from small reservoirs, such as those in Gunnerside Gill (Section 8). In the final stage, the crushed ore was allowed to settle out in water where, being heavier, it sank first before the other lighter waste material.

The final stage in the production process was the smelting of the dressed ore. This is a two-stage process. Firstly it is necessary to oxidise (burn) the lead thus:

$$\textbf{GALENA} + \text{oxygen} \longrightarrow \text{lead oxide} + \text{sulphur dioxide},$$
$$2PbS + 3O_2 \longrightarrow 2PbO + 2SO_2$$

Following oxidation, more galena was added to reduce ('de-oxidise') the lead oxide:

$$\text{lead oxide} + \textbf{GALENA} \longrightarrow \textbf{LEAD} + \text{sulphur dioxide}$$
$$2PbO + PbS \longrightarrow 3Pb + SO_2$$

Zinc is obtained from its ore, sphalerite (zinc sulphide), in a similar way and iron ore was also mined in the Alston area and smelted at Stanhope, using locally quarried limestone as flux.

Lead smelting was originally done in small peat furnaces where the lead ran out from between the dross (waste) into a sumpter pot, from which it was poured into moulds. In the larger smelt mills, reverbatory furnaces were introduced which could cope with larger amounts of lead, as they were bigger and designed to be run continuously, fuelled by a coal or coke fire. In total, it could be expected to obtain 0.87 tonnes of lead from a tonne of galena. However, since an average vein contained only between 5 and 10 per cent galena, it was necessary to mine about 15 tonnes of rock to obtain just one tonne of lead. The large costs involved in mining this relatively low-grade ore and the large cost of smelting led ultimately to the demise of the industry. At its heyday in the early part of the nineteenth century, the Old Gang Smelt Mill in the Gunnerside Gill area of Swaledale (Section 8) produced over 2,000 tonnes of lead each year but by 1880 the industry had all but collapsed due to competition from cheaper Spanish imports.

Today, the best mining remains are to be found in the valleys to the north of Swaledale, such as Gunnerside Gill (Section 8). However, much has been restored at Nenthead near Alston where there is a visitor centre and the old water wheel has been restored at Killhope (Weardale).

Another interesting feature of the North Pennines is the height to which land is enclosed. This, surprisingly, is a by-product of mining. Mine owners were obliged to provide their workers with farmsteads so all available land was enclosed and used to grow grass for grazing and hay production, grass being about the only crop which could be grown at this altitude.

In the Tertiary period, the North Sea basin was subsiding, which, in turn, pushed up the western Pennines as far as the western boundary faults. Further south along the Dent Fault, subsequent uplifts to the west have hidden the effect but here, along the Pennine Fault, there is a large escarpment above the Eden Valley which marks how the Pennines have been uplifted, despite the subsequent deposition of the Eden sandstones which are of Permian and Triassic age. However, there were some earth movements along the Pennine Fault, mainly a north–south shift. The subsidence of the North Sea basin also set a north-north-east dipping strata to the Yoredale Beds and the angle of the eastwards facing dip slope is a reflection of this.

The Ice Age was finally to define the North Pennines as a separate region. As well as the local ice sheet carving out the valleys and streams, the Lake District Ice breached the Pennines in the Tyne Gap to the north and in the Stainmore Gap to the south. Both were natural lines of weakness, the Tyne Gap being marked by the Stubblick Fault and the Stainmore Gap being the meeting point of the Dent and Pennine Faults. The Ice Age also left behind a thick coating of impervious boulder clay which helps to make the moorlands so notoriously wet.

Access

There are no rail services into the interior of the region but there are bus services to Alston from Penrith, to which there are West Coast main line services, to Haltwhistle, to which there are local services from Carlisle and Newcastle, and to Langwathby, from which there are local services from Leeds to Carlisle. There are stations at Appleby-in-Westmorland and Langwathby in the Eden Valley on the Settle–Carlisle line on which there is a frequent daily service between Leeds and Carlisle. On the Carlisle to Newcastle line, there are stations at Brampton, Haltwhistle, Bardon Mill, Haydon Bridge and Hexham; again there is a regular daily service between Carlisle and Newcastle. The best approach by road from the south is the B6277 up Teesdale from Barnard Castle, close to the A66 and approachable from Scotch Corner on the A1 up that road. Alston lies at the intersection of the A689 Brampton (near Carlisle) to Darlington road, and the A686 Penrith to Hexham road.

Accommodation

The starting point for the eastern mountains at Cow Green Reservoir is remote from sizeable habitations but lies almost equidistant from Alston and Middleton-in-Teesdale. Both towns support a variety of accommodation, although the closest base would be the small pleasant village of Garrigill just to the south of Alston where there is limited bed and breakfast accommodation. On the western side of the region, there is accommodation at Appleby and Penrith and also in many of the smaller villages, although it is advisable to book in advance. For Cold Fell, Brampton and Carlisle both have accommodation, although the Alston and Garrigill area would provide a good base for the entire section. There are youth hostels at Ninebanks (West Allendale), Alston, Langdon Beck (Forest-in-Teesdale – very close to Cow Green Reservoir), Dufton (near Appleby-in-Westmorland) and Carlisle.

Cross Fell

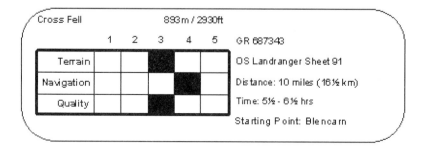

Cross Fell						893m / 2930ft
	1	2	3	4	5	GR 687343
Terrain			■			OS Landranger Sheet 91
Navigation				■		Distance: 10 miles (16½ km)
Quality			■			Time: 5½ - 6½ hrs
						Starting Point: Blencarn

Just to the north of Appleby, the Pennines rise to their highest point, the well-known flat-topped Cross Fell, the summit plateau completely surrounded by a band of scree. It is the fifth highest mountain in England and indeed the only mountain in the ten highest in England that is outside the Lake District.

It is possible to approach Cross Fell from the east but this is long and tedious in comparison with the fine western escarpment, affording continually fine views of the Lake District mountains, standing in stark contrast to the lush green Eden valley between. Park at Blencarn, a small village about six miles north of Appleby and approachable from there or the A66 at Temple Sowerby via Newbiggin. There are two streets in the village, a higher one and a lower one; the higher one is wider and it is best to park here. Walk initially north, soon turning down right onto the Kirkland road and following it up to that hamlet in about a mile. Keep straight on up to the very head of the tarmac at Kirkland Hall where a rough track, signposted to Garrigill, continues through two fields to emerge onto the open hill.

Rising across the hillside, it enters the valley of the Ardale Beck and stays on the southern side as it climbs past some old spoil tips to emerge onto less steep ground on the hillside above in the vicinity of a tin-built bothy to the south. At a cairn, the main track turns to the left but keep straight on up a cairned route, initially wet underfoot, which soon becomes drier and stonier once more. It reaches the ridge and then drops very slightly down the other side to reach a Pennine Way signpost and some shelters. The signpost points to the right and a vague track climbs

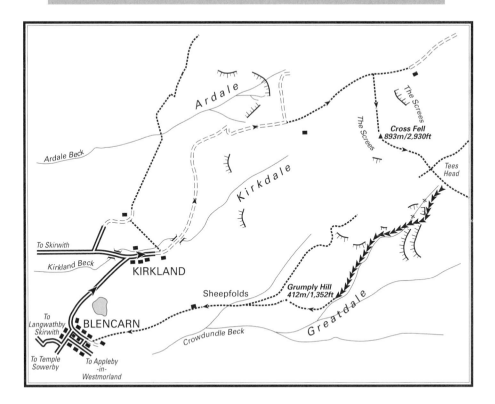

up the ridge, soon becoming very indistinct but reappearing further up along the same line to reach the screes. Some awkward progress follows over the large blocks but soon much flatter, greener ground is reached. In good weather, the onwards route is quite clear, rising slowly to some cairns and then up to the massive shelter and trig point on the summit. However, in mist it is far from obvious but a bearing of 161° will lead directly to the summit. The descent is a similar story; a line of small cairns leads off at a bearing of roughly 113° before becoming a much more distinct path as it drops down through the screes which are not as awkward on this side.

Some slabs help progress through the ensuing bog, but before too long the depression between Cross Fell and Little Dun Fell is reached. The head of the Tees is not a great distance away to the left but the car is down to the right. On the right, a narrow valley containing a small stream, the Crowdundle Beck, is the onwards guide and after falling over a couple of small cascades, best passed on the left, the beck resumes a more placid downwards course through some very good rocky gill scenery, but it is as well to cross to the right-hand bank as soon as possible.

Its steep descent ends by Wild Boar Scar on the right, when the valley opens out into Greatdale. A sheep track runs down through the valley and lower down, when the red sandstone soils are reached, the path runs across two little craglets where the beck is eroding the bank. Shortly after the second, the sheep track begins to contour along the hillside, rising only very slightly to reach a grassy area. Continue along, passing along the top of some rushes where another sheep track will be picked up which leads on, almost to the top of the grassy dome of Grumply Hill, which excels as a viewpoint.

A delightful, easily graded and quite narrow grassy ridge runs westwards and this should be followed until a green track leads a short distance onwards through the bracken to meet another track running along the valley on this side. Follow it to the left and down to and through some sheep pens. A wide, green lane with a track and a scattering of gorse bushes leads down all the way back to Blencarn.

Mickle Fell

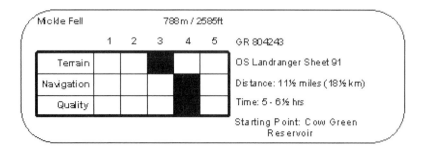

See also 'Access Arrangements in Sections 9 and 10' on page XX.

Mickle Fell is a dominant height in this area but is also quite remote from roads and habitations. Due to the access restrictions imposed by the Strathmore Estate, who own the land, a circular walk is unfortunately not possible but, nevertheless, there are plenty of interesting things to see in both directions on the up-and-back route described here.

Park at Cow Green Reservoir and leave the tiered car-park at the top level by walking back along the access road to the information boards covering climate, vegetation, wildlife and geology. It is also possible here to purchase a guide to the nature trail, which forms the initial stages of the route, for the sum of twenty pence, payable to the honesty box. The guide is highly recommended as it leads you through the different aspects of the flora and fauna that are seen along the route to the reservoir dam and the waterfall of Cauldron Snout beyond. The National Nature Reserve here in Upper Teesdale is important as the surrounding hills trap the cold air producing sub-arctic conditions (with a summer temperature similar to that of Reykjavik in Iceland) in which a unique flora, known as the Teesdale Assemblage, including the rare spring gentian found in the British Isles only here and on the west coast of Ireland, flourish partly due to the underlying sugar limestone which is as rare as some of the plants themselves.

The nature trail leaves the road a little further on down a gravel path on the right to reach a track, a left turn on which leads to a gate on the right marking the start of the Nature Reserve. Through the gate, a road runs

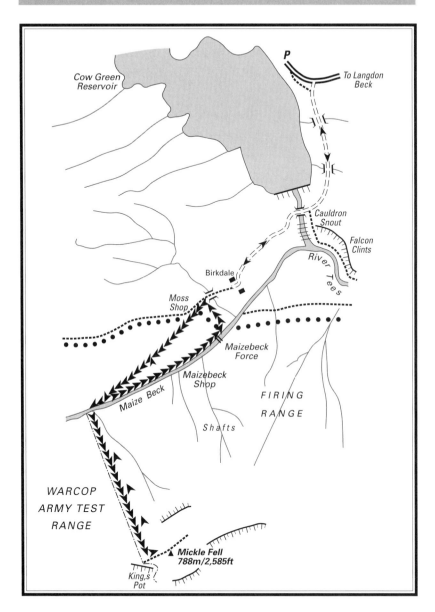

down to the dam, but do not cross it; instead, continue straight ahead to the top of the waterfall of Cauldron Snout. At this point it is worthwhile following the Pennine Way path to the foot of the waterfalls, as they will not be seen in their entirety elsewhere on the route. However, note that some scrambling is required which would lift the terrain grading to a level four.

From the top of the waterfalls, cross the bridge and follow the track onwards, turning left downhill to pass through the farmyard at Birkdale. The track continues on through the inbye, over a footbridge and up the hill to the spoil heaps at the ruined mine of Moss Shop. From here, the route enters the firing range. Walk up to the flagpole (note not to pass this point if the red flag is flying) and continue on over the shoulder of the hill on a bearing of 204° to reach the Maize Beck over rough, pathless country.

By looking to the right, up the beck, the bottom wooden part of a wire fence descending from Mickle Fell will be seen. Try to aim down to the beck until, about 50 yards short of the point where the fence meets the stream, a good crossing place should be found using natural stepping stones. Although the beck is no problem to cross in good weather, when it is in spate this crossing would be impossible, in which case a large detour of 10 km/6½ miles, in both directions, would have to be made to cross it at the bridge over Maizebeck Gorge at GR 749270 (add a total of 4–7½ hrs).

The fence line now stretches all the way to the skyline up a long slope, steep towards the top, there being no alternative but to follow the fence all the way to the summit ridge. Note the boundary stones on the other side of the fence – number 101 is by the stream (the number on the far side of the stone) and the others (some of which are missing) run along the other side of the fence, descending numerically to number 89 near to the ridge (the numbers on all the others are on the uphill-pointing faces). Eventually, at the top of the slope, the fence turns through a right angle to the left above a large corrie on the southern face, known as King's Pot. Beyond lies some very bleak terrain that the fence continues to traverse all the way to the cattle grid on the Brough to Middleton-in-Teesdale road. However, a left turn along a cart track leads, along the ridge, past two small cairns to the much larger but quite unshapely summit cairn.

Return back down by the fence side and cross the Maize Beck as on the ascent. However, instead of striking off over the moor to Moss Shop, follow down the bank of the beck to the right, picking up a cart track. On the other side of the beck the remains of another mine, Maizebeck Shop, are seen before, in about a mile, Maizebeck Force is reached. This is where the Maize Beck falls off the dolerite forming the Whin Sill and astute observers will note that this is at exactly the same height as Cauldron Snout where the infant Tees does likewise. Past the waterfalls, the cart track continues just above the beck before turning left just before the inbye. It then runs up the side of Grain Beck to the footbridge on the Pennine Way that was crossed earlier. From here on, there is no option but to follow the outward route back along the Pennine Way and Nature Trail to the reservoir car-park.

Burnhope Seat

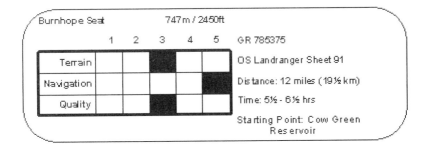

Between Teesdale and Weardale lies a high block of moorland with few large drops; the highest point is Burnhope Seat. However, there are no paths on the summit and the area is best left alone in mist.

At Cow Green Reservoir, there is a three-tier car-park (free) at the beginning of the nature trail to the dam and to Cauldron Snout (see Mickle Fell). However, our route leads away from the dam along a track that leaves the top tier of the car-park. Without any deviation, this track passes several mines, runs above the reservoir and then the valley above to eventually reach the Alston to Middleton-in-Teesdale road at almost 2,000ft (610m). Walk along it to the left to a cattle grid but, instead of crossing it, follow the fence on the right, and then back down into a stream valley. Note that there is parking for a few cars in a lay-by just beyond the cattle grid if a short up-and-back walk is desired. Follow the stream up into a rocky limestone gorge. About half-way up, a small stream discharges from a little cave on the right. By kneeling down, it is possible to see up the passage which, although small, is larger than would be imagined. Continue up the stream bank until a fence crosses it. Turn right and follow the fence up to the summit ridge, passing one or two boundary stones *en route.*

On Burnhope Seat, there were three mining areas, the mineral rights of each area being owned by an individual or company (not necessarily the landowner), known as the royalty owner; the three royalty owners here were the Greenwich Hospital, the Ecclesiastical Commissioners (for the Bishop of Durham) and the Duke of Cleveland. The London Lead

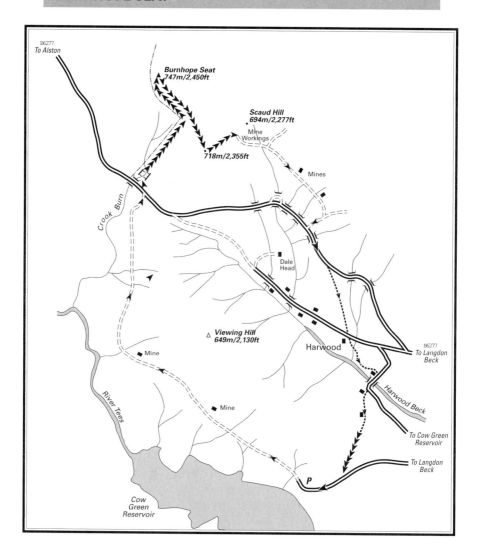

Company took out a lease on all three sections of land, paying a separate royalty to each of the royalty owners, which was proportional to the amount of the mineral removed. Needless to say, there was some confusion as the boundaries were difficult to determine on such an undefined section of moor. This resulted in a legal wrangle lasting many decades but eventually, in 1880, the royalty owners came to an agreement and a set of boundary stones was erected, bearing the letters GH, DC and EC as appropriate. The few boundary stones passed on the ascent are what remain of this boundary, each saying GH and DC. However, the final one, on the ridge, is marked with all three sets of initials and the date 1880.

From the final stone on the ridge, a walk to the left, along the fenceline, leads all the way to the summit cairn, although some peat hags have to be crossed in between. The trig point marks the summit, which has fine views of the Cross Fell group and Weardale.

Descend back down the ridge by the fence but, instead of following it back down to the road when it turns right, continue straight ahead along its line (a bearing of 146°) to climb to a small nameless summit with a small cairn but with excellent views down Teesdale. To continue, locate the sharp summit of Scauld Hill (56°) and walk in a straight line towards it or as near as is possible due to the rough ground and peat hags. However, when at the low point just before it, aim down to the right to a fenced area, which is a small pond. Continue a little further down the valley to another fenced enclosure, this time a mineshaft, which is flooded at depth, to reach a stony track leading down to the stream. Turn left and cross the stream to continue along the track up the opposite hillside and then follow it along to a gate into the inbye near some sheep pens. It continues along the top of the wall and through two more gates before meeting another track descending the hillside. A right turn, through a gate, leads down through a field to the road. Ignore a footpath almost straight ahead and instead walk down the road to the left.

Soon a deep gully (actually a mining hush) is reached and then, on the second left-hand bend in the road, a gate leads into a field on the right. Although there is nothing to mark it, this is a bridleway and on the next gate, at the bottom of the field, a small circular sign says so. It continues down to the road opposite the entrance to the farm that has been in view ever since leaving the main road. Along the road to the left is a river bridge but turn right down the riverbank before crossing the bridge until a wall comes close to the river.

Cross over the river here to a small stile marked by a yellow arrow in the opposite wall. Walk just along behind the wall to the right to another arrow by a telegraph pole where it is possible to cross the wall using a well-placed throughstone. Over the next field, aim for a small cliff where the river has cut into a hill and follow over the top of it, bearing in mind that it is somewhat undercut. The path keeps along the riverbank through a few more fields to the back of a house; it is possible to reach the road through a gate to its left.

Walk down the road to the right and over the river to reach a sharp left turn in the road in front of a small farm. Although the path lies through the farmyard and then over a ladder stile about half-way up the hillside, which can be clearly seen from the road, presently some dogs bar access and I have been informed that it is possible to walk along the road to the left, pass through a gate on the right and then ascend up to the ladder stile. However you reach it, aim up to the top of the field to a house that is clearly in view, crossing a stile behind a cattle feeder.

Beyond, the path leads up to and through the middle of the uninhabited complex of buildings to branch off right at the other side up to a gate. Cross the next field aiming for a gate but continue further up to a slit stile just to the left of a higher gate onto the open fell. A stake at the top of a steep slope marks the route onwards along a sheep track and then up a small hill just beyond. Although there is no path, continue on in a straight line over the shoulder of the moor to the road. A walk to the right leads back to the reservoir car-park.

Cold Fell

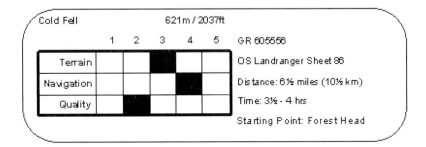

Cold Fell				621m / 2037ft			

North of Alston, on the western side of the South Tyne valley, there is a large tract of high land. Although initially it is all part of the Cross Fell massif, it soon drops into a large gash in the ridge before climbing once more into a remote and rough area of moor, the highest point of which is Cold Fell.

An interesting circular route can be made from the hamlet of Forest Head at the foot of the western slopes. It is possible to park on the large corner in the village but it is tactful to ask at one of the cottages before parking on the beautifully maintained verges. Even so, there is only room for about two cars, but as the hill is not popular, there are unlikely to be any major parking problems normally. Walk through a gate on the road corner and continue straight on down a track ahead, ignoring a footpath sign on the right pointing to Newbiggin, as it is rough and very difficult through the disused quarry.

Continue along the track to a ruined cottage on the left where there is a gate. Go through a stile to the right of the gate and now off the track, walk along the front of a series of old limekilns, noting the old railway sidings to the left. A stile ahead leaves the enclosure and in the next field keep to the right of the rushy area to reach a post with a waymarker on it. Continue ahead through the line of trees to an old gatepost (without a wall any longer), which is also waymarked. By keeping along the base of the old wall, a gate and a slit stile are reached, beyond which is a small field, on the other side of which is a cottage and rough road. Turn right on the road and walk up to the old miners' cottages and farm at Howgill.

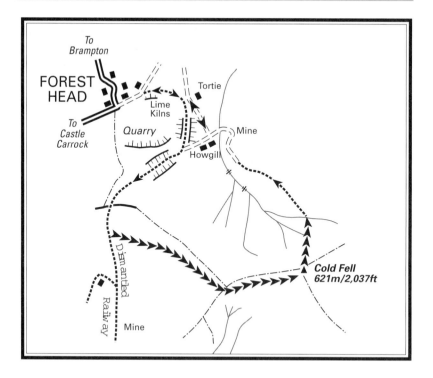

Turn right along the front of the cottages and along a track that bends to the left and passes through a gate onto the open hill beyond.

The track ascends the hill ahead but note the old railway cutting to the right, which is not as wet as it looks, and aim for that. The disused trackbed continues, gently ascending across the fellside to the head of the valley and then over a col into the head of a small valley beyond. A wall soon comes in on the right and runs back to the left. Just beyond this, the bracken ends and a slanting line up the fellside through the rough grass and heather should be taken. If the weather is clear, two stone pillars should be seen either side of the low point on the skyline; aim for the left one, which is on a bearing of 122°. When reached, it actually turns out to be two, but continue on past them to a fence beyond. Turn right and follow the fence, crossing another that joins from the right, all the way to the summit cairn, windshelters and trig point.

Despite the fact that there are three fences in the vicinity of the summit cairn, none of them now runs in the required direction. However, aim for a pillar on another smaller hill almost due north (4°), walking down the ridge to the intervening low point. Here, walk down to the left, well to the right of the stream, and a four-wheeled vehicle track should be picked up. This runs down the hillside to a ruined bothy, just after which it forks. Take the left fork, which then runs down the hill to a gate by the cottages at Howgill, where the outward route is rejoined and can then be followed back to Forest Head.

Section 10 – The Cheviot Hills

Union border between England and Scotland from the Solway Firth to Berwick-upon-Tweed, the east coast from there to Tynemouth and then the River Tyne, River South Tyne and Tipalt Burn to Holmhead. Hadrian's Wall from there to Gilsland and the rivers Irthing and Eden from there to the Solway Firth.

NAME	HEIGHT	IN SECTION	IN ENGLAND	IN BRITAIN
The Cheviot	815m/2,674ft	1 of 1	12 of 53	358 of 751

To the north of the Tyne Gap, which is one of the trans-Pennine glacial breeches by the Lake District Ice (see Section 9), the landscape subtly changes. So far, the Pennine landscapes have been dominated by rocks of the Carboniferous limestone group, mainly thin layers of limestone, shale and sandstone, capped by a topping of Millstone Grit. However, here, the Carboniferous sediments become thinner and eventually disappear after forming a few small hills in the south of the section. However, with the exception of Peel Fell, 1,975ft (602m), none of the more southern and western hills approach the 2,000ft (610m) mark.

However, the Cheviot range supports much ground above 2,000ft but, like in the North Pennines (Section 9), few large drops exist in the ridges and the range therefore only boasts one separate summit, The Cheviot. The geology of the range is, in fact, very different from the rest of the Pennines. Originally, there were hills here, formed from Lower Old Red Sandstone, deposited in the Devonian period and well seen in the Black Mountains (Section 2). However, later in the Devonian period, granite intruded into much of the Pennines, including the sandstone Cheviots. Further south, (see Sections 4, 8 and 9) this granite pushed up the basement rocks to form blocks of high ground and here it did likewise, forming a domed, uplifted area. This doming formed tensional cracks and the magma was forced into these, crystallising out into dykes of finely grained pink felsite. A good place to see these dykes is at Linhope Spout, where the Linhope Burn, a tributary of the River Breamish, has eroded the overlying rocks to expose them.

The Scafell Massif (Section 6) from Yewbarrow

Scafell as seen from near the summit of Scafell Pike (Section 6)

Great Gable (Section 6) and Sty Head from Yewbarrow

Bowfell (Section 6) and the Crinkle Crags at the head of Oxendale

The Old Man of Coniston (Section 6), seen across Broughton Moor

Looking along the summit ridge of Blencathra (Section 7)

The summit of Nine Standards Rigg (Section 8)

Cautely Spout and The Calf from the Ben End ridge of Yarlside (Section 8)

The summit of Mickle Fell (Section 9)

Maizebeck Force, as seen on the Mickle Fell route (Section 9)

The summit of Snaefell (Section 11)

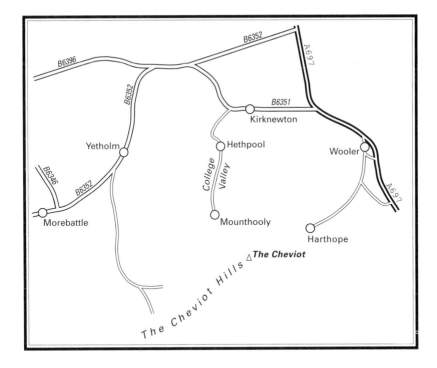

Large amounts of the igneous rock andesite are to be found as pebbles in streambeds, ranging in colour from grey and pink to black with red veining. This pyroclastic material and its wide distribution show that the volcanic activity was explosive. Where the andesite came into contact with the molten magma, it was baked into a harder rock containing crystals of mica and feldspar. It is this material that forms most of the rock outcrops to be seen in the Cheviots such as Braydon Crag on the northern slopes of the Cheviot and Housey Crag above the Harthope Valley on Hedgehope Hill.

By the Carboniferous period, the overlying sandstone on the granite dome had been eroded and the Cheviot granite formed an island in a warm Carboniferous sea. Fine material cemented together granite beach pebbles eroded from the dome to form a conglomerate found in the range away from the granite centre and exposed at Roddam Dene on the eastern side of the range. In deltas on this coastline, limestone and clay mixed together to form cementstone, which is to be found in bands with the conglomerate and exposed by the River Coquet in its gorge just above Alwinton. The next deposits were of Fell Sandstones, which form an outer ring around the range stretching from the Tweed down into the Simonside Hills south of Rothbury.

Since the Carboniferous period, any more recent rocks have been eroded and there has been extensive erosion of these Carboniferous sediments. The cementstones, which are easily weathered, tend to have largely disappeared around the outside giving rise to circular valleys. The Fell Sandstones have proved much more difficult to erode, so the greatest erosion of the cementstones occurs immediately behind them, leaving a sandstone ridge. The circular valley is first visible in the north where the northwards flowing streams, beginning with the Bowmont Water and including the College Burn, have been captured by the River Glen and forced eastwards to join the Till.

The River Till itself continues this capture down the eastern side as far south as the River Breamish. This circular valley, or, to be more accurate, trough, since it contains several valleys, has given the Fell Sandstone ridge a distinctive characteristic of having inward-facing escarpments whereas it generally slopes gently away on its eastern side. In fact so hard is the sandstone that only two rivers flow eastwards through the ridge. These are the Aln at Whittingham and the Coquet through its narrow valley at Rothbury. These two rivers have only been permitted to do so by the weakening of the Fell Sandstones at these two points by faulting.

The Ice Age finally shaped the Cheviots and, it is believed, also robbed them of the grandeur possessed by so many other ranges constructed from volcanic rock. It is thought that at the time of the Loch Lomond Readvancement, thick sheets, mainly of sandy clay and other solid material, known as till and regolith respectively, covered the hillsides hiding much of the granite underneath except where this coating has been worn away on the highest summits. However, here there is a thick coating of wet peat, due to the impermeable nature of granite, which also hides the rock. In fact, the only rock exposure in the range is where streams have eroded the surface sufficiently to uncover the granite below or where, at the metamorphic aureole, the andesite has been baked into a harder rock. Apart from that, the Ice Age appears to have left little mark, the only corrie being that of The Bizzle on The Cheviot's northern slopes.

Access

There are no east–west roads across the range so it takes a long time to travel from one side to the other as it is necessary to travel north into Scotland and through Yetholm or make an even longer detour south around Otterburn and Rothbury. Otherwise the area is well served, the A68 from Darlington to Edinburgh running up Redesdale and crossing over the range at Carter's Bar before descending to Jedburgh and the A697 which leaves the A1 at Morpeth and skirts the eastern fringes of the range, passing Wooler, before joining the A68 just to the north of Lauder. The A698 Hawick to Berwick road links Jedburgh and Coldstream via Kelso. There are daily rail services on the East Coast main line to Berwick-upon-Tweed and Alnmouth (near Alnwick). Some services do stop at Alnmouth and it may be necessary to change onto a local service at Newcastle (not Sundays). There are bus services to Wooler from Newcastle, Alnwick and Berwick and to Yetholm from Kelso. Buses to Kelso depart Berwick and pass through Coldstream *en route*.

Accommodation

Accommodation is more limited here than further south but the larger towns of Jedburgh, Kelso and Coldstream are the best places to look as there is very little in Wooler and Yetholm themselves. The best base for the whole range would probably be Yetholm or Kelso but if your expeditions are likely to be limited to the north-eastern and eastern sides of the range, then Coldstream and Wooler would be the best places to locate. There are youth hostels at Byrness (Redesdale), Wooler and Kirk Yetholm (SYHA).

The Cheviot

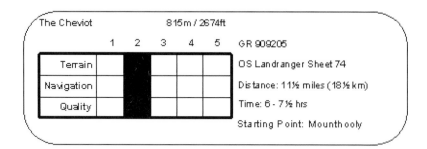

The Cheviot						815m / 2874ft
	1	2	3	4	5	GR 909205
Terrain		■				OS Landranger Sheet 74
Navigation		■				Distance: 11½ miles (18½ km)
Quality		■				Time: 6 - 7½ hrs
						Starting Point: Mounthooly

When driving around the edge of the Cheviot range, it is very difficult to see the parent mountain itself. The small foothills rise steeply from the surrounding valleys completely obliterating any views into the interior. In fact, given the dominating appearance of the range, the summit of The Cheviot itself is rather a letdown, being bleak and boggy.

Drive up the College Valley (see 'Access Arrangements in Sections 9 and 10' on page 257) for about 2½ miles above the end of the public road to where the road forks. Take the right fork and follow it up to a sign which says that there is no parking beyond this point; there is parking here on the right-hand verge just before the sign. From the parking area, a four-wheel-vehicle track ascends steeply up the hillside until it meets the ascending bridleway running from higher up the valley from left to right. Follow the bridleway to the right, through a gate, until it curves around into the valley of the Fleehope Burn and meets a conifer plantation.

It soon forks but, rather than following the left fork uphill, follow the right-hand fork along the top of the conifers and beyond up a waymarked path, through a gate, and up to the wall marking the summit ridge and the border between England and Scotland. At this point, the Pennine Way is reached and this should be followed to the left up the ridge to the summit of The Schil, which lies on the other side of the fence, which at this point does not mark the union border. From the fine, sharp, rocky summit, follow the ridge steeply downhill and over three small hills, past a mountain refuge hut, to the foot of the steep climb up to The Cheviot.

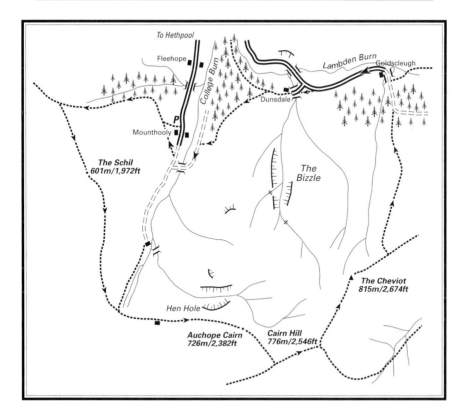

Passing the deep confines of Hen Hole on the left, continue along the Pennine Way up the very steep slope to the several cairns on Auchope Cairn. At this point, some relaxation may be had in the sure knowledge that the majority of the climbing has now been completed. A raised walkway now continues over the black bogs ahead to a stile over which there is a junction of paths. Turn left over another stile, signposted 'Cheviot Summit'. The footpath, almost always on slabs, continues without deviation, passing over Cairn Hill, all the way to the distinctive summit with its highly elevated trig point.

On past the summit, the slabs continue for some distance but then end in a terrible bog. It is best to keep away from the fence to the left where there is more vegetation but the worst is over before too long and the fenceline can once more be followed. However, the fence soon turns to the left and a cairn will be seen just up the slope to the left and another just to the right of the fence.

When equidistant between the cairns, take off left in a northerly direction along a track, not initially obvious, to a large shelter cairn and on beyond all the way down the slope until it enters a conifer plantation just above the valley. The track continues down to a crosstracks; go straight over and the track continues all the way down the hill, joining with a gravelled track swinging in from the right *en route* and then reaching the bottom of the plantation. Keep on down the track and along the front of the houses at Goldscleugh, swinging around to the left along their access road. In about a mile, a path (waymarked) continues straight ahead when the road bends to the right and this should be followed to join the drive to the cottage at Dunsdale.

The right of way passes through several gates behind the house to emerge onto the open hill at the corner of another conifer plantation. Follow a track up the hill to the left, keeping out of the conifer plantations. A waymarked right of way does run along the edge of and then a short distance into some impenetrable woods but, despite being waymarked, it is unlikely that the authorities intend it to be used as they provide a stile and a 'shut the gate' sign on the second gate on the track that is currently being followed.

Pass through the two gates and then follow the track to a deer fence, continuing along it as it bends downhill, still by the deer fence to a third gate. Here the 'true' path is crossed, but do not cross the stile to the right or the ladder stile to the left but follow the four-wheel-vehicle track down the hill to meet a forestry track, leaving the plantations just above valley level. Follow it to the left, over a bridge and up to the main valley track just above the farm below which the car is parked. The deer fencing marks an award-winning area of native broadleaved trees, planted to replace felled conifers and to improve the landscape. However, either the planting was extremely sparse (non-existent in some areas) or the trees have died; either way the project does not appear to have been very successful.

Section 11 – The Isle of Man

That island situated in the Irish Sea almost equidistant from Northern Ireland and England.

NAME	HEIGHT	IN SECTION	IN ENGLAND	IN BRITAIN
Snaefell	621m/2,036ft	1 of 1	52 of 53	727 of 751

The Isle of Man is neither a part of the UK, nor a member of the EU. It is in fact a Crown Dependency with its own parliament (the Tynwald) and its own high court and legal and financial systems. It remains a popular tourist destination because it is an island of contrasts. In the north, there is flat land but the central part of the island consists of a large upland massif rising straight up in some places from the sea. The coastline itself is incised with inlets and beautiful glens, such as Groudle Glen, on the east and west coasts. To the south-west of the island and at Maughold to the south of Ramsey, stupendous sea cliffs and grass slopes drop steeply to the crashing waves far below. In amongst the south-western cliffs are beautiful coves and bays, such as Fleshwick Bay to the north of Port Erin. Not surprisingly, one of the finest walks on the island is the coastal path, or the Raad ny Foillan as it is known.

The rocks of the Isle of Man were mainly deposited during the Ordovician period as part of a huge mountain chain that stretched from here through the Lake District and Yorkshire Dales into north-eastern England. As such, the sediments here are similar to those which make up parts of the non-volcanic Lake District (see Section 5), the Howgill Fells (see Section 8) and the basement rocks of the Pennines, exposed at Ingleton (see Section 4). However, despite their similar geological origins, the Isle of Man is much more reminiscent of parts of the Pennines than the Lake District, due to Lakeland's subsequent volcanic activity.

These old rocks are mainly flaggy greywackes – a rock consisting of fine to coarse sandy particles, cemented together by clay. They were laid down in beds, along which they now break, leading to them being

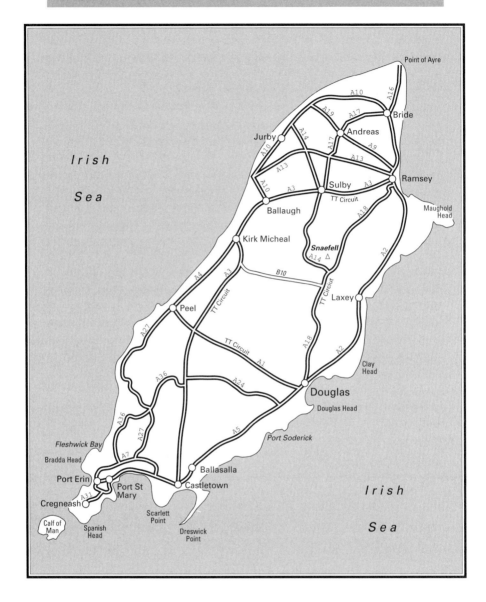

known as flaggy. The other type of rock that was deposited was the Manx slates. These form a bed around 2,000ft (610m) in thickness and consist of three layers: the Barrule Slates, quartz-veined Agneash Grits and the Lonan-Niarbyl Flags. The highest peaks are made of Barrule Slates which are well seen in and around the summit shelter on the small hill of South

Barrule, while underneath them, the Agneash Grits can be seen in the south of the island as well as on the eastern slopes of the central massif. Lowest of all, the Lonan-Niarbyl Flags exist as a coastal strip between Santon Head south of Douglas and Maughold Head south of Ramsey, straying inland in the Douglas area.

These rocks were then affected by the Caledonian earth movements, folding and crushing them, leading to highly inclined strata in places, whereas, at Spanish Head, near horizontal beds still exist. However, lateral pressure has also been exerted and the effect can be seen at The Chasms near Cregneash in the far south of the island, which are well worth a visit. Here, rock masses are in the process of detaching themselves from the hill, producing vertical clefts between the blocks up to 80ft (25m) in depth.

Later, as in many parts of the English Pennines, a granite intrusion occurred, which led to metamorphism of the surrounding clayey greywackes into schists. These are hard, gritty rocks, again bedded, differing in colour from blue to red and grey, depending on the chemical composition of the original clays and therefore tending to have a striped appearance. The general uplift and doming resulting from the granitic intrusion led to the formation of tension faults in the existing Ordovician sediments into which mineralising solutions, under intense pressure, could penetrate. As the pressure reduced, the solutions cooled and so minerals were deposited in the cracks, which then became veins. Where this occurred in the Pennines, lead and other useful minerals were deposited but here the veins consist mainly of quartz (silicon dioxide – SiO_2). This is seen in many rocks but is well viewed in those forming the summit cairn of Slieau Freoaghane.

The mountains had then been formed but other rocks, mainly sandstones on the western coast around Peel and under the northern plain, and limestone on the eastern coast between Port St Mary and Santon Burn, were formed in the lower Carboniferous period. The only other Carboniferous activity was a small coastal volcanic intrusion near Castletown between Poyllvaish and Scarlett Point.

In Permian times, sandstones were deposited in the north and then a thin layer of clay and lime (marl). Above that, St Bees Sandstone, seen on the western coast of the Lake District, was deposited in Triassic times as well as extensive salt deposits, again on the northern plains. These salt deposits have since been open-mined around the Point of Ayre but, today, many of the mining remains serve as landfill sites for the island's population.

The Ice Age has carved out the few U-shaped valleys that exist in the central massif but its lasting impression has been the deposition of large amounts of glacial drift or boulder clay, the northern plain being covered by about 150ft (45m) of it. However, at this time the island was still connected to the British mainland and it was not until a small amount of subsidence in the Pleistocene period, between about 5,000 and 10,000 BC, that the land-bridge was cut off. In fact, the deepest parts of the Irish Sea between the island and the British mainland are only covered by 140ft (40m) of water.

Access

National Express runs coach services to the island from departure points throughout the British mainland. Ferry services, run by the Isle of Man Steam Packet Company, depart Heysham, Liverpool (only Friday, Saturday and Sunday in winter), Belfast (not in winter) and Dublin (not in winter). The island's airport at Ronaldsway, near Ballasalla, is also well served. Emerald Airways run flights to the island from Liverpool while Manx Airlines flights depart Southampton, Newcastle, Manchester, London Luton, London Heathrow, Liverpool, Leeds/Bradford, Jersey (via Dublin), Glasgow, Dublin, Cardiff and Birmingham. However, it should be noted that the airport is at sea level, the runway ending only yards from the shore and, in the absence of high-tech equipment, delays due to sea fog can be a problem. Despite the fact that the island is not a part of the UK, it is not necessary to have a passport to travel to the island. United Kingdom currency is accepted although the island does have its own style of notes and coins.

On the island, there is an excellent public transport system. All the major towns, Ramsey, Douglas, Peel, Castletown and Port Erin, as well as other more rural areas, are linked by bus services. Regular services on the Isle of Man Steam Railway link Douglas, Ronaldsway Airport, Castletown, Port St Mary and Port Erin, while trams on the Manx Electric Railway connect Douglas, Laxey, Ramsey and stop at other local stations, such as Dhoon and Maughold *en route*. Of course, electric trams on the Snaefell Mountain Railway link the Manx Electric Railway station at Laxey with Snaefell summit.

The Manx road network, which has its own numbering system, is good, despite the fact that there is virtually no dual carriageway on the island, bar one short stretch near the airport. Many of the roads are much narrower than roads of the same class on the British mainland and, although signposting is generally good, it cannot be relied upon as road numbers are frequently omitted and sometimes disagree with those shown on the OS Landranger sheet. Please note that the island has its own laws and while those applying to motoring are the same as or similar to those in the UK, it should be noted that trailer caravans are prohibited, although motor caravans are permitted. Disc parking operates in many of the larger towns and some villages; discs are obtainable from car hire companies, local commissioners' offices, the sea terminal, airport and Isle of Man Steam Packet Company vessels. A list of telephone numbers for car hire companies is given on page 285.

Please also note that on the fortnight beginning around the end of May, the TT (Tourist Trophy) races take place. During the race times, the course is closed to traffic, which can mean lengthy diversions, and also heavy fines are payable by anybody who infringes upon the course. This means that it will be *impossible to cross the main Douglas to Ramsey mountain road on the ascent to Snaefell during the TT* races, except at the footbridge at The Bungalow. Many competing motorcyclists arrive prior to the event and practise by driving around the course at unnerving speeds with ordinary traffic. On Mad Sunday, which is the middle Sunday of the race period, there are no races but the competitors, with nothing else to do, joined by local enthusiasts, go 'mad', all driving around the course as if it were a normal race. On this date, the remainder of the local population keep well off the course and visitors are advised to do likewise.

Accommodation

All the main towns, Port Erin, Castletown, Peel, Douglas and Ramsey, support a wide variety of accommodation in plenty. However, there is much in the island's villages, though it would be wise to find somewhere in advance if you wish to stay outside the main towns. The best base for the whole island would probably be either Douglas or Peel due to their central position but in reality it is quite quick to reach anywhere by car on the island due to the good and quite quiet road network. Note, however, that during the TT races (see above), many hotels and guest houses apply a surcharge to all bookings for that period.

Snaefell

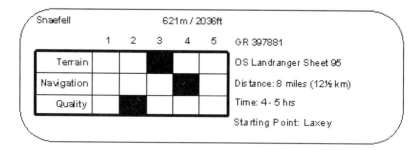

Snaefell				621m / 2036ft		
	1	2	3	4	5	GR 397881
Terrain			■			OS Landranger Sheet 95
Navigation				■		Distance: 8 miles (12½ km)
Quality		■				Time: 4 - 5 hrs
						Starting Point: Laxey

Since ancient Celtic times, it has been said that the seven kingdoms of England, Scotland, Wales, Ireland, Man (which, until the thirteenth century, included the Hebrides), sea and heaven can be seen from Snaefell's summit. In 1895, the Victorians built an electric railway over the 7 km/4½ miles from Laxey (where it joins with the Manx Electric Railway between Ramsey and Douglas, originally opened in 1893) to Snaefell, known as the Snaefell Mountain Railway. However, many of those who reach Snaefell's summit under their own propulsion begin the ascent at The Bungalow, on the A18, itself almost four fifths of the way up. However, here the ascent is started at Laxey, not on the shoreline exactly, but certainly at valley level.

Park in Laxey, where the A2 Douglas to Ramsey coast road and tram lines swing across the valley, in a car and coach park on the right. Walk up the side road, past the famous Laxey Wheel, to arrive at the end of the road in Agneash, situated on the ridge between Glen Laxey and Glen Mooar.

Turn left in the village, through a gate and up a track marked with a sign showing a horse and motorcycle. This is the old mine road which leads up the valley to the ruins of the old workings and associated spoil. Just before a small conifer wood, a path, starting by another sign, identical to the one in Agneash, leads steeply uphill, through bracken, to a ladder stile in the wall ahead. Over the wall, the path disappears. Walk half left (away from the wall) to arrive high on the slopes of a small side valley. Keep above the stream and gently make a rising traverse of the slopes to arrive at the valley head. A few paths may be found but these are more likely to be associated with sheep than humans.

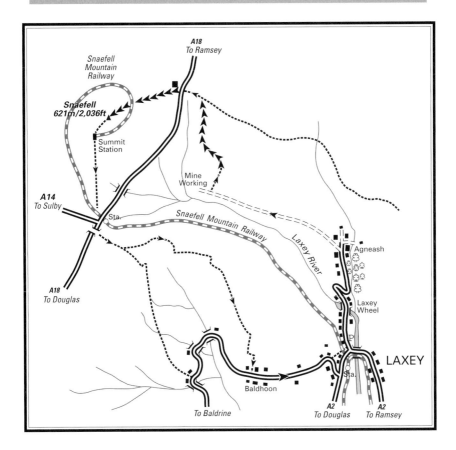

Turn left by the wall at the head of the valley to reach the A18 road over a stile, opposite the John Smyth Cabin, marked on the map as Black Hut. Behind the hut, another stile gives access to the open hill and, although a vague path may be found to begin with, this soon runs out and a beeline should be made for the prominent telecommunications mast, crossing the tram lines *en route*. Slightly beyond the mast is the trig point and associated viewfinder, which, on most days, is probably a little optimistic. A concrete path leads down to the café, bar and summit station.

For descent, there are three options; firstly, the route of ascent may be reversed, secondly, the tram may be caught down or thirdly (but maybe not quite legally), a circuit may be made.

To complete the circuit, begin by following the well-trodden path, indistinct at first, leading south-southwest from the station, to the road at The Bungalow. Over the tram crossing, a gate on the left (locked) gives access to what the Ordnance Survey terms a path (although not necessarily a right of way), which leads up and across the slopes of Mullagh Ouyr, by the fence. Pass through the first gate on the left and follow the slightly sunken but fairly pronounced groove all the way to a gate giving access to the inbye.

Climb the gate and walk down a rushy walled lane straight ahead, until a fence blocks it, beyond which are numerous gorse bushes that make the lane impenetrable. However, by following the headland of the left-hand field, parallel to the lane, the end of the walled lane and another gorsy field are reached. Aim half right down the field and the lane is picked up once more which, although somewhat overgrown, leads out to some large houses at Baldhoon. Turn left on the road and follow it down into the outskirts of Laxey; when the road bends sharply to the right, take a path straight ahead that leads down past one of the tram maintenance sheds, then over the tram lines, to arrive back at the car-park.

Scrambling Alternatives to the Walking Routes

In writing this guide, I have attempted to give what I consider to be the best route to the summit of a particular mountain. However, the best routes for walkers sometimes differ from those that would be recommended to scramblers. Therefore, this appendix is aimed at scramblers who, while following the walking routes described, have the urge to tackle the rock faces seen close to each route. The scrambles described all constitute only minor diversions from the walking route, the exception being the extra or alternative route on High Raise, which visits the Langdale Pikes and the famous cliff face of Pavey Ark. This route is included because its merits for scramblers make it far better than the best walking route up Easedale.

The best and most continuous mountain scrambling in England is to be found in the Lake District and it is here that the alternative routes all lie. The volcanic rocks that are found here lend themselves ideally to the purpose, having a good grip and being exposed in sufficient lengths so as to allow worthwhile scrambles. The rocks of the Pennines, limestones and grits, tend to lend themselves more to rock climbing than scrambling due to their smoother surfaces, while the tors of Dartmoor and the few exposures of the Cheviots are hardly worth mentioning.

Scrambling is, however, the next step up from walking and does therefore have its own inherent dangers. It is, at its simplest level, a natural progression from walking, in that it uses the hands and arms to aid the legs in providing forward motion. It is difficult to draw a boundary between scrambling and walking because there are so many different opinions. Most say that when the hands are used at all for forward progress then the route becomes a scramble and not a walk. I would agree with this but there are many simple scrambles, such as Striding Edge on Helvellyn, which can be comfortably undertaken by walkers. The scrambles included here are those that have been deemed too difficult to include in the walking descriptions but are nevertheless good natural approaches.

Just when scrambling becomes rock climbing is another grey area.

Rock climbing begins in theory when a rope is used but that depends largely on experience. A very experienced and competent rock climber may well choose to do the most difficult route here, Grey Crag via Harrow Buttress and the Chockstone Ridge, unroped, while I have seen people get roped up on Jack's Rake, a very popular and quite simple climb. The only safe way to do the most difficult 'scrambles' is as a roped climb using a belay system. This is not because they lie on sheer vertical faces, where to go climbing without a rope would be folly, but because they are exposed (they have a large drop below them) and therefore the consequences of a little slip would be as huge as if it were that vertical face.

Scrambling is one of the most dangerous of all mountain sports. It takes place on steep and difficult ground but the use of ropes is often not deemed necessary. However, this does not mean that it is not dangerous. The crags may not be sheer but the consequences of a slip while scrambling are almost certain to be much more severe than a similar slip while walking. Wet rock increases the danger as footholds, particularly sloping ones, become dangerously slippery but, when the rock is warm and dry, it is an exhilarating pleasure.

Winter, as well, spells danger on scrambles. Long ice-axes are usually not sufficient, the ice tools of the ice climber being more appropriate on many routes. Scrambling is normally undertaken as a summer sport and, in winter, those who are inexperienced in the use of ice tools and crampons are advised to think again.

Adventurous walkers can quite easily become good scramblers, provided that they are careful. To begin with, the scramble in Lower Dungeon Ghyll (described on page 251) is an ideal test piece and, if there are no problems with that, then perhaps go on to do Jack's Rake on Pavey Ark (also described here). Jack's Rake is more difficult than Lower Dungeon Ghyll but it is not exposed due to the fact that it runs in a groove. What is certainly not recommended is to start off by climbing Pillar Rock or even Pike Crag on Buckbarrow. These routes are more serious and the consequences of a slip severe. If, as an adventurous walker, you enjoy Lower Dungeon Ghyll and Jack's Rake, then the best way to progress further would be to do some more scrambles at the same grade to gain experience.

The books by R. Brian Evans *Scrambles in the Lake District* and *More Scrambles in the Lake District* (see Further Reading), are excellent for this purpose, containing many scrambles at all levels of difficulty and providing good, sensible advice. It is fairly safe to say that one can teach oneself to scramble for the main part, there being few rules and because the skills that are required cannot be taught by someone else, only learnt through practice. Once comfortable on a particular grade then it is simple to progress to the next, the art of ropework not being required except in exposed places and on the very highest grades.

One word of warning, though, for would-be scramblers. Most mountaineering accidents are caused by people who stray out of their depth and experience. Any walkers planning on undertaking the simplest scramble here (Lower Dungeon Ghyll and Jack's Rake) should be very comfortable on Striding Edge and have experience of all the grade four and five walking routes described in the main section of the book.

Unlike walking, fairly easy scrambling can lead into situations where retreat is intimidating, for example, climbing steep grass slopes interspersed with craglets is quite easy but a descent of the same slope can be very unnerving to even the most experienced scramblers. All, especially in the wet, should show caution, when greasy rocks can turn an easy expedition into a lethal misadventure. It should also be noted that descending scrambles is often much more difficult, sometimes frightening, and much less pleasing than an ascent.

Grading

Normally, there are three grades of scramble and a fourth reserved for routes that really are on the boundary with rock climbing. Here, five separate grades are used, the 'normal' ones placed in brackets afterwards. The reason for this is that, in my experience, many scrambles cannot be defined solely by using three grades, as there can be quite a difference between the lower and higher end of any particular grade.

Technical Difficulty (*replaces the terrain gradings given in the rest of the book*)

A grade five route in the main part of the book is in practice an easy scramble and would constitute the lower end of a normal scrambling grade 1.

1. Similar to a terrain grade 5 route in the main part of the book but the situation or technical difficulty has increased and cannot really be defined as walking (grade 1).
2. The scrambling is still quite straightforward but the described route can

still be varied and parts of it may even be avoidable (grade 1/2).

3. The route now involves more continuous stretches of scrambling and retreat may begin to become difficult once the route has begun. A rope is recommended for inexperienced parties (grade 2).

4. Some pitches may require easy rock climbing and the situation is increasingly exposed. Competent parties should have no fears but beginners should keep well away due to the severity of the route. The route is usually quite exposed and all but the most experienced should consider the use of a rope to safeguard against any slips, which would inevitably be severe if unroped (grade 3).

5. These routes are on the boundaries of true rock climbing and exposure is great. Poor rock or vegetation may hamper onwards progression or make it difficult and dangerous. A rope is essential for security for all (grade 3S).

Navigation

The navigation gradings are the same as those used in the main part of the book but only describe the diversion to and from the scramble and not the rest of the route.

Quality

The quality gradings are different but again only refer to the scramble and not the remainder of the route:

1. The scramble only marks a slight improvement on the main route and is hampered by various defects such as vegetation and poor and continually damp rock.

2. The route includes several good points but overall is not continuous in its quality, containing some sections of grade 1.

3. Interest is sustained throughout and the scrambling is good and continuous.

4. The scrambling is generally excellent although it is not given a grade 5 due to some poor sections.

5. Grade 5 marks a classic route with excellent rock and interesting scrambling throughout.

The grid reference given is that of the start of the scramble and unlike elsewhere is an eight-figure reference to help give added clarity to the position of a route.

Use of a rope in scrambling

A rope is highly recommended either for security or protection on several routes and this is mentioned in the grading system as well as with the routes themselves. Scrambling retains much of its appeal due to the fact that the complex ropework of climbers is avoided but complete beginners should only attempt grade 3 scrambles with the comfort of a rope. In general, a kernmantel rope of 9mm (0.35 inches) in diameter and of about 36m (120ft) in length is sufficient for scrambling purposes. A seat harness is advised for comfort where the rope is likely to be used for a long period of time on routes of grades 4 and 5. However, a makeshift harness can be made from a long sling and this should suffice on grade 3 routes where the rope will be used, if at all, for shorter periods of time. In addition, it is essential to be able to use the rope properly and the instruction of a qualified mountain guide or climbing instructor is the easiest way to do this. It is possible to teach yourself by using a good quality book (*Mountaineering: The Freedom of the Hills* is recommended – see Further Reading). However, if you do teach yourself, it is essential to practise the techniques well in advance, preferably in the company of an experienced person.

As well as a rope, a selection of about five chocks of varying sizes, a selection of long and short slings and about seven locking karabiners will be required to anchor the rope in belay stances and for leader protection on exposed pitches. Whether or not to wear a helmet is a grey area; there is a danger of having rocks kicked down from above but most scramblers acknowledge the risk and do without.

The Routes

NAME	TECHNICAL GRADE	SECTION	AS AN ADDITION TO THE DESCRIBED ROUTE ON	PAGE No
Broad Stand	4	6	Scafell Pike	244
Eagle's Nest Gully	3	6	Great Gable	245
Pillar Rock	4	6	Pillar	247
Grey Crag	5	6	High Stile	249
High Raise[1]	1–2	6	High Raise	251
Pike Crag	3	6	Seatallan	256

[1] The scrambling route described is a complete alternative to the walking route described in the main part of the book.

Broad Stand

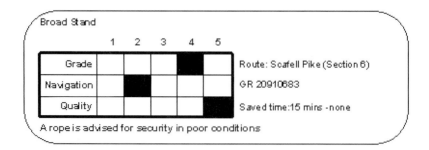

Broad Stand is notorious for casualties as the rock is often wet. In addition, many walkers are tempted into its ascent, believing it to be a quick and easy way from Mickledore to the summit of Scafell. In reality it is not and walkers not sure of their abilities should avoid it and take the delightful route described earlier via Lord's Rake. However, for scramblers, it is the best, most direct and most pleasing way to Scafell's summit from Mickledore.

A short way down on the Eskdale side of the col, there is a narrow crack, known as Fat Man's Agony. Squeeze through this and then proceed to climb an awkward corner on the left, using a small crack for help. This is the crux and it remains damp long after rain causing most parties to rope up in such conditions. The rest of the way now unfolds as a broad platform with a set of steps rising upward to the right. The first step is also quite tricky but it is best surmounted on the left where it adjoins Scafell's crags. Ahead, more steps are easily climbed to leave a fairly pleasant stroll to Scafell's summit cairn along the path to the left. Note that in mist, the first cairn reached away from the cliff edge, at a junction of paths, is not the summit.

Those attempting the whole route in reverse are warned not to embark upon the descent of Broad Stand unless they are confident and experienced. The top 'steps' can be swung down quite easily but the lowest one is different. A narrow ledge awaits those who are successful, while a nasty, possibly fatal, accident awaits those who miss. The crux is more difficult to downclimb than to ascend and those steps which were so easily swung down are much more difficult to climb up.

The Napes and Eagle's Nest Gully

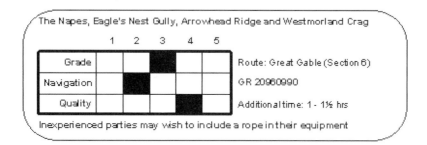

Gable's most interesting and certainly most hidden secret is the rarely explored recesses of its southern crags, the Great Napes, and its famous needle. They are located on the traverse path along its southern and western slopes between Beck Head and Sty Head and, although difficult for walkers to combine the traverse with an ascent of the mountain, scramblers can see the best part of the mountain and then reach the summit via an interesting scramble. However, the gully is best avoided in or after rain when the grass becomes very slippery.

Leave the Kirk Fell and Great Gable route at Beck Head by turning right. Two footpaths leave the col in this direction; one descends down to Wasdale Head and the other is the traverse path. The traverse is the higher of the two and can be found above the level of the col by about 30ft (10m). It maintains a fairly level course, so if the path that is being followed starts dropping continuously, leave it and ascend the screes to find the traverse. The path first comes under the rocky crags of White Napes where, above Moses Finger, the path turns the corner onto Gable's southern face. Ascending slightly, it crosses the red scree run of Little Hell Gate and then starts to traverse below the Napes.

It is now necessary to pick out the Needle and this should be done without delay as it soon merges into the crag behind (in mist, this may be impossible). Once found (at the foot of the fourth ridge along for those who still have not located it), it should be passed by until a faint path is found, ascending rough ground back up to it. A sloping chimney now runs up to the col between the Needle and the crag and this should be ascended, a process known as 'threading the Needle' (awkward with a large rucksack). Beyond, a large drop should be swung down into Needle Gully. On the far side, quite easy rocks lead up to the Dress Circle, the traditional standpoint for viewing climbers ascending the Needle. Above now is Eagle's Nest Ridge and after contouring around its base, crossing a minor gully and passing through a narrow gap between a large detached flake and the cliff, Eagle's Nest Gully is reached.

The gully looks awkward but this is more to do with its vegetative appearance than its technical difficulty. The first pitch is easy enough, best taken towards the left, but then a large chockstone blocks the main part of the gully. Climb around it on the left-hand side to rejoin the base of the gully beyond. A small amount of scree follows before the gully narrows and then rises steeply. However, a terrace up on the left avoids the direct climb, and then another steep place is bypassed on the left. Now the gully splits; take the right-hand gully, marked at first by near vertical grass, but soon the crest of Arrowhead Ridge appears on the left and this should be joined. The ridge, previously a sharp arête, now widens and, after a first awkward pitch, easier scrambling follows to where the Napes ridges join into a single narrow grass arête.

However, in a matter of yards the grassy ridge turns into a much broader stonier ridge descending from Gable. Westmorland Crag lies ahead. It is possible to scramble up the ridge behind a prominent square-crested block at the base of the crag. It is an interesting route which initially keeps to the right-hand side of the crest up a series of steps but keeping out of the gully to the right by traversing back left to a pinnacle on the arête. From here on, keep on the apex of the ridge all the way to the top. Alternatively, if you have had enough, a loose path avoids the crags on the left before joining with the scrambling route at the top and continuing the short distance to Gable's summit where the walking route is rejoined.

Pillar Rock via the Slab and Notch

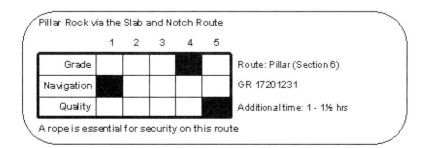

Pillar Rock via the Slab and Notch Route	1	2	3	4	5	
Grade				■		Route: Pillar (Section 6)
Navigation	■					GR 1720 1231
Quality					■	Additional time: 1 - 1½ hrs

A rope is essential for security on this route

First ascended by John Atkinson, an Ennerdale shepherd, on 9 July 1826, the summit of Pillar Rock is one of the most sought after scrambling objectives in Lakeland. The easiest way to the summit is via the Slab and Notch, a popular and enjoyable route. However, the exposure is great, the consequences of a slip while unroped easily fatal and parts greasy after rain, which all together make this no place for the novice.

The ascent of the rock can easily be included in the route described earlier in the book, despite the fact that the scramble is an up and a back, there being no route from the summit of the Rock to the neck between it and the mountain. Follow the route along Robinson's Traverse, past Robinson's Cairn and along the Shamrock Traverse (see Pillar). However, before the track rises to the neck between Pisgah (Pillar Rock's lower neighbour) and the main mountain, take off at a small cairn on a path to the right that contours around the amphitheatre at the head of Jordan's Gully. A few awkward steps are found along the path but, soon, at the end of the path, the start of the route is reached.

A few small steps lead up to the top of the slab, which should then be descended to the right, to reach the small path at its foot. Walk along the path to its end a few yards to the left. Now look up; the notch can now be seen between a rock tower just above on the arête and the main crag. Good holds lead up a steep section (the crux) to gain the notch itself, beyond which a ledge leads on to the next arête. Climb this to find a path on the right, leading into a gully (Great Chimney).

Much easier scrambling now follows up that gully to the top of the rock.

The same route must now be followed in descent, where a rope is even more comforting than it was on the ascent, especially when dropping down from the notch.

Grey Crag via Harrow Buttress

and the Chockstone Ridge

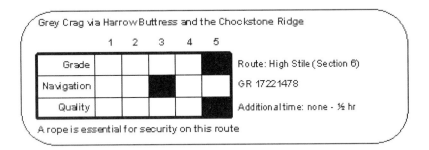

Grey Crag via Harrow Buttress and the Chockstone Ridge

	1	2	3	4	5	
Grade					■	Route: High Stile (Section 6)
Navigation			■			GR 1722 1478
Quality					■	Additional time: none - ½ hr

A rope is essential for security on this route

Birkness Comb sits between High Stile and High Crag and is a very impressive corrie, its walls being bounded by impressive crags on all sides. All the crags in the corrie are, in rock climbing terms, fairly easy but, for the scrambler, provide some serious and exposed expeditions. This route should not be attempted while the rock is damp and not by anybody who is not thoroughly experienced in the art of scrambling. However, for those able to undertake it, this route is one of the best scrambles around Buttermere and avoids the tough pull up Gamlin End on High Crag – an advantage indeed.

Start off by following the walking route over the outflow from Buttermere Lake but after that, rather than following the lakeside path, take a broad forest track. In fact, there are three paths and the required track is the gently rising middle one. Continue on through the wood but, after passing through a wall, look out for a rising path on the right, which leads up out of the wood and on to the open fell. It continues on above the wall into the corrie, at which point Grey Crag should be located. It is on the right-hand side of the corrie, below High Stile and of the two sets of crags there, Eagle Crag and Grey Crag, Grey Crag has the lighter rocks.

Go onwards through the corrie and climb the scree to reach its lowest rocks; this is Harrow Buttress. Begin by continuing a short distance up the right edge of the buttress until it is possible to traverse back left on a ledge to a chimney. This can be climbed on the right but, when possible, move out left on ledges to find a worn corrugation leading up to a platform at its head. Ahead is a prominent overhang but continue up towards it before making a tricky move to the left into a small depression and then following an arête up to the top of a crag. A more broken ridge now leads onwards from the top of the buttress and this should be followed as far as a poised block. Here, take off right into the gully and descend it to the narrow pillar of the Chockstone Ridge, just beyond a vegetated gully.

The ridge now rears impressively ahead and should be followed up to a tower that can be climbed or alternatively avoided at will on the left. The next part of the ridge is difficult to climb direct but a groove to the right provides the key and should be followed until it is once more possible to regain the crest. Ahead, the ridge should be left to rock climbers, scramblers escaping into the gully on the left and then avoiding a chockstone by traversing a ledge on its right. A grassy terrace is now reached before the final upper part of the crag is climbed. The key to its ascent is the bouldery gully in a fairly central position. However, initially it is awkward due to its damp, greasy rocks, which are best avoided by moving to the left, to pass between two towers blocked by a chockstone, before working back right into the gully, which can now be followed up to arrive at the summit of High Stile. Note that of the three cairns on its northern ridge, the central, smallest one is the highest and not the largest one on the left as might be expected.

High Stile marks roughly the central point of the described walking route so which way it is followed back to Buttermere is largely a matter of choice. To the south-east lies High Crag and this, following the ridge around Birkness Comb, provides the most pleasing route, but tired knees will be put to the test in descending Gamlin End and then walking back along the length of Buttermere Lake. In which case, continue over Red Pike to the north-west, following the walking route onwards in the direction in which it is described.

High Raise via Dungeon Ghyll and Jack's Rake

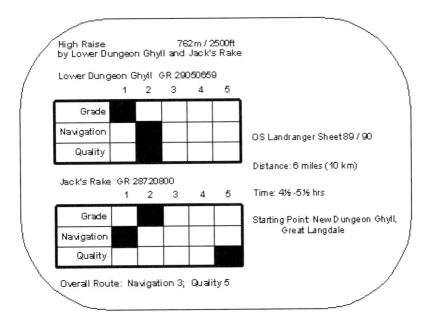

High Raise   762m / 2500ft
by Lower Dungeon Ghyll and Jack's Rake

Lower Dungeon Ghyll   GR 29050659

	1	2	3	4	5
Grade	■				
Navigation		■			
Quality			■		

OS Landranger Sheet 89 / 90

Distance: 6 miles (10 km)

Jack's Rake   GR 28720800

	1	2	3	4	5
Grade		■			
Navigation	■				
Quality					■

Time: 4½ - 5½ hrs

Starting Point: New Dungeon Ghyll,
Great Langdale

Overall Route: Navigation 3; Quality 5

Pavey Ark is one of the greatest cliff faces in England and has a wealth of rock routes on its face. A diagonally slanting rake, Jack's Rake, from bottom right to top left, divides the cliff into two segments, an upper and a lower. The rake is not difficult and is well recommended for anyone who is new to scrambling or progressing from the grade 5 walking routes described in the main section of the book. Although dramatic, there is curiously little sense of exposure, as for a large part the rake forms a groove, which renders the route difficult in wet conditions, as it acts as a drainage channel for water from the upper cliff. Dungeon Ghyll is well known but few penetrate into its depths to see its delights and a walk with some easy scrambling thrown in for good measure allows these delights to be discovered by the few discerning explorers who venture into its depths.

Pavey Ark is one of the many crags and cliffs that the comparatively dull moor of High Raise throws down on its Langdale flank, the best known of all being the Langdale Pikes, of which only Pike of Stickle is suitably impressive from the moor behind. Although the quiet Easedale is probably the best route up the mountain, a walking route by the Langdale Pikes is a very close second, even if it is very busy for most of the year. As such, walkers wishing to use this as an extra or alternative to that described in the main part of the book should use the footnotes to avoid the scrambling sections, rejoining the main route at the next * in the text.

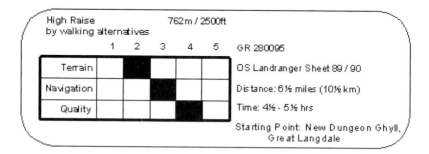

High Raise by walking alternatives			762m / 2500ft			GR 280095
	1	2	3	4	5	
Terrain		■				OS Landranger Sheet 89 / 90
Navigation			■			Distance: 6½ miles (10½ km)
Quality				■		Time: 4½ - 5½ hrs

Starting Point: New Dungeon Ghyll, Great at Langdale

Park near the New Dungeon Ghyll Hotel, the one lower down the valley, either in the Lake District National Park car-park opposite the hotel, which is the cheaper, or the National Trust car-park on the right a short distance further on, which is free to NT members with their membership cards. From the National Park car-park, walk up through the hotel, or, from the National Trust car-park, leave it at the top along a path through trees to the back of the hotel, where the routes meet and lead onwards to a fork in a very short distance. Go left and up to a gate, through which a right turn leads up to a bench and then over a stile to another fork. Another left turn leads over Dungeon Ghyll; it is possible to walk up the stream to a small cascade that, although impassable, is nevertheless quite pretty. The path climbs alongside the ravine and soon a small path through bracken leads to a set of natural steps leading down into the gorge, from where Dungeon Ghyll force, a fine 80ft (25m) cascade, can be seen.

Another small path leads from the top of the steps to the main path higher up, where, in a short distance, another small path, in bracken, leads off to the right. This leads to the top of a natural bridge, actually a wedged boulder, which may have been seen while inspecting the waterfall. It is possible to cross although not really worth the risk as it goes nowhere and is difficult and very dangerous to negotiate since it is

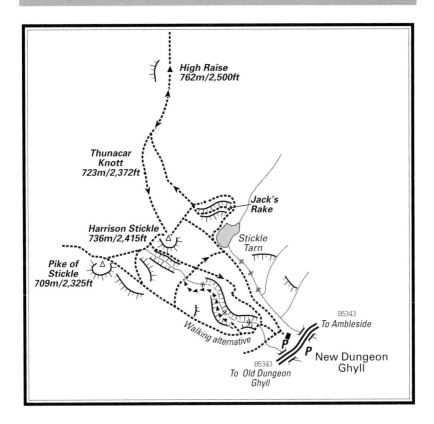

domed. Again, a small path leads up to the main track at a higher level[1].
A little further up, the summit cone of Harrison Stickle comes into view
on the right and it is here that a small grassy path in bracken, not to be
confused with a stony one just above, which is only a diversion of the
main path, leads along into the middle section of the gill just above the
narrow gorge.

Start off on the left bank but, just around the corner, a fine 40ft (12m)
cascade necessitates a crossing to the right bank where a path climbs up
some rock steps to reach the top. Stay on the right bank until a crag bars
progress and the path crosses the stream before running up to a choke of
very large boulders ahead. The easiest route starts off on their left-hand
side and then moves back to the stream's edge before moving back to the
left again. Above, a walk, still on the left bank, leads up to bigger 50ft
(15m) cascade at the end of the ravine that is not directly passable. A
rocky gully on the left at a good angle provides the key and an escape
may be made up it to reach grass slopes above, which can then be

followed around to the head of the waterfall. Continue by the stream to reach the point where a small path crosses and follow it to the right *. The path goes on to cross over one of the descent paths from Harrison Stickle, before contouring around the hillside to the dam at Stickle Tarn.

Ahead lies the imposing face of Pavey Ark and Jack's Rake should be located beginning at the bottom of Easy Gully to the right and running obliquely up the face to top left. Take the path along the left-hand shore of the tarn, where it soon forks.[2] Take the right-hand fork, which continues to some scree at the back, up which it climbs to the foot of the rake. In total, the ascent of the rake will take about an hour and the section that can now be seen at the beginning is the worst. Start off up the groove, easy at first, until it steepens, when parts of the groove are difficult, the rock rib on the left then being a better alternative.

There are no route-finding difficulties and soon the groove ends and a path runs along a grass terrace ahead. However, it is not over yet as an awkward rock step must be climbed to reach an easy terrace, beyond which a much deeper groove runs up to an exposed corner above Great Gully. It takes about 40 minutes to here and it is possible to stop and sit on the grass on the right to admire the blue waters of Stickle Tarn from what must be one of the most impressive viewpoints in England. The rake ends here and a path leads up the right-hand side of Great Gully before crossing it to the left on a terrace and then dropping a few feet to reach some large but easily climbable rock steps that lead to the end of the scramble at the discontinuous summit wall, just near a wet depression between craglets. The highest point of Pavey Ark is up to the right but a return to this point should be made to go onwards**.

At the far end of the wet area, a path runs half left, gradually rising until it forks. Keep right, traversing just below the summit of Thunacar Knott and then up the long hill to the large shelter cairn and trig point on High Raise.

Follow the track back down to the depression between High Raise and Thunacar Knott but keep straight ahead on a less distinct path when the main track curves around to the left. This path leads onwards to the summit cairn on Thunacar Knott, although it disappears on the final stage. A little to the left of the summit cairn, the path can be picked up again, which leads down to the col between Thunacar Knott and the rocky summit of Harrison Stickle, at which point the path swings right. Keep straight ahead and a distinct path will be found that climbs up to the summit. A path, indistinct at first, leads away south-west and descends to the head of Dungeon Ghyll, just before which it forks.

Straight ahead is the rocky peak of Pike of Stickle that can be visited if desired but the descent route lies down to the left. A path leads high above the upper ravine, before descending steeply down to more grassy pastures behind the knoll of Pike How. It then hairpins down to the right (note the fine view back to the final cascade of the Dungeon Ghyll middle ravine), around the base of Pike How and then down to the foot of the lower ravine where the outward route is rejoined.

Walking alternatives to the scrambles

[1] Continue up the main track, past where the ravine turns away to the right, and up through some small craglets. When more level grassy ground is reached, look out for a small path on the right, which contours along to cross Dungeon Ghyll above the ravine.

[2] Take the left-hand fork, which is the tourist path to Harrison Stickle from the tarn. It is steep and arduous but not difficult and there are nice retrospective views of Stickle Tarn. When the ground becomes less stony and craggy, cut across the rough grass half right to meet a faint path running along from Harrison Stickle to Pavey Ark. Just before the path runs into rocks on the final ascent to Pavey Ark's summit, a wet depression is passed between craglets and, after the fine rocky summit of Pavey Ark has been visited, this point must be returned to before travelling onwards.

Pike Crag

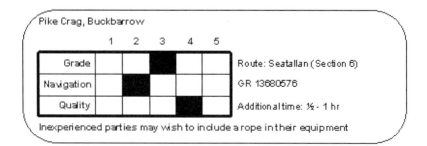

Pike Crag, Buckbarrow

	1	2	3	4	5	
Grade			■			Route: Seatallan (Section 6)
Navigation		■				GR 13680576
Quality				■		Additional time: ½ - 1 hr

Inexperienced parties may wish to include a rope in their equipment

The front face of Buckbarrow is impressive when viewed from below and the scramble up one of its ridges, Pike Crag, is far better than the walking route that reveals little of this spectacular place.

Park at Greendale as described in the main description but begin by walking along the road towards Gosforth. Looking up to the right, the face of Buckbarrow should be studied. It consists of three crags; the furthest one, separated from the others by a large scree gully, is Pike Crag. It is best approached by a faint path that is found just before a wall running up the fellside, just beyond the crag. Another faint path branches right in due course over loose rock before ending. Here, a number of terraces lead along below the crags and these should be followed before climbing up to a prominent holly tree at the foot of the cliff. Start on the right of the holly and climb just above it to gain a terrace running back to the left. Follow this terrace and then cross a small rib to a ledge with a number of delicately balanced blocks. Here, climb some small rock steps on the right-hand side of a moss-covered slab before traversing to the right below a rock wall. Another heather traverse now runs back left to a detached block that should be squeezed behind. A short distance further on, a small ridge is reached and this should be climbed until it is possible to traverse back to the edge of the gully.

The angle of the crag now relents and an interesting route high above the gully is revealed. In practice, after one airy move above the gully, the arête should be followed all the way to Buckbarrow's summit cairn, avoiding any awkward moves on the left if desired. The walking route can now be followed to Seatallan's summit and beyond.

Access Arrangements for
Sections 9 and 10

1. Mickle Fell (Section 9)

Mickle Fell has always been very difficult to climb due to access restrictions. Some old books refer to the need to gain permission from the then Nature Conservancy Council to climb to the summit, as the fell lies within the National Nature Reserve of Upper Teesdale. However, today no such restrictions apply but it is necessary to gain permission from Strathmore Estates of which Mickle Fell is a part. Not only that, but part of the route is also within the Warcop army firing range so additional care must be taken to ensure that firing is not taking place.

Firstly, to ascertain the dates upon which firing is not taking place, contact the Commandant at Warcop Camp:

> The Commandant
> Warcop Training Area
> Warcop
> Appleby-in-Westmorland
> Cumbria.
> CA16 6PA
> Tel: 01768 341661

If you are planning a walking trip a long time in advance, precise details may not be known but, currently, firing never takes place on a Monday and usually not on a Sunday afternoon but it is still necessary to check the day before doing the walk that firing will not be taking place on Mickle Fell.

Secondly, with a date in mind, write to the land agent acting on behalf of the Earl of Strathmore:

> Land Agent – Strathmore Estate
> Youngs Chartered Surveyors
> 3 Wentworth Place
> Hexham
> Northumberland
> NE46 1XB

They will wish to know, as well as the proposed date, the number in the party and the proposed route. They will send you a permit that will allow you to climb the fell following 'the boundary route'. In practice, this means that they will allow you to follow the fence line and county boundary from Maize Beck (GR 791263) to the summit ridge (GR 801243) and then deviate from the fence, along the ridge, to the true summit (GR 804244), as described in the description earlier in the book. The trig point (of lower elevation) is strictly out of bounds but they do allow an alternative route of ascent from the cattle grid on the B6267 Middleton-in-Teesdale to Brough road at GR 832199, following the fence and county boundary from there. However, as anybody who has looked out over that direction from the summit of Mickle Fell knows, it is a long, arduous, dull and difficult approach over the aptly named Lune Head Moss, not to be preferred to the approach from the north.

If you decide at short notice you wish to climb the fell or have to make an alteration to the programme, then it is possible to telephone the agent on 01434 609600 or the head keeper on 01833 640721 during office hours to arrange an alternative date and a place to collect the permit.

As the fell is a managed grouse moor, Strathmore Estates refuse permission for dogs (as they pose a threat to ground-nesting birds), smoking, lighting matches or fires and camping. They also assert that the walk must take place in daylight hours. Between 12 August and February, permission may be refused due to shoots and in spring due to the presence of young birds. Permission may also be refused on days when there is a high fire risk or when sheep are being gathered.

Although the access arrangements are restrictive, for example in not allowing a circular route, it is imperative that they are respected, as limited access is better than no access at all. One other point should be mentioned: access to other high ground in the estate is expressly forbidden. Luckily, this does not involve any other separate mountains but it does include the top of Bink Moss. Therefore, anybody wishing to bag the tops (I say bag because few people will enjoy those in the North Pennines) will have to negotiate with the land agent in the hope that they will relent.

2. College Valley (The Cheviot) (Section 10)

The best approach to The Cheviot is as a part of a circuit of the head of the College Valley, which extends into the heart of the range from Westnewton on the B6351 Akeld to Town Yetholm road. The valley road begins as a public road, at Westnewton, signposted to Hethpool, where there is a car-park but, beyond that point, it becomes a private road. However, the College Valley Estates do allow twelve cars to drive further up the road each day, except under snow conditions, but they do insist that fishing is not allowed and that cars containing dogs will not be given a permit.

To gain a permit, contact Sale and Partners, agents for College Valley Estates:

> Sale and Partners
> 18–20 Glendale Road
> Wooler
> Northumberland
> Tel: 01668 281611

If it is not possible to gain a permit on a particular day, it is possible to start at the head of Harthope valley and then cross to the College Valley on a footpath, signposted to Goldscleugh, and from there to the suggested car-parking point in the College Valley on the described route. From here, ascend The Cheviot as described, via The Schil. However, beyond the summit of The Cheviot, rather than following a track to the left as described, continue by the fence side until a path leads off to the right back down into the Harthope valley. Parking in the valley is permitted at and around GR 955226 on the large grassy meadows next to the road. This would be a shorter alternative than the 6 km/3½ mile walk up the valley to Mounthooly and then a return of similar length back down the tributary valley from Dunsdale.

English Mountain Names and their Meanings

The knowledge of the meaning of a mountain name gives a fascinating insight into not only the topography of the mountain but to how our ancestors saw it and used it. The birch trees on Birks Fell have long since been felled and the pigs have disappeared from Grisedale. Nevertheless, to many people, there is a curiosity into why Blencathra is called such and what caused somebody to give Whernside its name. This section is intended to answer those questions and has been simplified greatly to give the information in a concise and clear way without giving all the evidence that the experts have used to come to their decisions.

Each mountain name is given a translation and the words and languages from which its name originates. These place-name elements are given in the order of the translation and not in the order of the original name. The following abbreviations have been used to show the languages from which the elements originate:

ON	Old Norse
OIce.	Old Icelandic
OE	Old English (*c.*450–*c.*1100)
ME	Middle English (*c.*1100–*c.*1500)
Eng.	Modern English (*c.*1500–present)
OWel.	Old Welsh
Wel.	Welsh
Bret.	Breton
Lat.	Latin
Dial.	Local dialect English

Again, the Ordnance Survey names have been used as the standard modern form of the name, which is not necessarily that used locally.

Where appropriate, an older name has also been given where the modern name has changed beyond recognition.

The Names and their Meanings

The number in brackets after the name is the section in which that mountain lies.

BIRKS FELL (4) – the fell of the birch trees, ON fjall + ON birki.

BLACK MOUNTAIN (2) – takes its name from the Black Mountains (Wel. Y Mynyddoedd Duon), so named due to their dark appearance from their cover of heather and bilberries.

BLENCATHRA (7) – hill-shaped like a chair (which it does appear to be from some angles, hence the alternative name 'Saddleback'), Wel. blaen + Wel. cateir.

BUCKDEN PIKE (4) – the peak of the narrow, wooded valley frequented by bucks, OE pic + OE bucc + OE denu.

BURNHOPE SEAT (9) – hill of the slope with a small enclosed stream valley, OE side + OE burna + OE hop.

COLD FELL (9) – the bleak or exposed fell, OE cald + ON fjall.

CROSS FELL (9) – originally Fendesfell (1340) – the fiend's fell (according to local legend, the fell top is haunted by evil spirits), OE feond + ON fjall. Renamed Cross Fell by 1608 to give Christian association to the fell under the influence of evil powers, Eng. cross + ON fjall.

DALE HEAD (6) – the fell at the head of the Newlands Valley (the new lands), ON dalr.

DODD FELL HILL (4) – the hill of a fell with a rounded, grassy hill, ON fjall + ME dodde.

FAIRFIELD (5) – the fair or pleasant fell (field is an alternative word for fell). Previously known as Rydale Head – the head of the valley where rye is grown, OE ryge + ON dalr.

FOUNTAINS FELL (4) – the fell belonging to Fountains Abbey, ON fjall.

GRASMOOR (6) – the grassy upland, OE grass + OE mor.

GREAT SHUNNER FELL (8) – the large lookout hill, ON sjón + ON fjall.

GREAT KNOUTBERRY HILL (4) – the large hill of the cloudberries (dwarf mountain brambles), Dial. knoutberry.

GREAT COUM (4) – the hill of the large cirque, corrie or coombe (relates to the corrie of Great Coombe on the north-eastern slopes), OE cumb.

GREAT WHERNSIDE (4) – large hill of the slope where millstones are found, OE cweorn + OE side.

GREAT GABLE (6) – Mykelgavel (fourteenth century), the large fell which resembles a gable, ON mikill + ON gafl.

GRISEDALE PIKE (6) – the peak above the valley of the pigs, ON pík +

ON dalr + ON gríss.

HARTER FELL (6) – The fell of the hart, ON fjall + ON hjartar (of the hart).

HELVELLYN (5) – meaning unknown.

HIGH RAISE (6) – the high cairn (a reference most probably to the rocky summit named High White Stones), OE heah + ON hreysi.

HIGH STILE (6) – the high path, OE heah + OE stigel.

HIGH STREET (5) – named after the Roman Road between Ambleside and Brougham, which runs close to the summit of the fell.

HIGH WILLHAYS (1) – The high enclosure near or with a well or spring, OE heah + OE heg + OE wella. The hill is often named after its lower summit Yes Tor – the eagle's rock, OE earn + OE torr.

INGLEBOROUGH (4) – meaning is obscure, but either fortification on the peaked hill, OE burh + OE ing-hyll, or Ingjaldr's fort, ON personal name Ingjaldr + OE burh.

KINDER SCOUT (3) – the first element, *Kinder*, is unknown but its origin is pre-English. The second element, *Scout*, means craggy ridge, ON skúti.

KIRK FELL (6) – the fell above the church (the church at Wasdale Head stands at its foot), ON fjall + ON kirkja.

KNOTT (7) – the hill (it is the main height of the Caldbeck and Uldale fells which form one large massif without many significant drops), ON knútr.

LOVELY SEAT (8) – the meaning of this name is obscure. It may be derived from an older name, although it does not appear in many place-name books. As such, it appears likely that it is a recent name given to the mountain with a self-explanatory, on some days somewhat ironic, modern English derivation.

MICKLE FELL (9) – large fell, ON mikill + ON fjall.

NINE STANDARDS RIGG (8) – ridge of the nine piles of stones, Dial. standard, ON hryggr.

PEN-Y-GHENT (4) – meaning is obscure, possibly open hill, OWel. penn + Wel. y + Wel. caint.

PIKE OF BLISCO (6) – meaning unknown.

PILLAR (6) – renamed after the famous rock on its Ennerdale slopes that resembles a pillar. Its earlier name is obscure.

PLACE FELL (5) – the fell with an open, marshy area (most probably the summit plateau), ON fjall + OE plaesce.

RED SCREES (5) – named after the red colour of the screes that it throws down to Kirkstone Pass.

ROBINSON (6) – named after the sixteenth-century landowner, Richard Robinson.

ROGAN'S SEAT (8) – meaning obscure, possibly Rugga's mountain shieling, OE personal name Rugga + ON saetr.

SAINT SUNDAY CRAG (5) – St Dominic's Crag (Sunday = dies Dominica [Lat.]) + ME cragge.

SCAFELL PIKE (6) – meaning obscure, either the peak of the fell with the shieling, ON pïk + ON fjall + ON skáli, or the peak of the fell with the bare summit, ON pïk + ON fjall + ON skalli.

SEAT SANDAL (5) – Sandulfr's mountain shieling, ON personal name Sandulfr + ON saetr.

SEATALLAN (6) – Alein's mountain shieling, Bret. personal name Alein + ON saetr.

SKIDDAW (7) – meaning is obscure. Possibly archer's hill, ON skyti + ON haugr, hill of the craggy ridge, ON skúti + ON haugr, or the chopped billets of wood or bundle of firewood (in reference to shape), OIce. skitha, but more likely the hill where firewood is found, ON skith + ON haugr.

SNAEFELL (11) – snow fell, ON snjae + ON fjall. The name may have originally had a Manx name, such as others in the area, such as snow mountain, Manx Slieau Sniaghtey.

STONY COVE PIKE (5) – peak of the stony cove. The fell is generally known as Caudale Moor – the upland of the valley of the calves, OE mor + OE calf + ON dalr.

TARN RIGG HILL (8) – the high point of the ridge with a tarn, ON hryggr + ON tjorn. Part of Baugh Fell – the rounded fell, OE balg + ON fjall.

TARN CRAG (5) – crag of the tarn, ME cragge + ON tjorn, in reference to Greycrag Tarn, south-east of the summit. Tarngowe (1622) – cove of the tarn, OE cofa + ON tjorn.

THE CALF (8) – derived from calf but in some transferred sense. It could be a reference perhaps to two rocks or hills, a large one and a small one (the cow and calf), OE calf.

THE OLD MAN OF CONISTON (6) – the old, large cairn of Coniston (the king's farm, OE cyning/ON konungr + OE tun), Dial. man.

THE CHEVIOT (10) – meaning unknown but of pre-English origin.

WHERNSIDE (4) – hill of the slope where millstones are found, OE cweorn + OE side.

WILD BOAR FELL (8) – fell where tusked wild pigs are found, ON fjall + OE bar.

YARLSIDE (8) – either the earl's slope, ON jarl + OE side, or the earl's mountain shieling, ON jarl + ON saetr.

The Mountains and Tops of England and the Isle of Man

This section is intended as a 'mopping up' operation. It lists all the summits in England that qualify as separate mountains and/or tops. The same criterion of a 500ft (152m) drop on all sides that is used throughout the book to assess what qualifies as a separate mountain is also used here. The tops are the subsidiary summits, not given a separate description earlier in the book, which appear as small eminences but that cannot really be called separate. Each top must have a descent of 100ft (30m) on all sides, therefore making them Hewitts also. Any minor eminence with a descent of less than 100ft (30m) on all sides is considered as nothing more than a part of the parent mountain and therefore not worth inclusion. The names given are those that appear on the most recent edition of the appropriate Ordnance Survey Landranger map. Where summits are not named on that map but are named on smaller-scale maps, these names are given. However, as the tops are only subsidiary summits of higher mountains, some of them are completely nameless and it is therefore necessary to use points of the compass to define them from other summits on the same mountain. The following symbols are therefore used:

N = north top
S = south top   Sometimes it is necessary to combine
W = west top   symbols: e.g. NE = northeast top
E = east top

A top indicated by a * is included in the descriptions for the ascent of the parent mountain as it is passed over *en route*.

NAME	HEIGHT		NO. IN ORDER OF ALTITUDE		OS LANDRANGER SHEET NO.	GRID REFERENCE
	METRES	FEET	MTN.	TOP		

Section 1 – Dartmoor

NAME	METRES	FEET	MTN.	TOP	SHEET	GRID
High Willhays	621	2038	50	167	191	SX 580892

Section 2 – The Black Mountains

NAME	METRES	FEET	MTN.	TOP	SHEET	GRID
Black Mountain	703	2306	32	103	161	SO 255350

Section 3 – The Peak District

NAME	METRES	FEET	MTN.	TOP	SHEET	GRID
Kinder Scout	636	2088	49	157	110	SK 086875
Bleaklow Head	633	2077	–	159	110	SK 092959

Section 4 – South Yorkshire Dales

NAME	METRES	FEET	MTN.	TOP	SHEET	GRID
Whernside	736	2416	24	76	98	SD 738814
Ingleborough	724	2376	26	84	98	SD 740745
Great Whernside	704	2309	31	102	98	SE 001739
Buckden Pike	702	2302	33	105	98	SD 960787
Pen-y-ghent	694	2278	34	109	98	SD 838733
Great Coum	687	2255	36	112	98	SD 700835
Plover Hill	680	2231	–	116	98	SD 848752
Great Knoutberry Hill	672	2205	40	125	98	SD 788871
Dodd Fell Hill	668	2192	42	129	98	SD 840845
Fountains Fell	668	2191	43	130	98	SD 864715
Simon Fell	650	2132	–	146	98	SD 754751
Yockenthwaite Moor	643	2109	–	150	98	SD 909810
Gragareth*	627	2057	–	164	98	SD 687792
Darnbrook Fell	624	2048	–	165	98	SD 884727
Drumaldrace*	614	2015	–	175	98	SD 873866
Potts Moor	610	2001	–	179	98	SD 918763

Section 5 – Eastern Lakeland

NAME	METRES	FEET	MTN.	TOP	SHEET	GRID
Helvellyn	950	3116	2	3	90	NY 341151
Catstye Cam*	890	2920	–	12	90	NY 348158
Raise	883	2896	–	14	90	NY 342174

NAME	HEIGHT		NO. IN ORDER OF ALTITUDE		OS LANDRANGER SHEET NO.	GRID REFERENCE
	METRES	FEET	MTN.	TOP		
Fairfield	873	2863	7	15	90	NY 358117
White Side	863	2832	–	18	90	NY 337166
Dollywaggon Pike	858	2815	–	20	90	NY 345130
Great Dodd	857	2811	–	21	90	NY 342206
Stybarrow Dodd	843	2765	–	24	90	NY 343189
St Sunday Crag	841	2760	10	26	90	NY 369134
High Street	828	2718	11	30	90	NY 440110
Hart Crag	822	2698	–	33	90	NY 368112
High Raise (Mardale)	802	2630	–	40	90	NY 448134
Green Side	795	2608	–	44	90	NY 352187
Dove Crag	792	2600	–	46	90	NY 374104
Rampsgill Head	792	2598	–	47	90	NY 442127
Thornthwaite Crag	784	2572	–	52	90	NY 431100
Harter Fell (Mardale)*	778	2552	–	55	90	NY 459092
Red Screes	776	2547	15	56	90	NY 396087
Great Rigg	766	2513	–	62	90	NY 355104
Stony Cove Pike	763	2502	19	63	90	NY 417100
Ill Bell	757	2485	–	66	90	NY 436077
Seat Sandal	736	2415	25	77	90	NY 343115
Kentmere Pike	730	2396	–	80	90	NY 465077
Clough Head	726	2382	–	82	90	NY 333225
Froswick	720	2362	–	86	90	NY 435085
Branstree	713	2340	–	92	90	NY 477100
Yoke	706	2315	–	100	90	NY 437067
Rest Dodd	696	2283	–	108	90	NY 432136
Sheffield Pike	675	2215	–	120	90	NY 369181
Loadpot Hill	671	2200	–	128	90	NY 456181
Tarn Crag	664	2178	44	133	90	NY 488078
Place Fell	657	2154	46	138	90	NY 405169
Selside Pike	655	2150	–	140	90	NY 490111
Grey Crag	638	2093	–	154	90	NY 496072

NAME	HEIGHT		NO. IN ORDER OF ALTITUDE		OS LANDRANGER SHEET NO.	GRID REFERENCE
	METRES	FEET	MTN.	TOP		
Little Hart Crag	637	2091	–	155	90	NY 387100

Section 6 – Western Lakeland

NAME	METRES	FEET	MTN.	TOP	Sheet No.	Grid Ref.
Scafell Pike	978	3210	1	1	89/90	NY 215072
Scafell*	964	3162	–	2	89/90	NY 206064
Ill Crag	935	3067	–	4	89/90	NY 223073
Broad Crag	934	3063	–	5	89/90	NY 218075
Great End	910	2984	–	7	89/90	NY 226084
Bow Fell[1]	902	2960	–	8	89/90	NY 244064
Great Gable	899	2949	4	9	89/90	NY 211103
Pillar	892	2927	6	11	89/90	NY 171120
Esk Pike	885	2903	–	13	89/90	NY 236075
Crinkle Crags – Long Top*	859	2817	–	19	89/90	NY 248048
Grasmoor	852	2795	9	22	89/90	NY 174203
Little Scoat Fell – W Top	841	2760	–	26	89/90	NY 159113
Crag Hill*[2]	839	2753	–	28	89/90	NY 192203
Crinkle Crags – S Top	834	2735	–	29	89/90	NY 249045
Little Scoat Fell – E Top*	828	2716	–	31	89	NY 166117
Red Pike (Wasdale)*	826	2710	–	32	89	NY 165106
Crinkle Crags – Shelter Crags	815	2673	–	35	89/90	NY 249053
Lingmell	807	2649	–	36	89/90	NY 209081
High Stile	807	2648	13	37	89	NY 170148
The Old Man of Coniston	803	2635	14	38	96/97	SD 272978
Kirk Fell – W Top	802	2631	15	39	89/90	NY 194104
Swirl How*	802	2630	–	40	89/90	NY 272005
Green Gable	801	2628	–	42	89/90	NY 241107

NAME	HEIGHT		NO. IN ORDER OF ALTITUDE		OS LANDRANGER SHEET NO.	GRID REFERENCE
	METRES	FEET	MTN.	TOP		
Haycock	797	2615	–	43	89	NY 144107
Grisedale Pike – NE Top	791	2595	16	48	89/90	NY 198225
Kirk Fell – E Top*	787	2582	–	50	89/90	NY 199106
Allen Crags	785	2575	–	51	89/90	NY 236085
Glaramara – N Top	783	2570	–	53	89/90	NY 246104
Dow Crag	779	2555	–	54	96/97	SD 262978
Grey Friar	773	2536	–	57	89/90	NY 259003
Sail*	773	2535	–	58	89/90	NY 198202
Wandope	772	2533	–	59	89/90	NY 188197
Hopegill Head	770	2525	–	60	89/90	NY 185221
Wetherlam*	763	2502	–	63	89/90	NY 288011
High Raise (Langdale)	762	2500	20	65	89/90	NY 280095
Red Pike (Buttermere)*	755	2478	–	67	89	NY 160154
Dale Head	753	2470	21	68	89/90	NY 223153
Black Sails*3	745	2443	–	72	89/90	NY 282007
High Crag*	744	2442	–	73	89/90	NY 180140
Grisedale Pike – SW Top*	739	2424	–	74	89/90	NY 194220
Robinson	737	2417	23	75	89/90	NY 201168
Harrison Stickle*4	736	2415	–	77	89/90	NY 281073
Hindscarth	727	2385	–	81	89/90	NY 215165
Ullscarf	726	2381	–	83	89/90	NY 291121
Glaramara – S Top	721	2365	–	85	89/90	NY 242097
Whiteside	719	2360	–	87	89/90	NY 175221
Brandreth	715	2345	–	89	89/90	NY 214119
Pike of Stickle*5	709	2325	–	97	89/90	NY 273073
Pike of Blisco	705	2313	30	101	89/90	NY 271042
Cold Pike	701	2300	–	107	89/90	NY 262035
Seatallan	692	2270	35	110	89	NY 139083

NAME	HEIGHT		NO. IN ORDER OF ALTITUDE		OS LANDRANGER SHEET NO.	GRID REFERENCE
	METRES	FEET	MTN.	TOP		
Scar Crags*	672	2205	–	125	89/90	NY 208206
Whiteless Pike	660	2165	–	135	89/90	NY 180189
Harter Fell (Eskdale)	653	2143	47	141	96	SD 218997
High Spy	653	2143	–	141	89/90	NY 234162
Rossett Pike	651	2135	–	144	89/90	NY 249075
Fleetwith Pike	648	2126	–	148	89/90	NY 205141
Base Brown	646	2120	–	149	89/90	NY 225114
Iron Crag	642	2105	–	151	89	NY 123119
Causey Pike	637	2089	–	156	89/90	NY 218208
Starling Dodd	633	2076	–	160	89	NY 141157
Seathwaite Fell	632	2073	–	161	89/90	NY 227096
Dovenest Crag Top	632	2072	–	162	89/90	NY 255113
Yewbarrow – S Top	628	2060	–	163	89/90	NY 173084
Great Borne	616	2020	–	172	89	NY 123163
Yewbarrow – N Top	616	2020	–	172	89/90	NY 176092

Section 7 – Northern Lakeland

NAME	HEIGHT		NO. IN ORDER OF ALTITUDE		OS LANDRANGER SHEET NO.	GRID REFERENCE
Skiddaw	931	3054	3	6	89/90	NY 260290
Blencathra	868	2847	8	16	90	NY 323277
Skiddaw Little Man*	865	2838	-	17	89/90	NY 266278
Carl Side*	746	2446	–	71	89/90	NY 254280
Long Side	734	2408	–	79	89/90	NY 248284
Lonscale Fell	715	2345	–	89	89/90	NY 285270
Knott	710	2329	28	93	89/90	NY 296329
Bowscale Fell	702	2303	–	105	90	NY 333305
Great Calva	690	2265	–	111	89/90	NY 290311
Bannerdale Crags	683	2240	–	114	90	NY 335290
Carrock Fell	660	2165	–	135	90	NY 341336
High Pike	658	2159	–	137	90	NY 318350

NAME	HEIGHT		NO. IN ORDER		OS LANDRANGER	GRID
			OF ALTITUDE		SHEET NO.	REFERENCE
	METRES	FEET	MTN.	TOP		

Section 8 – North Yorkshire Dales and the Howgill Fells

NAME	METRES	FEET	MTN.	TOP	SHEET NO.	GRID REFERENCE
Great Shunner Fell	716	2349	27	88	98	SD 848973
High Seat	709	2327	–	95	91/92	NY 802013
Wild Boar Fell	708	2324	29	98	98	SD 758988
Swarth Fell*	681	2235	–	115	98	SD 755966
Tarn Rigg Hill (Baugh Fell)	678	2224	37	117	98	SD 740916
The Calf	676	2219	38	118	98	SD 667970
Lovely Seat	675	2213	39	122	98	SD 879950
Calders*	674	2211	–	123	98	SD 671960
Rogan's Seat	672	2205	40J	125	91/92	NY 919030
Sails	667	2188	–	131	98	SD 808971
Nine Standards Rigg	662	2171	45	134	91/92	NY 825061
Fell Head	640	2100	–	152	97	SD 649981
Yarlside	639	2096	48	153	98	SD 685985
Randygill Top	624	2047	–	166	91	NY 686000

Section 9 – The North Pennines

NAME	METRES	FEET	MTN.	TOP	SHEET NO.	GRID REFERENCE
Cross Fell	893	2930	5	10	91	NY 687343
Great Dun Fell	848	2781	–	23	91	NY 710321
Little Dun Fell	842	2761	–	25	91	NY 704330
Knock Fell	794	2604	–	45	91	NY 721302
Mickle Fell	788	2585	17	49	91/92	NY 804243
Meldon Hill	767	2517	–	61	91	NY 771290
Little Fell	748	2455	–	69	91	NY 781224
Burnhope Seat	747	2450	22	70	91	NY 785375
Dead Stones	710	2329	–	93	91	NY 793399
Melmerby Fell	709	2326	–	96	91	NY 652380
Great Stony Hill	708	2322	–	99	91/92	NY 823359
Chapelfell Top	703	2305	–	104	91/92	NY 875346
Round Hill	686	2250	–	113	91	NY 744361
James' Hill	675	2216	–	119	91/92	NY 923325
Murton Fell	675	2215	–	120	91	NY 753246

NAME	HEIGHT		NO. IN ORDER OF ALTITUDE		OS LANDRANGER SHEET NO.	GRID REFERENCE
	METRES	FEET	MTN.	TOP		
Killhope Law	673	2207	–	124	86	NY 819448
Black Fell	664	2179	–	132	86	NY 648444
Grey Nag	656	2153	–	139	86	NY 664476
Three Pikes	651	2135	–	144J	91/92	NY 833343
Viewing Hill	649	2130	–	147	91	NY 788332
Fiend's Fell	634	2079	–	158	86	NY 643406
Cold Fell	621	2037	51	168	86	NY 605556
Bink Moss	619	2030	–	171	91/92	NY 875243
The Dodd	614	2014	–	176	86/87	NY 791457
Flinty Fell	614	2013	–	177	86/87	NY 771419
Burtree Fell	612	2007	–	178	87	NY 862432
Section 10 – The Cheviots						
The Cheviot	815	2674	12	34	74/75	NT 909205
Hedgehope Hill	714	2342	–	91	80	NT 943197
Comb Fell	652	2139	–	143	80	NT 924187
Windy Gyle	619	2031	–	170	80	NT 855152
Cushat Law	615	2018	–	174	80	NT 928137
Bloodybush Edge	610	2001	–	179J	80	NT 902143
Section 11 – The Isle of Man						
Snaefell	621	2036	52	169	95	SC 397881

Notes

1. Bowfell is included in the book as a separate entry in Section 6 (Western Lakeland) as it is such a major and well-known summit.
2. Crag Hill is named Eel Crag in the text.
3. Black Sails is the summit contoured around on its Greenburn side between Wetherlam and Swirl How on the route that ascends The Old Man of Coniston.
4. Harrison Stickle is included in the scrambling route (with walking alternatives to the scrambles detailed also) that ascends High Raise.
5. Pike of Stickle is mentioned as an optional extra to the route mentioned in 4.

Personal Log

NAME	HEIGHT	GRID REFERENCE	DATE OF FIRST ASCENT
Section 1 – Dartmoor			
High Willhays	621m 2,038ft	SX 580892	
Section 2 – The Black Mountain			
Black Mountain	703m 2,306ft	SO 255350	
Section 3 – The Peak District			
Kinder Scout	636m 2,087ft	SK 086875	
Section 4 – South Yorkshire Dales			
Whernside	736m 2,416ft	SD 738814	
Ingleborough	724m 2,376ft	SD 740745	
Great Whernside	704m 2,309ft	SE 001739	
Buckden Pike	702m 2,302ft	SD 960787	
Pen-y-ghent	694m 2,278ft	SD 838733	
Great Coum	687m 2,255ft	SD 700835	
Great Knoutberry Hill	672m 2,205ft	SD 788871	
Dodd Fell Hill	668m 2,192ft	SD 840845	
Fountains Fell	668m 2,191ft	SD 864715	
Potts Moor	610m 2,001ft	SD 893768	
Section 5 – Eastern Lakeland			
Helvellyn	950m 3,116ft	NY 341151	
Fairfield	873m 2,863ft	NY 358117	
St Sunday Crag	841m 2,760ft	NY 369134	
High Street	828m 2,718ft	NY 440110	
Red Screes	776m 2,547ft	NY 396087	
Stony Cove Pike	763m 2,502ft	NY 417100	
Seat Sandal	736m 2,415ft	NY 343115	
Tarn Crag	664m 2,178ft	NY 488078	
Place Fell	657m 2,154ft	NY 405169	

NAME	HEIGHT	GRID REFERENCE	DATE OF FIRST ASCENT
Section 6 – Western Lakeland			
Scafell Pike	978m 3,210ft	NY 215072	
Great Gable	899m 2,949ft	NY 211103	
Pillar	892m 2,927ft	NY 171120	
Grasmoor	852m 2,795ft	NY 174203	
High Stile	807m 2,648ft	NY 170148	
The Old Man of Coniston	803m 2,635ft	SD 272978	
Kirk Fell	802m 2,631ft	NY 194104	
Grisedale Pike	791m 2,595ft	NY 198225	
High Raise	762m 2,500ft	NY 280095	
Dale Head	753m 2,470ft	NY 223153	
Robinson	737m 2,417ft	NY 201168	
Pike of Blisco	705m 2,313ft	NY 271042	
Seatallan	692m 2,270ft	NY 139083	
Harter Fell	653m 2,143ft	SD 218997	
Bow Fell*	902m 2,959ft	NY 244064	
Section 7 – Northern Lakeland			
Skiddaw	931m 3,054ft	NY 260290	
Blencathra	868m 2,847ft	NY 323277	
Knott	710m 2,329ft	NY 296329	
Section 8 – North Yorkshire Dales and the Howgill Fells			
Great Shunner Fell	716m 2,349ft	SD 848973	
Wild Boar Fell	708m 2,324ft	SD 758988	
Tarn Rigg Hill	678m 2,224ft	SD 740916	
The Calf	676m 2,219ft	SD 667970	
Lovely Seat	675m 2,215ft	SD 879950	
Rogan's Seat	672m 2,205ft	NY 919030	
Nine Standard's Rigg	662m 2,171ft	NY 825061	
Yarlside	639m 2,096ft	SD 685985	
Section 9 – The North Pennines			
Cross Fell	893m 2,930ft	NY 687343	
Mickle Fell	788m 2,585ft	NY 804243	
Burnhope Seat	747m 2,450ft	NY 785375	
Cold Fell	621m 2,037ft	NY 605556	

NAME	HEIGHT	GRID REFERENCE	DATE OF FIRST ASCENT

Section 10 – The Cheviots

The Cheviot	815m 2,674ft	NT 909205	

Section 11 – The Isle of Man

Snaefell	621m 2,036ft	SC 397881	

	SECTION	TOTAL	DONE
1	Dartmoor	1	
2	The Black Mountains	1	
3	The Peak District	1	
4	South Yorkshire Dales	10	
5	Eastern Lakeland	9	
6	Western Lakeland	14	
7	Northern Lakeland	3	
8	Northern Yorkshire Dales and the Howgill Fells	8	
9	The North Pennines	4	
10	The Cheviots	1	
11	The Isle of Man	1	
	TOTAL	**53**	

Glossary

ADIT A horizontal entrance to a mine. See also *level*.

ALSTON BLOCK A section of the basement rocks of the Pennines, underlying Section 9, as defined by its boundary faults (see Section 9). See also *Askrigg Block*.

ANDESITE An *igneous* rock containing less than 50 per cent silica, also called basic, cf. *rhyolite*.

ANTICLINE A type of fold in rock formations resembling an n-shape, cf. *syncline*.

ARÊTE A knife-edged ridge formed as a result of glaciation.

ARUNDIAN Period of the lower *Carboniferous*.

ASKRIGG BLOCK A section of the basement rocks of the Pennines underlying Sections 4 and 8, as defined by its boundary faults (see Section 4). See also *Alston Block*.

AUREOLE, METAMORPHIC A circle of surrounding rocks that have been baked as a result of a *metamorphic* intrusion.

BASALT A dark *andesitic igneous* rock, the *strata* of which often form columns.

BEDDED Rocks that were deposited in definite beds and usually split easily along their *strata*.

BELL PIT A type of colliery working which resembles a bell. A narrow shaft was bored down into the earth and then excavated outwards at its foot until it became too dangerous to work further; many today are blocked.

BLUE JOHN An extremely rare gemstone found in the Castleton area of the Peak District (Section 3).

BORROWDALE SERIES Type of volcanic rock deposited in the upper *Ordovician* period in the Lake District (see Section 5).

BOULDER CLAY Material deposited on valley floors as a result of glaciation. Also known as glacial drift.

BRECCIA A fragmented rock. See also *fault-breccia*.

BRIDLEWAY Right of way on which horses, cyclists and walkers are legally permitted to travel.

BYWAY A right of way on which all modes of transport are legally permitted to travel.

CARBONIFEROUS See geological timescale (page 364).

CHIMNEY A steeply angled groove in a cliff face that provides an easy way of ascent of that crag.

CHINA CLAY A white powder formed from the decomposition of granitic feldspars, *kaolinite* being a major constituent. Also known as kaolin.

CLINT A separate block of limestone in a *limestone pavement*, cf. *grike*.

CLITTER Granite blocks found on hillsides, particularly on Dartmoor (Section 1), as a result of *exfoliation.*

COAL A deposit consisting of the compacted remains of plants that grew in tropical swamps.

COMBE See *corrie.*

CONCAVE SLOPE A hillside curved like the interior of a saucer, cf. *convex.*

CONGLOMERATE A rock containing stones and pebbles, cemented together by finer material.

CONVECTION A process of the circular movement of molecules within a liquid or gas. Warmer, less dense molecules are drawn in on the surface to replace colder, denser molecules that have sunk. In turn, these cold molecules move back at a lower level to replace the warm molecules that have risen. For convection to work, an object or influence must warm the molecules at some point so that they rise. This is how the *Mid Atlantic Drift* operates, the warming influence being the hot equatorial seas in the Gulf of Mexico.

CONVEX SLOPE A hillside curved like the exterior of an upturned saucer, cf. *concave.*

CORAL The external skeletons of sea-creatures, known as polyps, which live on reefs in warm, tropical seas.

CORBETT A Scottish hill between 2,500ft and 3,000ft in altitude with a descent of 500ft on all sides.

CORRIE Coming from the Scottish Gaelic, coire, meaning a cauldron, it is the most commonly accepted term for a glacial hollow in a hillside shaped like an armchair. Known also in England as combes and in Wales as cwms (see Section 5).

CRETACEOUS see the geological timescale (page 34).

CRUST, EARTH'S The solid surface on the Earth, which floats upon the liquid *mantel* and is subdivided into *tectonic plates.*

CWM See *corrie.*

CYCLOTHEM One cycle of a repetitive sequence.

DEVONIAN See the geological timescale (page 34).

DIMINGTON STADIAL One of the most recent cold periods in British history lasting about 10,000 years, reaching its peak between 15,000 and 21,000 years ago.

DINANTIAN Another name for the lower *Carboniferous* period.

DOLERITE A medium-grained *igneous* rock, mainly consisting of ferro-magnesian metals and lime *feldspars.*

ESCARPMENT A steep hill slope all along one side of a hill or mountain range, often shortened to scarp. Where hills form circular or semi-circular rings, the scarps may be either inward-facing (i.e. they face in to the centre of the circle) or outward-facing (i.e. they face out from the centre of the circle).

EXFOLIATION A form of weathering due to extremes of temperature, such as are found in deserts. During very hot conditions (such as during the day in a desert), the rock expands and then, at night, it cools rapidly and shrinks. This causes the outer layers of the rock to peel or flake away, hence its alternative name 'onion-skin weathering'.

FAULT The boundary between divisions of the Earth's crust, breaking the continuity of rock *strata*.

FAULT-BRECCIA An area of shattered rock near a *fault*, caused by the scraping that has taken or is taking place there. See also *breccia*.

FELDSPAR Aluminosilicates that naturally occur in *igneous* intrusions.

FELL WALL See *inbye wall*.

FLOWSTONE A rock deposited in caves and under bridges in limestone areas. Formed by the slow flow of an aqueous solution of calcium carbonate (limestone) over rock.

FOOTPATH A right of way along which only pedestrians are legally permitted to travel.

FOSSIL The impression of a dead marine creature that has since decomposed or skeleton left behind in the rock.

FOSSIL FUEL A combustible material formed from the fossilised remains of dead plants and animals. Examples include *coal*, oil, gas and *peat*.

FROST FAIRS Fairs held on the frozen Thames in 1683–84 during the *Little Ice Age*.

GABBRO A dark, granular *igneous* rock.

GALENA Lead sulphide (PbS). Mined in parts of the Pennines, particularly Sections 3, 8 and 9, to be dressed and smelted to produce lead.

GENDARME a pinnacle or rock tower found on a ridge or *arête*.

GLACIAL DRIFT See *boulder clay*.

GLOBAL WARMING The artificial warming of the Earth's climate by man's release of greenhouse gases, including carbon dioxide (CO_2) and methane (CH_4).

GRAHAM A Scottish hill between 2,000ft and 2,500ft in altitude with a descent of 500ft on all sides.

GRANITE A coarsely grained intrusive *igneous* rock, mainly consisting of *mica*, *quartz* and *feldspar*.

GRIKE A cleft found between *clints* on *limestone pavements*, cf. *clint*.

GRITSTONE A coarse-grained *sedimentary* rock deposited on beaches and in deserts.

GULF STREAM An ocean current that brings warm water out of the Gulf of Mexico and into the Atlantic Ocean. See also *Mid Atlantic Drift*.

HANGING VALLEY A tributary valley that ends at a higher elevation than the valley into which it is flowing (see Section 5).

HEWITT A hill in England, Wales or Ireland above 2,000ft that has a descent of 100ft on all sides.

HUSH An artificial ravine carved by water into the hillside for mining purposes (see Section 9).

ICE AGE The last period of extreme coldness in the Earth's climate, in which Britain underwent extensive glaciation, see also *Little Ice Age*.

IGNEOUS A rock formed from molten magma.

INBYE The enclosed land in a valley or on the lower slopes of a hill, cf. *open fell*.

INBYE WALL The wall between the enclosed land or *inbye* and the *open fell*. Also called the fell wall.

INTERGLACIAL PERIOD A period of warmth between ice ages.

KAOLIN See *China clay*.

KAOLINITE $Al_2(OH)_4SiO_5$. A major constituent of *China clay*.

KISSING-GATE A gate that is able to swing in a V-shaped enclosure.

LEAT A small canal conducting water to a mining works or mill.

LEVEL A horizontal passage in a mine. See also *adit*.

LIMESTONE A *sedimentary* rock formed from the skeletons of dead sea creatures.

LIMESTONE PAVEMENT An area of limestone separated into *clints* and *grikes*.

LITTLE ICE AGE A cooling of the British climate during the Middle Ages lasting from AD 1450 to AD 1850, reaching a peak around AD 1680 when *frost fairs* were held on the frozen Thames.

LOCH LOMOND STADIAL A periodic readvancement of the ice sheets at the end of the *Dimlington Stadial*, lasting about 1,000 years, also called the Loch Lomond Readvance.

MAM TOR BEDS A repetitive sequence of limestones, shales and sandstones in the Pennines.

MANTEL, EARTH'S A layer of the Earth below the *crust* and above the core, which is made up of molten magma.

MARBLE The *metamorphic* version of limestone.

MARILYN A British hill that rises 500ft or more from its surrounding landscape.

METAMORPHIC A *sedimentary* or *igneous* rock baked by an *igneous* intrusion or subjected to intense pressure.

MICA Aluminosilicates with linked layers of silicon and aluminium oxide tetrahedra. Micas occur naturally in *igneous* rocks including *granite*.

MID ATLANTIC DRIFT The northwards continuation of the *Gulf Stream*, which brings warm water from the Gulf of Mexico into the North Atlantic.

MUDSTONE A sedimentary rock formed by the compression of muddy deposits.

MUNRO A Scottish hill over 3,000ft in altitude as defined in the publication 'Munro's Tables'.

NAMURIAN Another name for the upper *Carboniferous* period.

OPEN FELL Unenclosed and unimproved land lying above valley level on the slopes and summits of hills and mountains.

ORDOVICIAN See geological timescale (page 34).

PALAEOZOIC See geological timescale (page 34).

PANGAEA A large landmass, which comprised all the continents of the modern world that existed about 270 million years ago.

PATH Used in this book to define an area of ground eroded by the passage of feet, which is too narrow to drive an all-terrain vehicle along, cf. *track*.

PEAT Undecomposed plant remains.

PEAT HAG An area of denudation in a *peat* bog where the surface vegetation has been removed to expose the black peaty soil below. Some are wet and 'bottomless' while others are dry and firm.

PERMIAN See the geological timescale (page 34).

POT-HOLE A vertical shaft formed by the erosion of *limestone* by water.

PSEUDO-JOINTS Horizontal and vertical cracks that appear in cooling *granite* due to shrinkage.

QUARTZ Silicon dioxide (SiO_2); a naturally occurring white mineral found in *igneous* rocks.

RESURGENCE The point at which a subterranean stream appears on the surface.

RHYOLITE An *igneous* rock containing more than 50 per cent silica, also called acidic, cf. *andesite*.

ROCHES MOUTONNÉES A polished rock, formed as a result of glacial action (see Section 5).

SANDSTONE A *sedimentary* rock formed by the compression of sand on beaches or in deserts.

SCAR A vertical *limestone* cliff.

SCARP See *escarpment*.

SCRAMBLING A method of motion up or down a mountainside or rock face when the arms (and other parts of the anatomy) must be used in conjunction with the legs to project the body forwards. However, ropes are not used, except for security on some routes, so it is not difficult enough to be a rock climb.

SEDIMENTARY A rock formed from the compression of sediments on land or under water.

SERPENTINE (ROCK) Hydrated magnesium silicate; a soft and rare dark-green rock found on the Lizard Peninsula of Cornwall, which is shaped into decorative ornaments.

SHAFT A vertical entrance to a mine or a vent to allow the movement of air through mine workings.

SHAKE HOLE A depression on the surface that is either a blocked *pot-hole* or where a cave has collapsed.

SHALE A *sedimentary* rock formed from fine particles.

SHEEP TRACK A faint, narrow path, usually thought of as formed by the passage of sheep.

SILURIAN See the geological timescale (page 34).

SLATE The *metamorphic* version of *shale*. Sometimes compacted, *bedded* mudstones form false slates.

SPECIFIC HEAT CAPACITY The resistance of a body to a change in temperature, measured in joules per degree centigrade per kilogram.

STRATA Layers in rocks.

SWALLOW HOLE The point at which a stream disappears below ground in *limestone* terrain.

SYNCLINE A U-shaped fold in a series of rocks, cf. *anticline*.

TARN A small lake.

TECTONIC PLATE A part of the Earth's *crust* that moves around due to *convection* currents in the Earth's *mantel*, colliding with some tectonic plates while pulling away from others.

TERTIARY See the geological timescale (page 34).

THREE PEAKS The three summits of Ingleborough, Whernside and Pen-y-ghent, which surround Ribblehead in the South Yorkshire Dales (Section 4).

THREE PEAKS WALK A long and arduous walk of around 24½ miles/38½ km in length and involving around 5,500ft (1,700m) of ascent which links the summits of the *Three Peaks*.

TOR A rocky peak or summit, particularly on Dartmoor (Section 1).

TRACK Used in this guide to refer to an area of ground eroded by either feet or vehicles so that is wide enough to drive an all-terrain vehicle along, cf. *path*.

TRIASSIC See the geological timescale (page 34).

TRIGONOMETRIC POINT A concrete pillar constructed by the Ordnance Survey to conduct trigonometrical surveys. Often abbreviated to trig point.

TROD A faint or narrow *path* or *sheep track*, usually on grass.

WATERSHED A ridge that marks the boundary of the water catchment area of a valley.

WHIN SILL An *igneous* intrusion of *dolerite* under the North Pennines (Section 9) and parts of north-eastern England.

YOREDALE BEDS A cyclical series of limestones, shales, sandstones and coal seams found in the Pennines (see Section 8).

Further Reading

Walking

General

Dawson, Alan, *The Relative Hills of Britain* (Cicerone Press, 1992)
(Amended by subsequent update sheets, up to and including 1999.)

Gilbert, Richard, *200 Challenging Walks in Britain and Ireland* (Diadem Books, 1992)

England and Wales

Nuttall, J. and Nuttall, A., *The Mountains of England and Wales* Volumes 1 and 2 (Cicerone Press, 1989, 1990)

Section 1

Ordnance Survey Leisure Guide 6: Devon and Exmoor (Automobile Association and Ordnance Survey, 1999)

Ordnance Survey Pathfinder Guide 1: South Devon and Dartmoor Walks (Ordnance Survey, 1998)

Ordnance Survey Pathfinder Guide 26: Dartmoor Walks (Ordnance Survey, 1997)

Section 3

Hanks, Martyn, *The Peak District Youth Hosteller's Walking Guide* (Landmark Publishing, 1998)

Hunt, Charles and Williams, Mike, *On Foot in the Peak District* (David & Charles, 1996)

Ordnance Survey Landranger Guidebook: The Peak District (Ordnance Survey, 1990)

Ordnance Survey Leisure Guide 15: Peak District (Automobile Association and Ordnance Survey, 1999)

Ordnance Survey Pathfinder Guide 16: Peak District (Ordnance Survey, 1997)

Sections 4 and 8

Hanks, Martyn, *The Yorkshire Dales and Moors Youth Hosteller's Guide* (Landmark Publishing, 1997)

Ordnance Survey Leisure Guide 20: Yorkshire Dales (Automobile Association and Ordnance Survey, 1999)

Ordnance Survey Pathfinder Guide 15: Yorkshire Dales Walks (Ordnance Survey, 1999)

Sellers, Gladys, *The Yorkshire Dales – A Walker's Guide to the National Park* (Cicerone Press, 1992)

Smith, Roland and Cleare, John, *On Foot in the Yorkshire Dales* (David & Charles, 1996)

Wainwright, A.W., *A Coast to Coast Walk* (Westmorland Gazette, 1972)

Wainwright, A.W., *Walks on the Howgill Fells and Adjoining Fells* (Westmorland Gazette, undated)

Wainwright, A.W. and Geldard, Ed., *Wainwright in the Limestone Dales* (Michael Joseph, 1994)

Sections 5, 6 and 7

Boardman, John, *Classic Landforms of the Lake District,* (Geographical Association, 1996)

Ordnance Survey Leisure Guide 11: Lake District (Automobile Association and Ordnance Survey, 1999)

Ordnance Survey Pathfinder Guide 13: Lake District Walks (Ordnance Survey, 1998)

Ordnance Survey Pathfinder Guide 22: More Lake District Walks; (Jarrold Publishing and Ordnance Survey, 1997)

Wainwright A.W., *A Pictorial Guide to the Lakeland Fells*:
  Book One: *The Eastern Fells* (Michael Joseph, 1992)
  Book Two: *The Far Eastern Fells* (Michael Joseph, 1994)
  Book Three: *The Central Fells* (Michael Joseph, 1992)
  Book Four: *The Southern Fells* (Michael Joseph, 1994)
  Book Five: *The Northern Fells* (Michael Joseph, 1996)
  Book Six: *The North-Western Fells* (Michael Joseph, 1992)
  Book Seven: *The Western Fells* (Michael Joseph, 1994)

Wainwright A.W., *The Outlying Fells of Lakeland* (Michael Joseph, 1992)

Section 10

Ordnance Survey Leisure Guide 13: Northumbria (Automobile Association and Ordnance Survey, 1999)

Ordnance Survey Pathfinder Guide: Northumbria (Ordnance Survey, 1991)

Section 11

Corran, H.S., *The Isle of Man* (David & Charles, 1977)

Evans, Aileen, *Isle of Man Coastal Path: Raad ny Foillan* (Cicerone Press, 1991)

Scrambling

Ashton, Steve, *Rock Climbing Techniques* (Crowood Press, 1995)

Evans, R.B., *Scrambles in the Lake District* (Cicerone Press, 1996)

Evans, R.B., *More Scrambles in the Lake District* (Cicerone Press, 1994)

O'Connor, Bill, *50 Best Scrambles in the Lake District* (David & Charles, 1995)

Geology

Adams, John, *Mines of the Lake District Fells* (Dalesman Publishing, 1995)

Brumhead, Derek, *Geology Explained in the Yorkshire Dales and on the Yorkshire Coast* (David & Charles, 1979)

Holland, Eric G., *Coniston Copper – A History* (Cicerone Press, 1987)

Holland, Eric G., *Coniston Copper Mines – A Field Guide* (Cicerone Press, 1989)

Marr, J.E., *Geology of the Lake District* (Cambridge University Press, 1916)

Whittow, John, *Geology and Scenery in Britain* (Chapman and Hall, 1992)

Other

Bondi, Alice, Leech, Daniel and Leech, Marilyn, *Widdybank Fell Nature Trail* (English Nature, 1994)

Graydon, Don and Hanson, Kurt (eds), *Mountaineering: The Freedom of the Hills* (Swan Hill Press, 1997)

Pearsall, Judy and Trumble, Bill (eds), *The Oxford English Reference Dictionary* (Oxford University Press, 1995)

Sharp, D.W.A., *The Penguin Dictionary of Chemistry* (Penguin Books, 1990)

The YHA Guide 1998 (Youth Hostels Association, 1997)

Uvarov E.B. and Isaacs, Alan, *The Penguin Dictionary of Science* (Penguin Books, 1993)

Useful Telephone Numbers

Several places and attractions are mentioned in the main part of the book but telephone numbers are not given to avoid breaking up the text. Instead, they are given here along with other useful numbers, for tourist information centres, for example. Where the section lies partly or wholly within a National Park, the numbers for the National Parks Centres may also be given under the heading 'Tourist Information Centres' as the two generally perform very similar services in relation to, for example, accommodation booking. It should also be noted that some attractions and information centres are closed during the winter months although generally those in and around large towns are more likely to remain open.

General

National rail enquiry service (advanced timetable and fare information, 24hr service)
0345 484950

Section 1 – Dartmoor

Commandant of Dartmoor Rangers' telephone answering service –
Torquay (01803) 24592
Exeter (01392) 70164
Plymouth (01752) 701924
Okehampton (01837) 52939
Morwellham Quay (Historic Port and Copper Mine) (01822) 833808
Tourist Information Centres –
Ashburton (01364) 653426
Bovey Tracey (01626) 832047
Chagford (01647) 432080
Exeter (01392) 265700
Haytor (01364) 661520
Ivybridge (01752) 897035
Moretonhampstead (01647) 440043
Newbridge (01364) 631305
Newton Abbott (01626) 367494
Okehampton (01837) 53020
Plymouth (01752) 264849
Postbridge (01822) 880272
Tavistock (01822) 890414
Torquay (01803) 297428
Totnes (01803) 863168
Youth Hostels (YHA) –
Bellever (01822) 880227
Dartington (01803) 862303
Exeter (01392) 873329
Maypool (01803) 842444
Okehampton (01837) 53916
Plymouth (01752) 562189
Steps Bridge (01647) 2524351 (For bookings at Steps Bridge YH more than seven days in advance ring (01629) 825983)

Section 2 – The Black Mountains

Tourist Information Centres –
Abergavenny (01873) 857588
Brecon (01874) 622485
Talgarth (01874) 712226
Youth Hostels (YHA)

Capel-y-Ffin (01873) 890650
Llanddeusant (01550) 740218 (For bookings at Llanddeusant YH more than seven days in advance ring (01629) 581399)
Llwyn-y-Celyn (01874) 624261
Ty'n-y-Caeau (01874) 665270
Ystradfellte (01639) 720301

Section 3 – The Peak District

Blue John Cavern, Castleton (01433) 620638
Peak Cavern, Castleton (01433) 620285
Poole's Cavern, Buxton (01298) 26978
Speedwell Cavern, Castleton (01433) 620512
Treak Cliff Cavern, Castleton (01433) 620571
Tourist Information Centres –
  Ashbourne (01335) 343666
  Bakewell (01629) 816200
  Buxton (01298) 25106
  Castleton (01433) 620679
  Edale (01433) 670207
  Glossop (01457) 855920
  Hayfield (01663) 746222
  Leek (01538) 483741
  Macclesfield (01625) 504114
  Matlock (01629) 583388
Youth Hostels (YHA) –
  Bakewell (01629) 812313
  Bretton (01433) 631856 (For bookings more than seven days in advance ring (01629) 825983)
  Buxton (01298) 22287
  Castleton (01433) 620235
  Edale (01433) 670302
  Elton (01629) 650394
  Eyam (01433) 630335
  Gradbach Mill (01260) 227625
  Hartington Hall (01298) 84223
  Hathersage (01433) 650493
  Ilam Hall (01335) 350212
  Matlock (01629) 582983
  Meerbrook (01538) 300174
  Ravenstor (01298) 871826
  Shining Cliff (07788) 725938

Youlgreave (01629) 636518

Section 4 – South Yorkshire Dales

Ingleborough Cave (015242) 51242
Tourist Information Centres –
  White Scar Cave (015242) 41244
  Aysgarth Falls (01969) 663424
  Bentham (01524) 262549
  Clapham (01524) 251419
  Grassington (01756) 752774
  Hawes (01969) 667450
  Horton-in-Ribblesdale (01729) 860333
  Ingleton (01524) 241049
  Leyburn (01969) 623069
  Malham (01729) 830363
  Sedbergh (015396) 20125
  Settle (01729) 825192
  Skipton (01756) 792809
Youth Hostels (YHA) –
  Aysgarth Falls (01969) 663260
  Dentdale (015396) 25251
  Hawes (01969) 667368
  Ingleton (01524) 241444
  Kettlewell (01756) 760232
  Linton (01756) 752400
  Malham (01729) 830321
  Stainforth (01729) 823577

Sections 5, 6 and 7 – The Lake District

Honister Slate Mine (Visitor Centre and Shop) (01768) 777230
Ravenglass and Eskdale Railway (01229) 717171
Tourist Information Centres –
  Ambleside (01539) 432582
  Bowness Bay (01539) 442895
  Broughton in Furness (01229) 716115
  Cockermouth (01900) 822634
  Coniston (01539) 441533
  Glenridding (01768) 482414
  Grasmere (01539) 435245
  Hawkshead (01539) 436525
  Kendal (01539) 725758

Keswick (01768) 772645
Penrith (01768) 867466
Pooley Bridge (01768) 486530
Seatoller Barn (01768) 777294
Waterhead (nr. Ambleside) (01539) 432729
Windermere (01539) 446499
Youth Hostels (YHA)
Ambleside (01539) 432304
Borrowdale (Longthwaite) (01768) 777257
Buttermere (01768) 770245
Carlisle (01228) 597352
Carrock Fell (016974) 78325
Coniston Coppermines (01539) 441261
Coniston (Holly How) (01539) 441323
Derwentwater (01768) 777246
Elterwater (01539) 437245
Ennerdale (Black Sail) (0411) 108450
Ennerdale (Gillerthwaite) (01946) 861237
Eskdale (019467) 23219
Grasmere (01539) 4353164
(Butterlip How and Thorney How)
Hawkshead (01539) 436293
Helvellyn (01768) 482269
Honister Hause (01768) 777267
Keswick (01768) 772484
Langdale (High Close) (01539) 437313
Patterdale (017684) 82394
Skiddaw House No telephone service (Enquiries by telephone to Carrock Fell YH. Postal bookings to: Youth Hostel, Skiddaw Forest, Bassenthwaite, Keswick, Cumbria CA12 4QX. Book well in advance due to the poor postal service.)
Thirlmere (01768) 773224
Wastwater (01946) 726222
Windermere (01539) 443543

Section 8 – North Yorkshire Dales

Tourist Information Centres –
Aysgarth Falls (01969) 663424
Hawes (01969) 667450
Kirkby Lonsdale (015242) 71437
Kirkby Stephen (017683) 71199
Leyburn (01969) 623069
Reeth (01748) 884059
Richmond (01748) 850252
Sedbergh (015396) 20125
Youth Hostels (YHA) –
Aysgarth Falls (01969) 663260
Grinton Lodge (01748) 884206
Hawes (01969) 667368
Keld (01748) 886259
Kirkby Stephen (017683) 71793

Section 9 – North Pennines

Commandant at Warcop Camp (01768) 341661
Youngs Chartered Surveyors (land agents) (01434) 609600
Killhope Wheel (01388) 537505
Nenthead Mines (Heritage Centre and Historic Site) – (01434) 382037
Tourist Information Centres –
Alston (01434) 381696
Appleby-in-Westmorland (017683) 51177
Barnard Castle (01833) 690909
Brampton (016977) 3433
Corbridge (01434) 632815
Haltwhistle (01434) 322002
Hexham (01434) 605225
Penrith (01768) 867466
Stanhope (01388) 527650
Youth Hostels (YHA) –
Alston (01434) 381509
Carlisle (01228) 597352
Dufton (017683) 51236
Langdon Beck (01833) 622228
Ninebanks (01434) 345288

Section 10 – The Cheviots

Sale and Partners (Land Agents) (01668) 281611
Tourist Information Centres –
Adderstone (01668) 213678
Alnwick (01665) 510665
Bellingham (01434) 220616
Berwick-upon-Tweed (01289) 330733
Coldstream (01890) 882607
Jedburgh (01835) 863435
Kelso (01573) 223464
Rothbury (01669) 620887
Wooler (01668) 282123
Youth Hostels (YHA) –
Byrness (01830) 520425 (For bookings more than seven days in advance ring (01629) 581399.)
Wooler (01668) 281365
Youth Hostels (SYHA) –
Kirk Yetholm (01573) 420631

Section 11 – The Isle of Man

Car Hire –
Athol Car Hire (Europcar) (01624) 623232
Rent Ocean Ford (01624) 662211
Hertz -Ronaldsway Airport (01624) 825855
Douglas (01624) 621844
Mylchreests Car Rental (0500) 823533
Emerald Airways (0500) 600748
Isle of Man Railways (01624) 670077
Isle of Man Steam Packet Company (0990) 523523
Isle of Man Steam Railway (01624) 661661
Manx Airlines (0345) 256256
National Express (0990) 010104
Tourist Information Centres –
Airport (01624) 821600
Ballasalla (01624) 822531
Castletown (01624) 825005
Douglas (01624) 686766
Laxey Heritage Trust (01624) 862007
Onchan (01624) 621228
Peel (01624) 842341
Port Erin (01624) 832298
Port St Mary (01624) 832101
Ramsey (01624) 817025